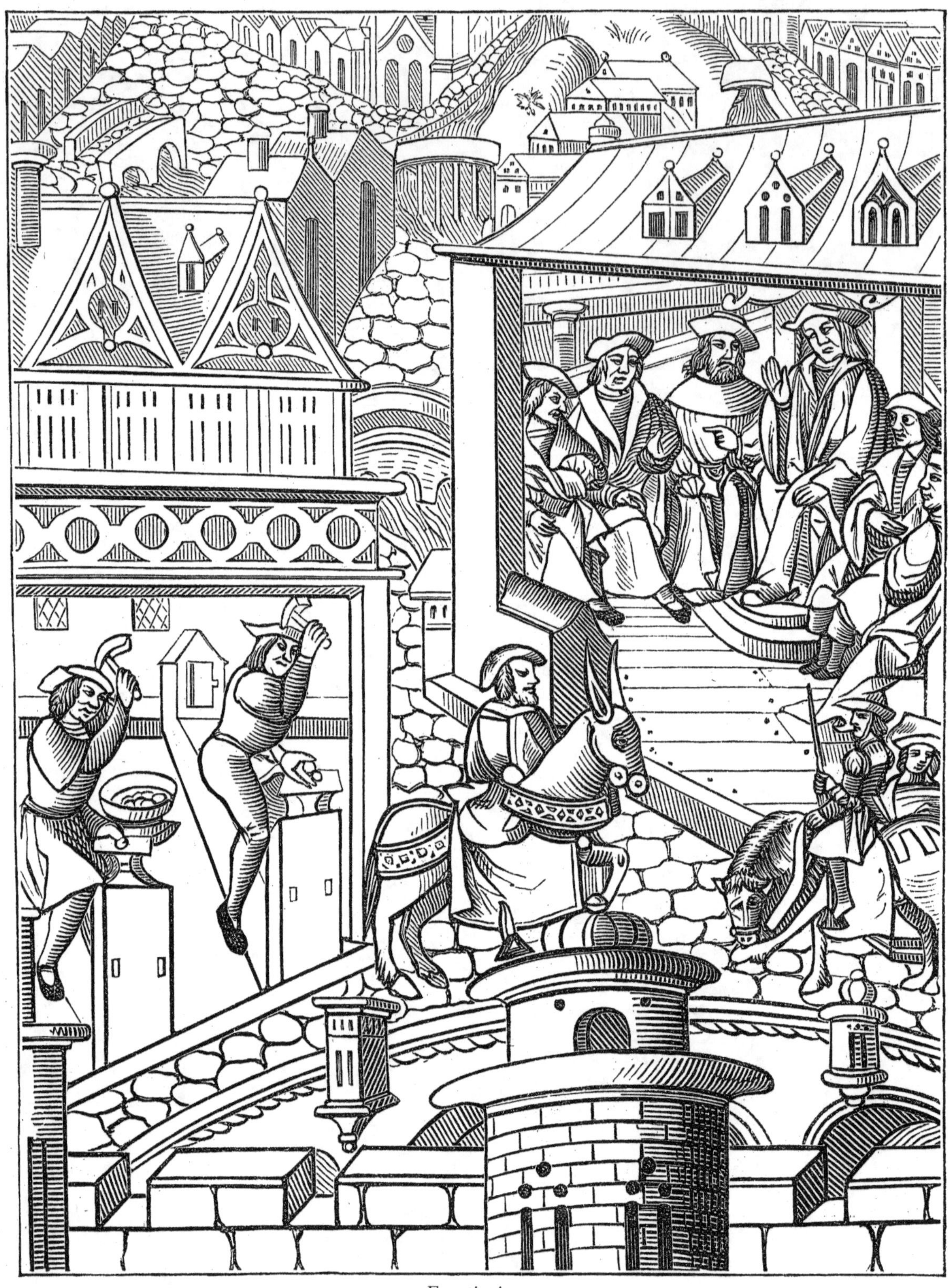

Frontispiece
The mint, 1520
[page 9]

TREASURY OF

Medieval Illustrations

Paul Lacroix

Selected and Arranged by
CAROL BELANGER GRAFTON

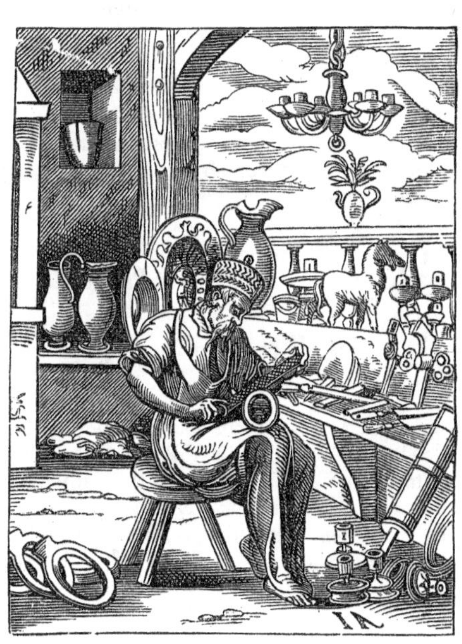

DOVER PUBLICATIONS, INC.
Mineola, New York

Bibliographical Note

This Dover edition, first published in 2008, is a new compilation of illustrations from the following works by Paul Lacroix: *The Arts in the Middle Ages and the Renaissance* (Chapman & Hall, London, 1870); *Manners, Customs, and Dress During the Middle Ages and During the Renaissance Period* (D. Appleton and Co., New York, 1874); *Military and Religious Life in the Middle Ages and at the Period of the Renaissance* (Chapman & Hall, London, 1874); and *Science and Literature in the Middle Ages and the Renaissance* (Bickers and Son, London, 1878).

DOVER *Pictorial Archive* SERIES

Library of Congress Cataloging-in-Publication Data

Jacob, P. L., 1806–1884.
Treasury of medieval illustrations / Paul Lacroix ; selected and arranged by Carol Grafton.
p. cm.
"This Dover edition, first published in 2008, is a new compilation of illustrations from the following works by Paul Lacroix: The arts in the Middle Ages and the Renaissance (Chapman & Hall, London, 1870); Manners, customs, and dress during the Middle Ages and during the Renaissance period (D. Appleton and Co., New York, 1874); Military and religious life in the Middle Ages and at the period of the Renaissance (Chapman & Hall, London, 1874); and Science and literature in the Middle Ages and the Renaissance (Bickers and Son, London, 1878)."
ISBN-13: 978-0-486-46012-3
ISBN-10: 0-486-46012-6
1. Civilization, Medieval—Pictorial works. I. Grafton, Carol Belanger. II. Title.

CB351.J23 2008
909.07022'2—dc22

2007049442

www.doverpublications.com

Publisher's Note

THE ILLUSTRATIONS IN THIS EXTENSIVE COMPILATION are drawn from four late-nineteenth-century works by Paul Lacroix: *The Arts in the Middle Ages and the Renaissance* (1870); *Manners, Customs, and Dress During the Middle Ages and During the Renaissance Period* (1874); *Military and Religious Life in the Middle Ages and at the Period of the Renaissance* (1874); and *Science and Literature in the Middle Ages and the Renaissance* (1878). Carol Belanger Grafton has selected more than 750 images from these highly regarded sources and arranged them thematically to reflect the essential topics of medieval life, from trades, occupations, and commerce to architecture and costume. The scope of this treasury includes the lands of France, Germany, Belgium, Italy, Russia, England, and Spain, as well as other evolving nations.

Medieval times in Western Europe—the period of roughly the fifth to the fifteenth centuries (some sixteenth-century images are included here as well)—continue to fascinate the modern sensibility. The dissolution of Rome in the fifth century gave way to the rise of the Christian church. This church, persecuted at its start, continued to develop until it arrived at a state of influence and wealth that made it supremely powerful among European nations. The societal organization and material progress—"civilization" in the true sense of the word—created by the Roman Empire was undermined by repeated invasions by nomadic tribes from eastern and central Asia, as well as invaders such as the Angles, Jutes, Saxons, Visigoths, Ostrogoths, and Vandals. The unifying effect of the Roman administration was increasingly threatened by the tribal nature of these disruptive people, traditionally referred to as "barbarians"; it is helpful to keep in mind that "barbarian" originally was a word used by the Greeks to refer to non-Greeks—foreigners or outsiders. The network of roads built by the Romans—a symbol of their strides in unifying the European lands—fell into ruins, further damaging their empire. Nevertheless, by the seventh century, the Roman model began to reappear, and an increasingly orderly society re-formed in the wasted lands of Western Europe. The growth of cities and towns and cultivation of the land led to a new framework for stability and prosperity.

The cornerstones of the medieval world—monasticism and chivalry—are included in great detail in this book. Images of popes, clerics, and other religious figures proliferated as Christianity came to predominate over paganism in Western Europe. But at the heart of the medieval world are its people, and among the numerous depictions are those of workers such as a shoemaker [Plate 1], a carpenter's apprentice [Plate 55], a poultry dealer [Plate 146], and a swineherd [Plate 168], as well as the upper classes: noble ladies and children [Plate 346], a knight and his lady [Plate 356]; and women of the court [Plate 371]. The gulf between the peasant and the aristocrat was wide indeed; the occupants of a Venetian gondola [Plate 5] represent a class that, although few in number, had incalculable influence over laborers such as the scantily clad baker shown in Plate 169. The medieval period was marked by the lurking presence of death, due to pestilence and unsanitary conditions. During the mid-1300s, a catastrophic plague—the Black Death—wiped out one-quarter to a third of the European population. Plates 506, 510, 511, and 515 through 518 provide striking imagery of the Grim Reaper, waiting to take the old and the sick.

Rounding out the gallery are scenes of the hunt ["How to shout and blow horns," Plate 90]; typical pastimes ["French card for a game of piquet," Plate 117]; meal preparation ["Interior of a kitchen," Plate 130]; the enjoyment of music ["German musicians playing the lute and guitar, 16th century," Plate 217]; the advance of literacy ["Scribe or copyist in his workroom, 15th century," Plate 234]; scientific research ["A lesson in astronomy, 13th century," Plate 271]; worship ["Jewish ceremony before the ark," Plate 468]; battle ["Man-of-war, 1520," Plate 540]; royalty ["Robert Chamberlain, esquire to Henry V," Plate 547]; armor ["Frankish warrior, 9th century," Plate 606]; and architecture ["Porte de Hal, Brussels," Plate 706]. An informative selection of costumes and jewelry indicate the styles adopted by various classes in medieval society over the centuries. These images, and hundreds more, weave a remarkable tapestry of medieval life.

The scope and breadth of this exhaustive work presents medieval people in all of their contrasting aspects: rich and well-born, or poor and toiling; hungry for knowledge, yet bound by superstition; warlike and combat-ready, but eager to join an increasingly well-regulated world—one thousand years of society-building, leading to the threshold of the Renaissance.

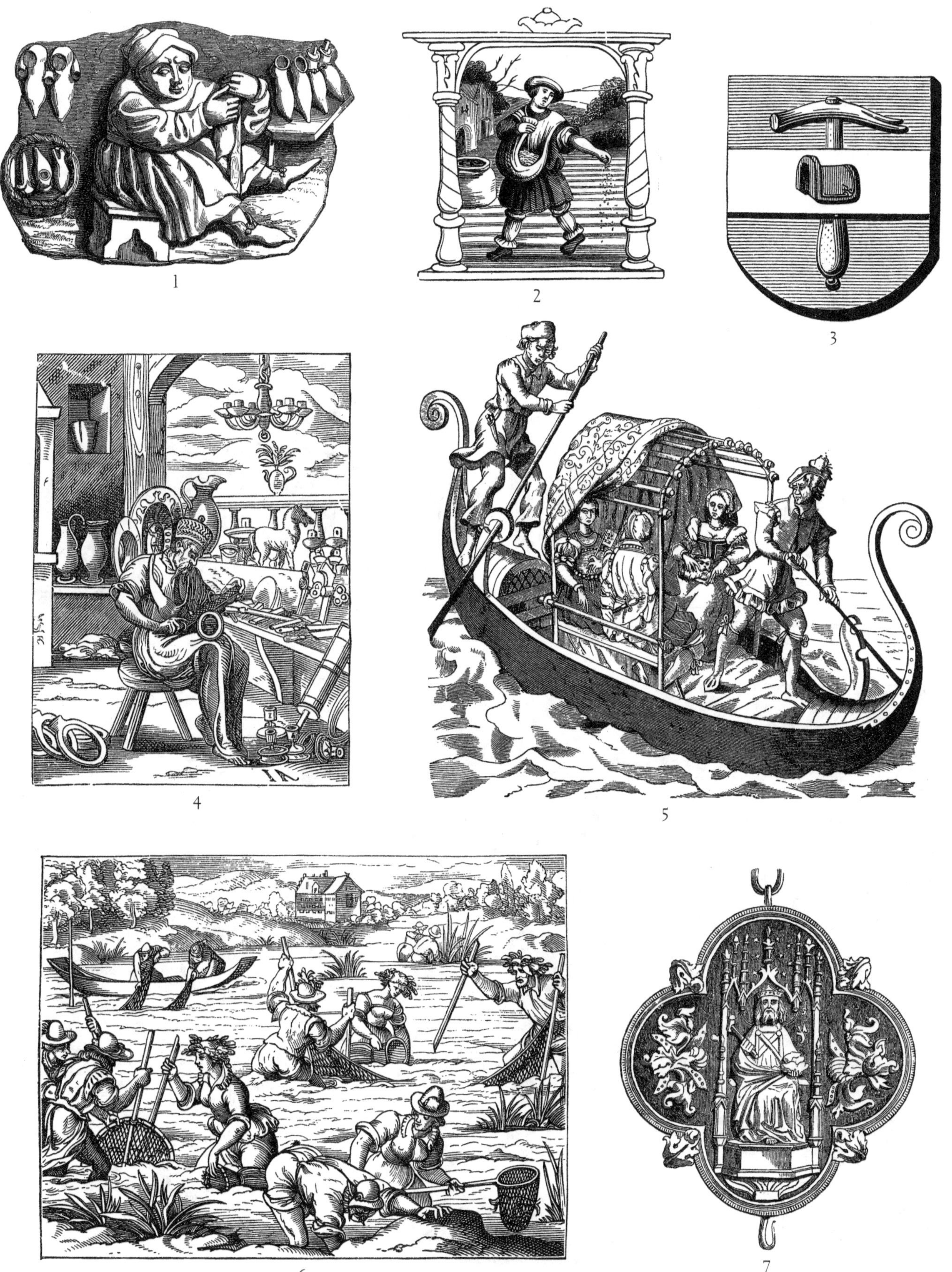

1. Shoemaker fitting a shoe. 2. An operator. From the *Book of Hours*. 3. Banner of the Corporation of the Saddlers of Tonnerre. 4. Coppersmith. 5. Venetian gondola. 6. River fishing. 7. The Ensign of the Collar of the Goldsmiths of Ghent, 15th century.

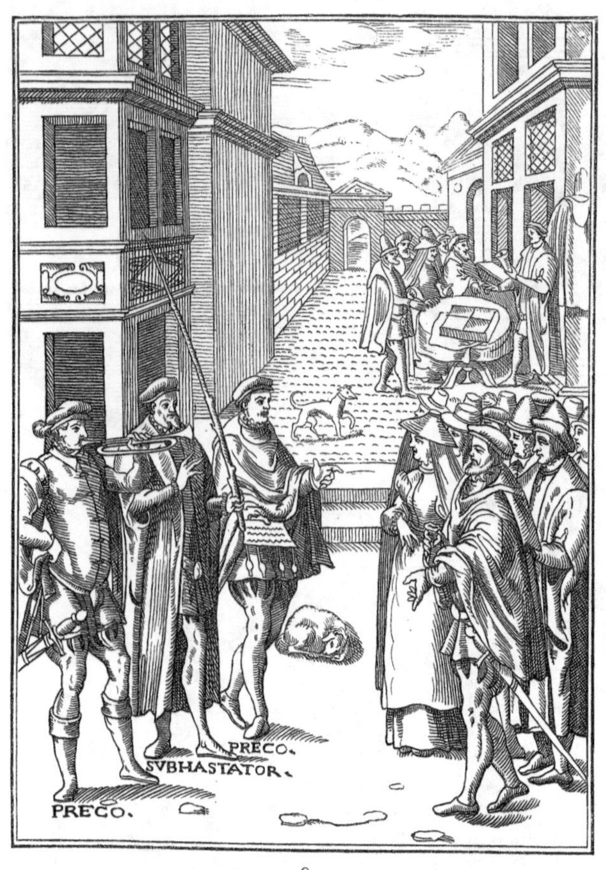

8

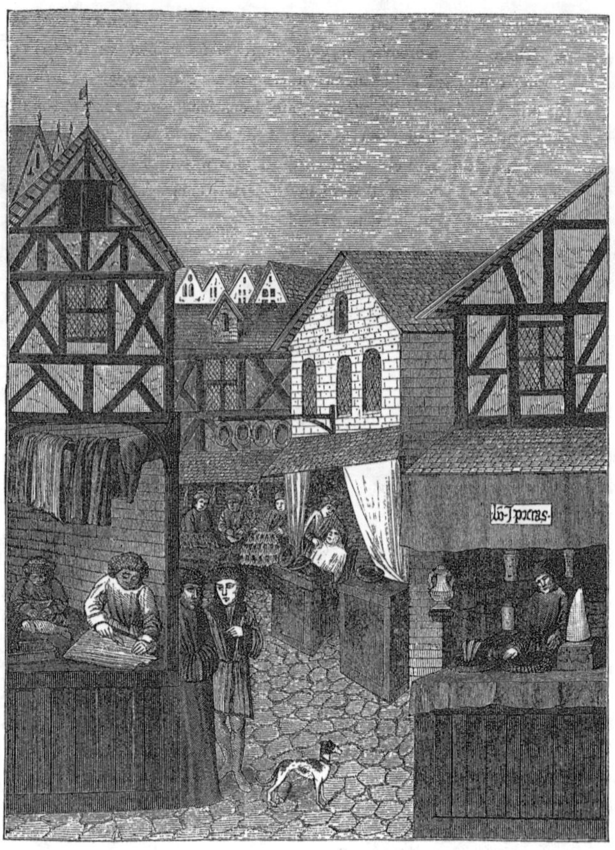

9

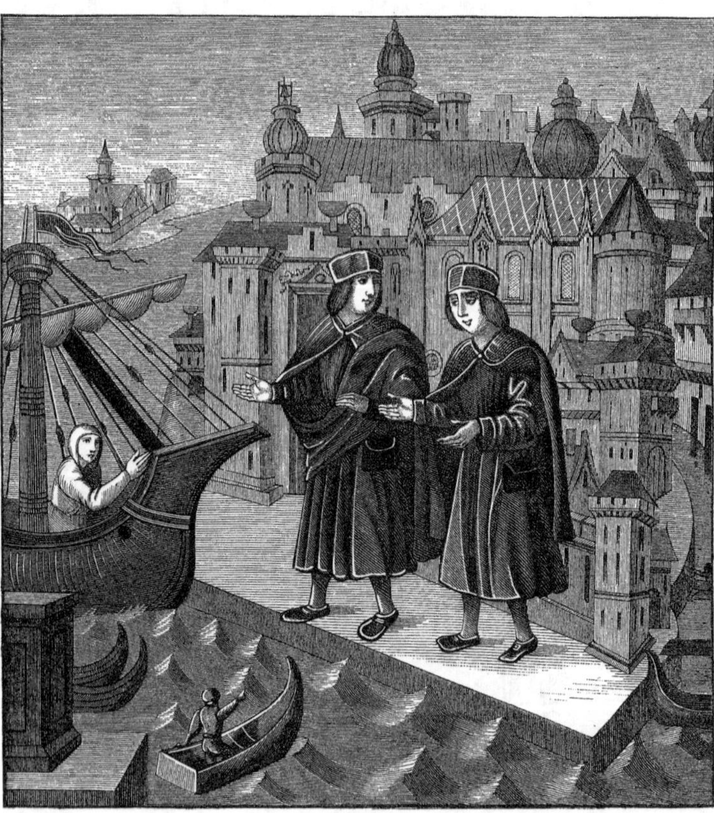

10

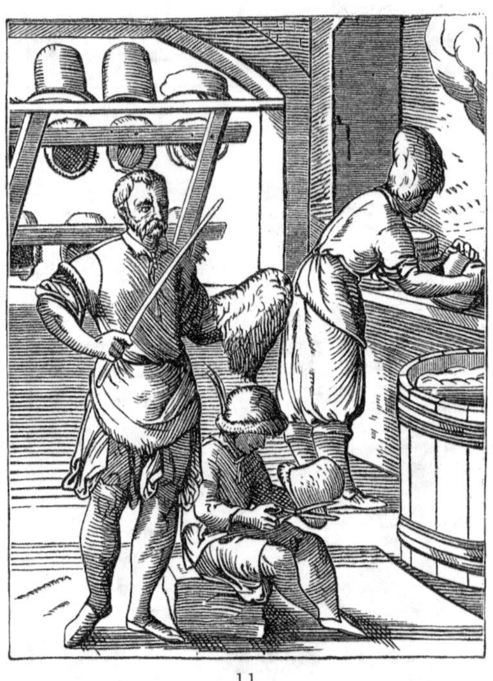

11

8. Sale by town-crier. **9.** Shops in an apothecary's street, 15th century. **10.** Trade on the seaports of the Levant. **11.** Hatter.

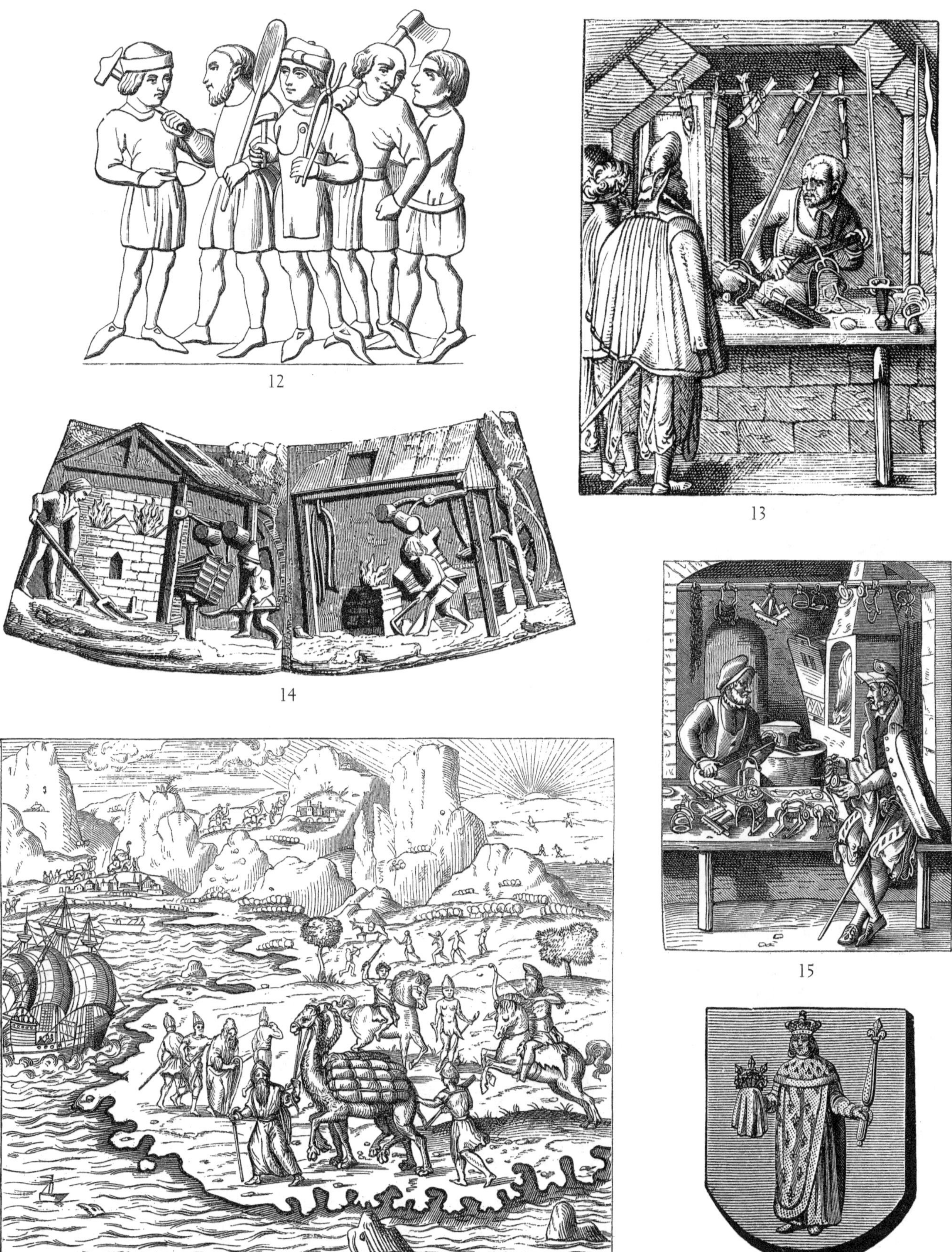

12 13 14 15 16 17

12. Craftsmen in the 14th century. **13.** Sword maker. **14.** The Foundry of Precious Metals. Piece in the ceremonial collar of the senior member of the goldsmiths at Ghent. **15.** Spur maker. **16.** Transport of merchandise on the backs of camels, 1575. **17.** Banner of the tapestry workers of Lyons.

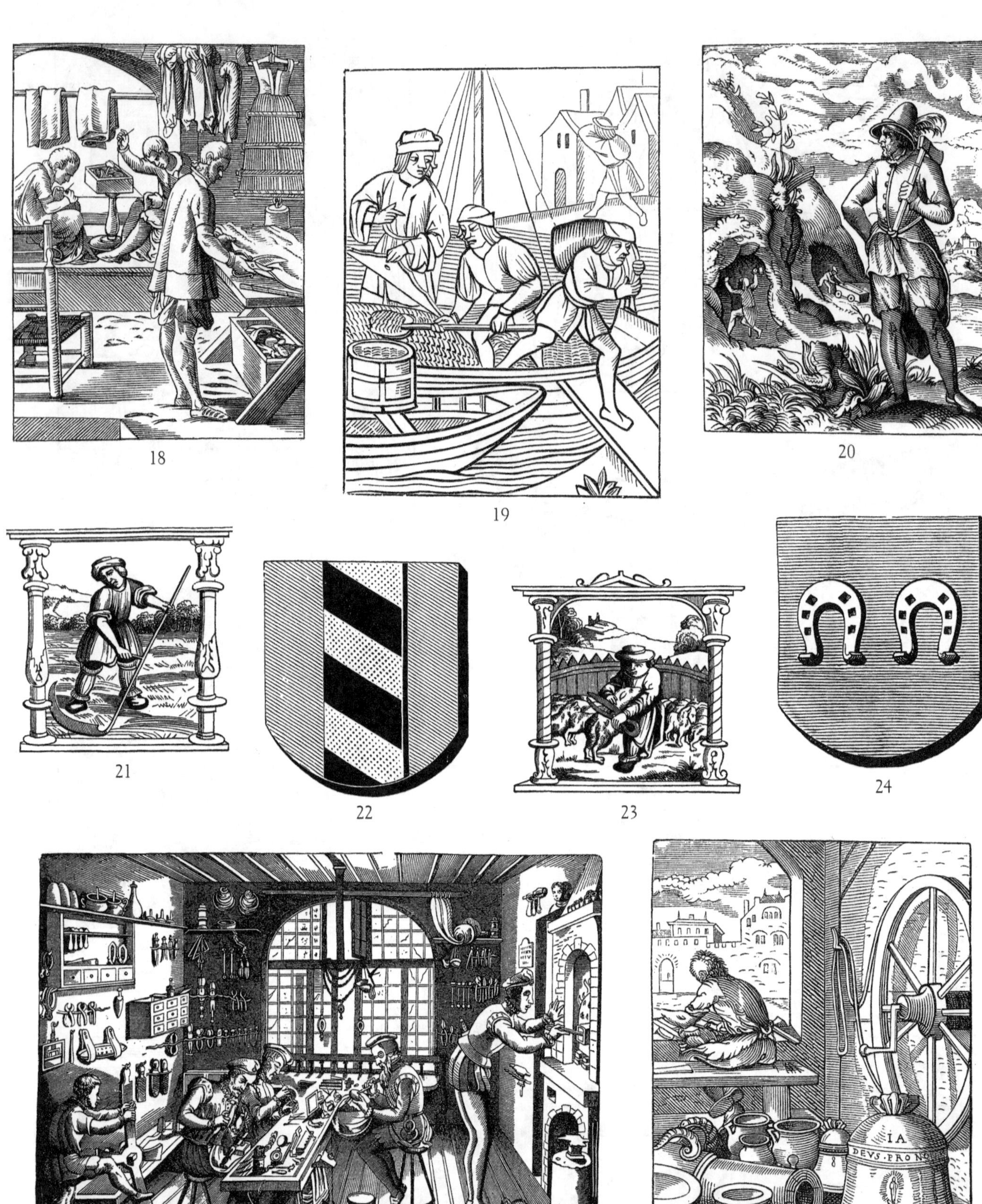

18. Tailor. **19.** Measuring salt, 1500. **20.** Miner. **21.** An operator. From the *Book of Hours*. **22.** Banner of the Calais innkeepers. **23.** From the *Book of Hours*. **24.** Banner of the St. Lô blacksmiths. **25.** Interior of the atelier of Etienne Delaulne, a celebrated goldsmith of Paris, 16th century. **26.** Bell and cannon caster.

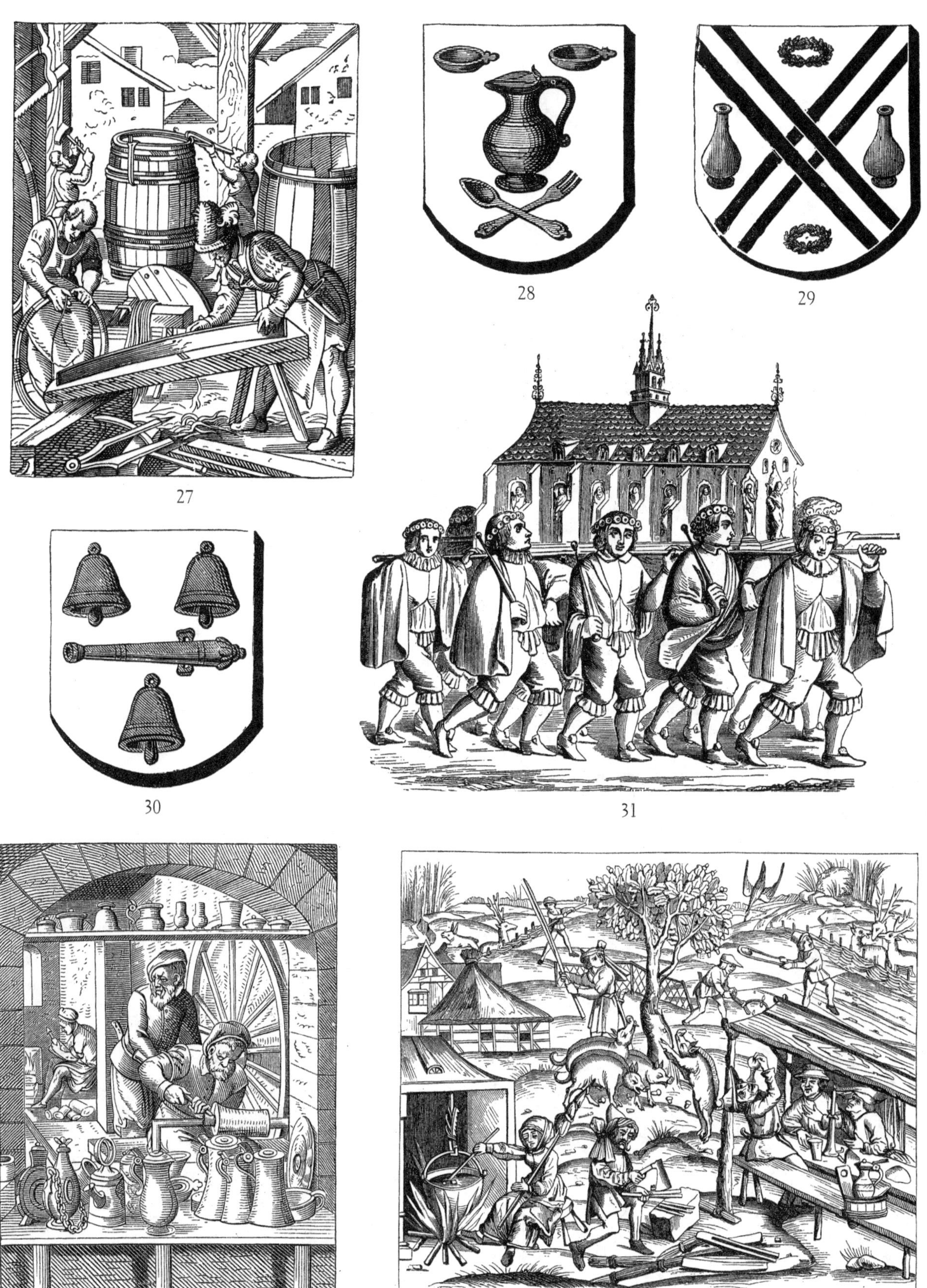

27. A cooper's workshop, 16th century. **28.** Banner of the Lyons tinmen. **29.** Banner of the corporation of the public housekeepers of Tonnerre. **30.** Banner of the Paris founders. **31.** The Corporation of the Goldsmiths of Paris carrying the shrine of St. Geneviève, 17th century. **32.** Tinman. **33.** Country life.

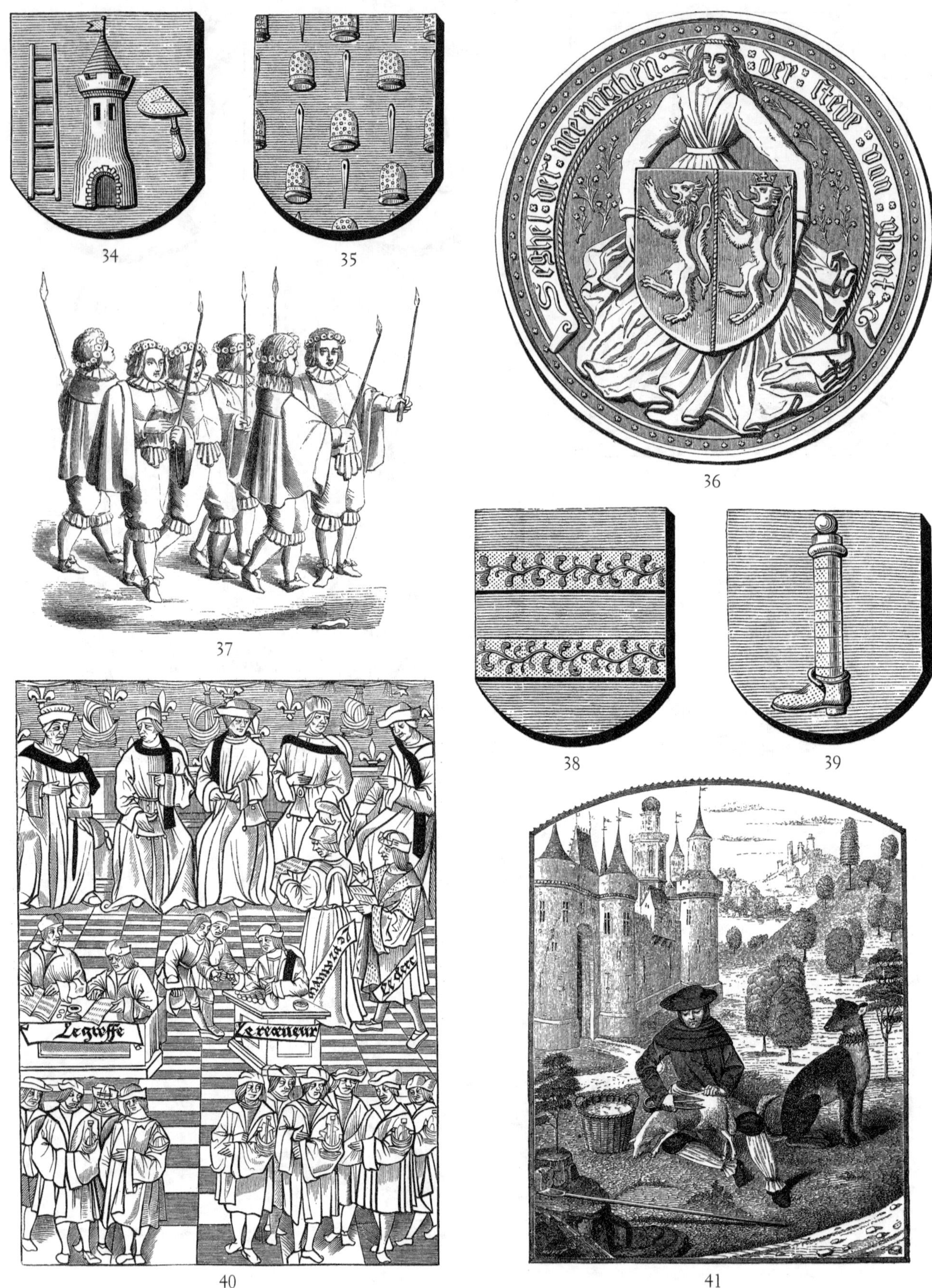

34. Banner of the tours slaters. **35.** Banner of the pin and needle makers. **36.** Seal of the United Trades of Ghent, 15th century. **37.** Group of goldsmiths. **38.** Banner of the Bordeaux upholsterers. **39.** Banner of the Douai shoemakers. **40.** Assembly of the provostship of the merchants of Paris, 1528. **41.** Sheep shearing.

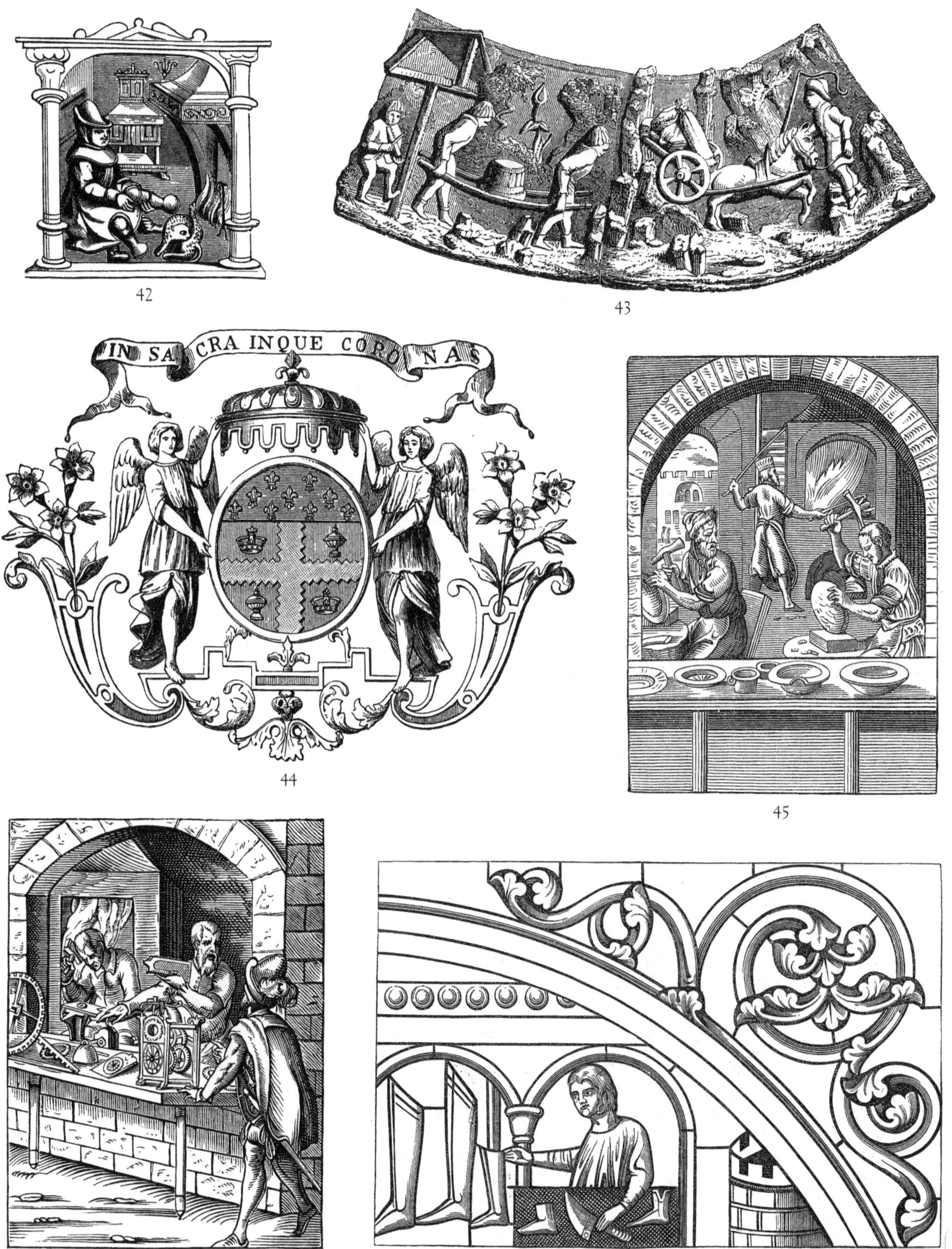

42. From the *Book of Hours.* 43. Extraction of precious metals. 44. Arms of the Corporation of Goldsmiths of Paris. 45. Basin-maker. 46. The clockmaker. 47. Bootmaker's apprentice working at a trial piece.

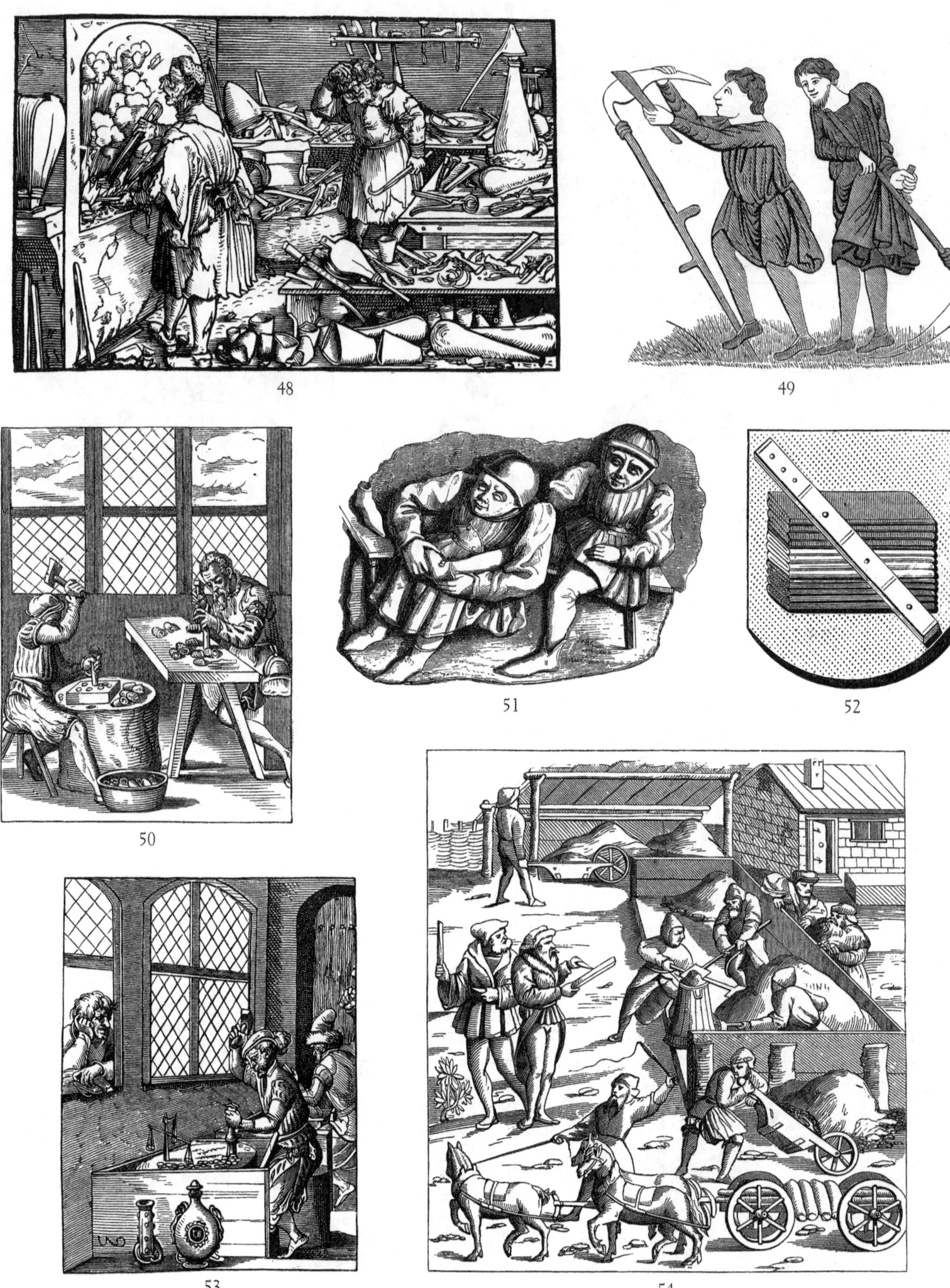

48 49 50 51 52 53 54

48. German alchemist. **49.** Laboring colons, 12th century. **50.** Dice maker. **51.** The shoemaker and his customer, 15th century. **52.** Banner of the drapers of Caen. **53.** The officer of the Mint, 16th century. **54.** The extraction of metals, 1552.

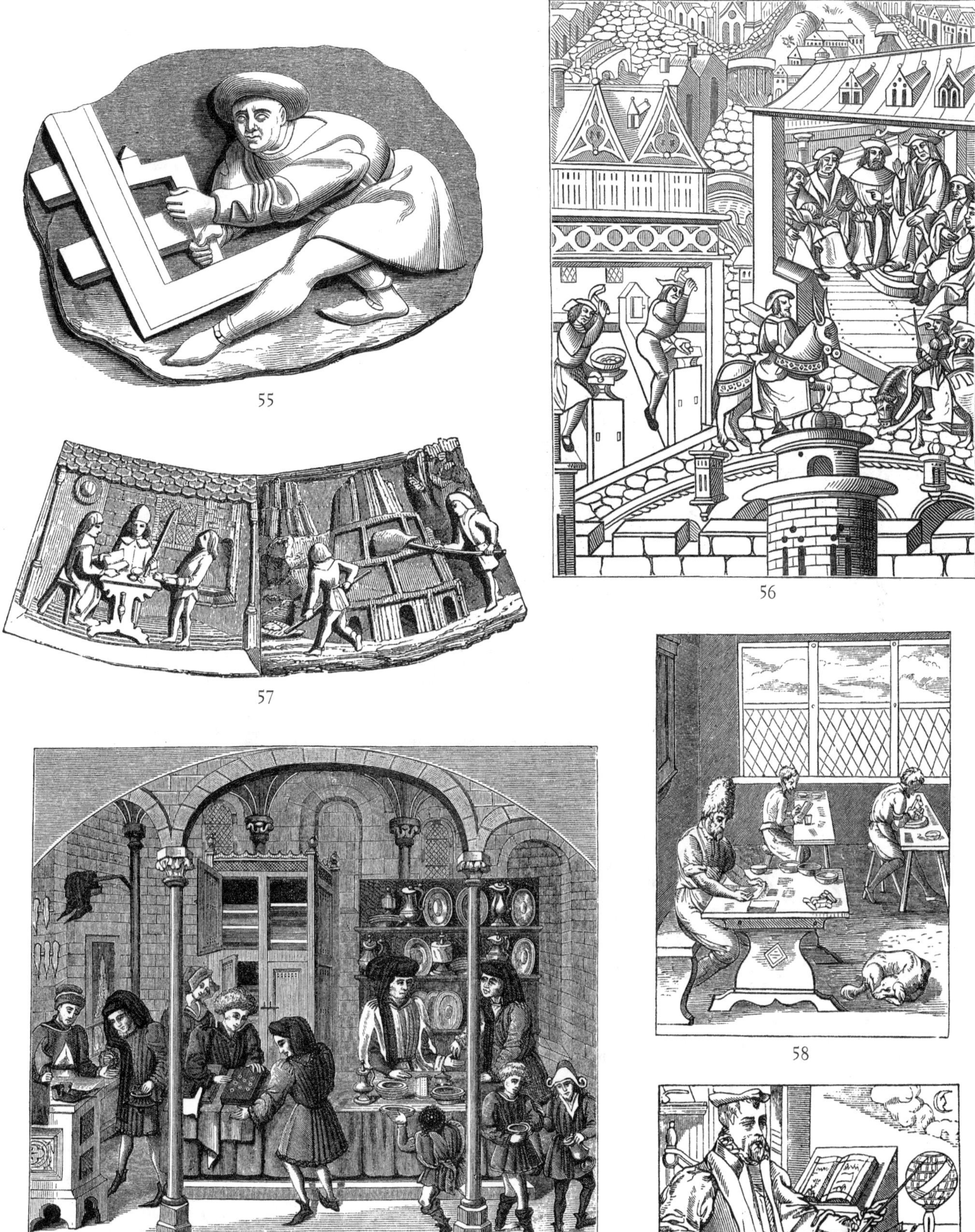

55
56
57
58
59
60

55. Carpenter's apprentice working at a trial piece. **56.** The mint, 1520. **57.** The Foundry of precious metals, 15th century. **58.** Pin and needle maker. **59.** Shops under covered market, 15th century. **60.** Bernard Abbatia, astronomer to the king.

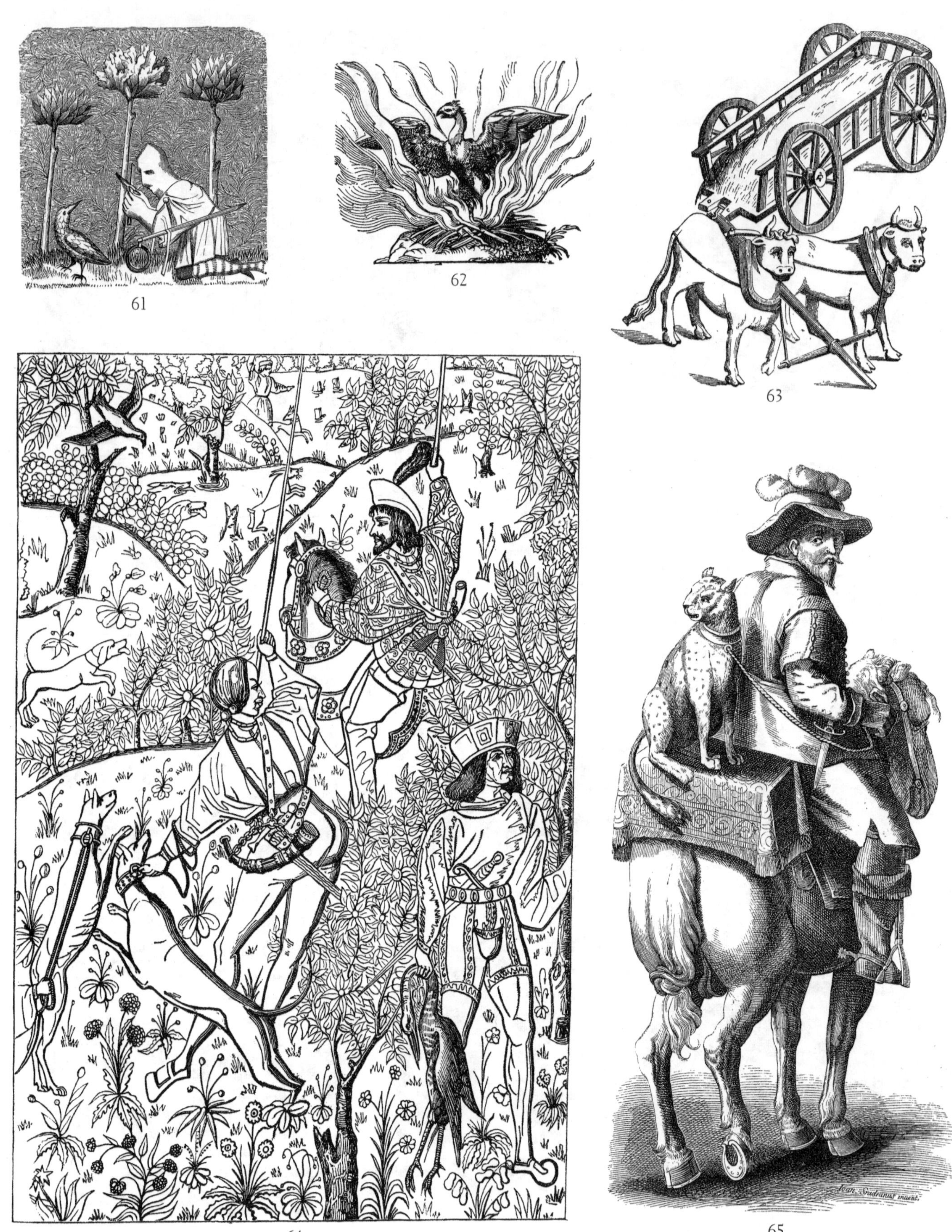

61. Mode of catching a woodcock. **62.** The phoenix rising from his ashes, 1602. **63.** Cart drawn by oxen, 15th century. **64.** Tapestry representing a hunting scene. **65.** Hunting with the leopard.

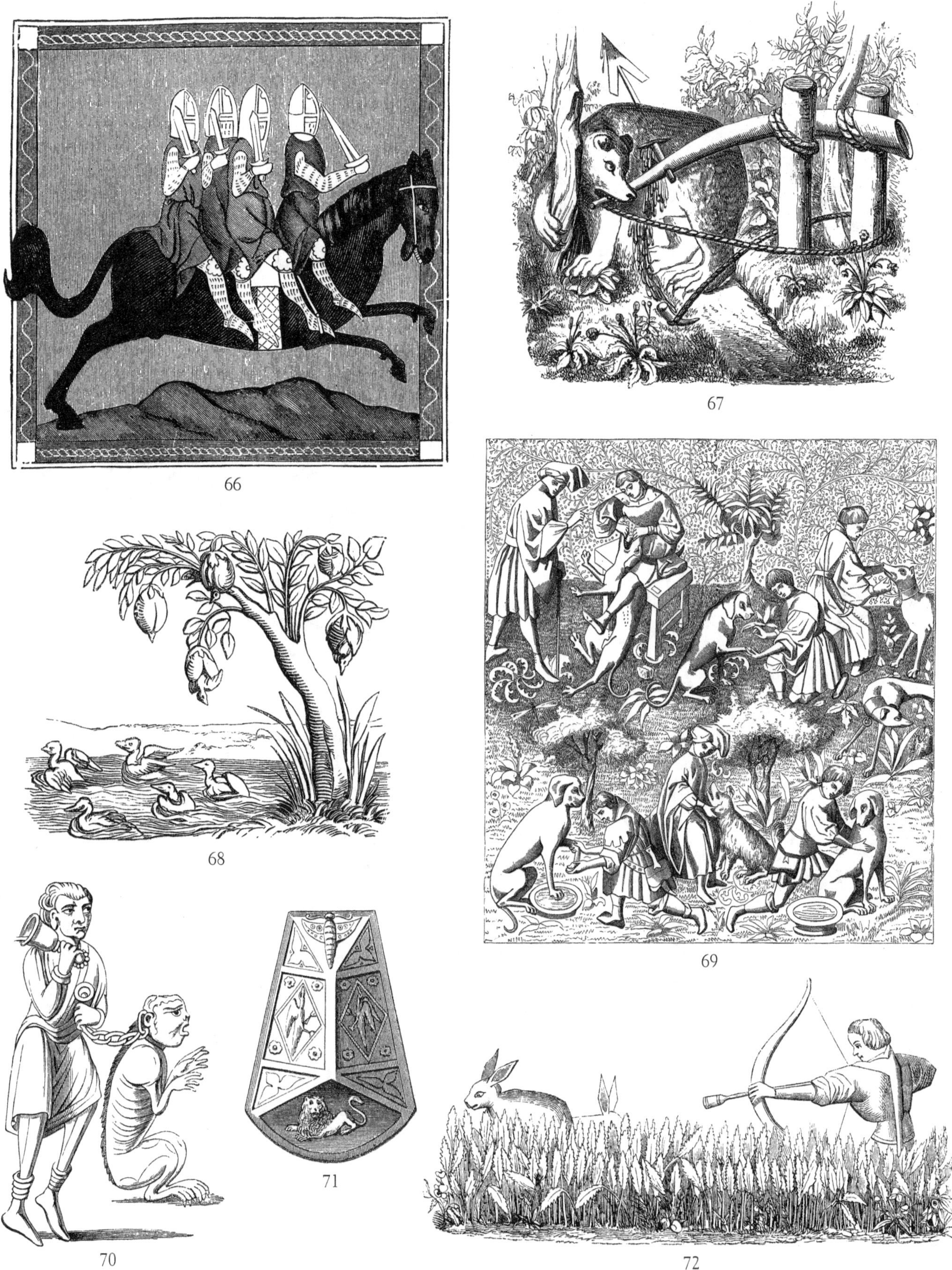

66. The four sons of Aymon on their good steed, Bayart, 13th century. 67. How bears and other beasts may be caught with a dart. 68. Barnacle geese. 69. Diseases of dogs and their cure, 14th century. 70. The exhibitor of strange animals, 12th century. 71. Detail of hunting horn. 72. How to allure the hare.

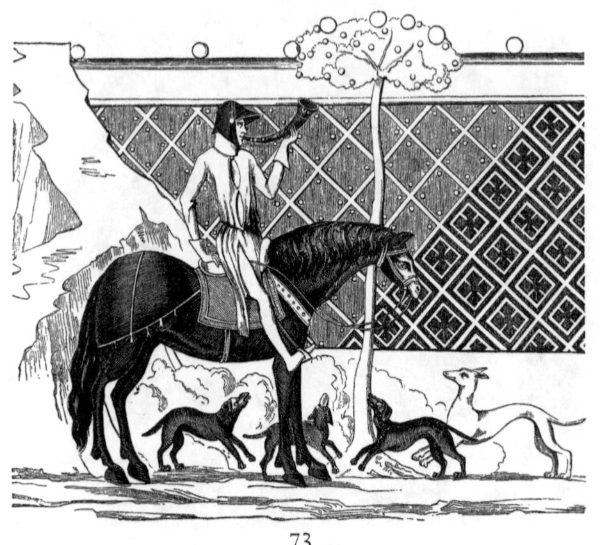

73

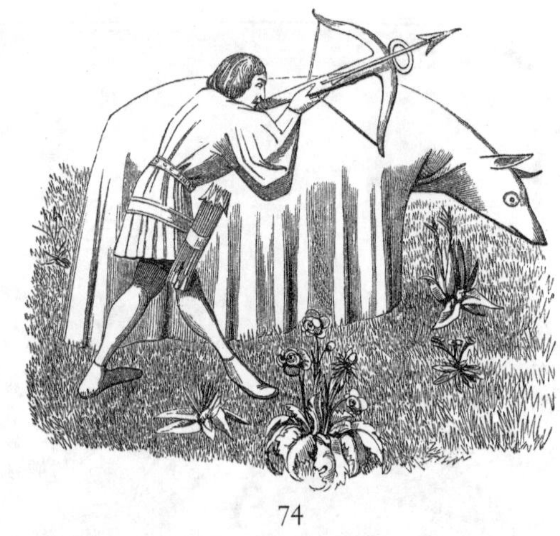

74

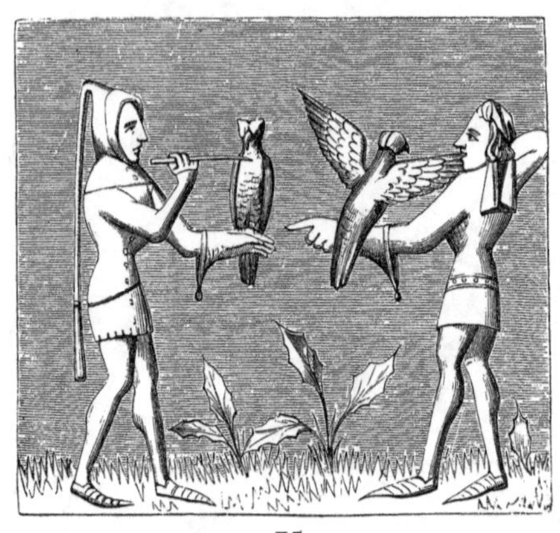

75

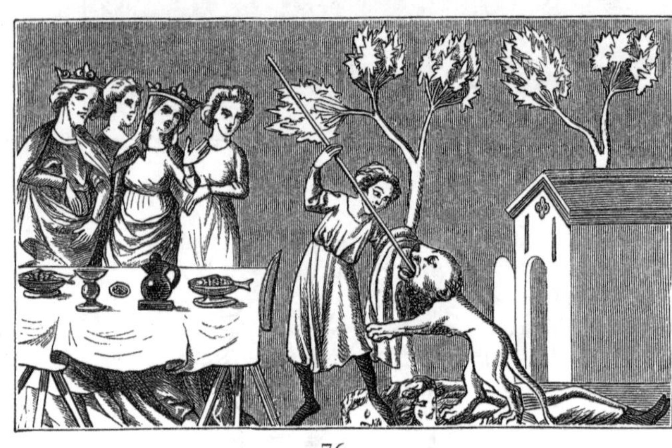

76

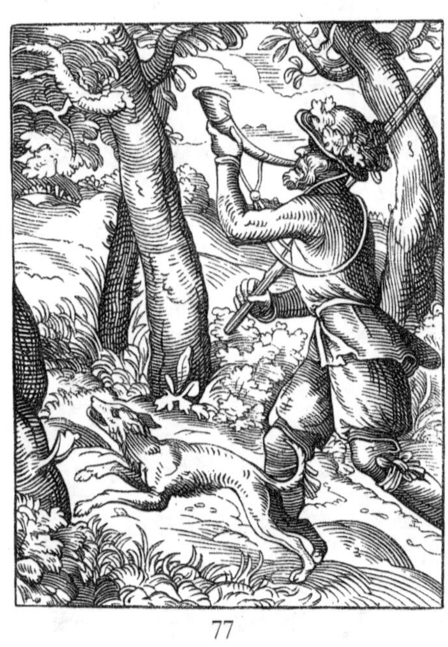

77

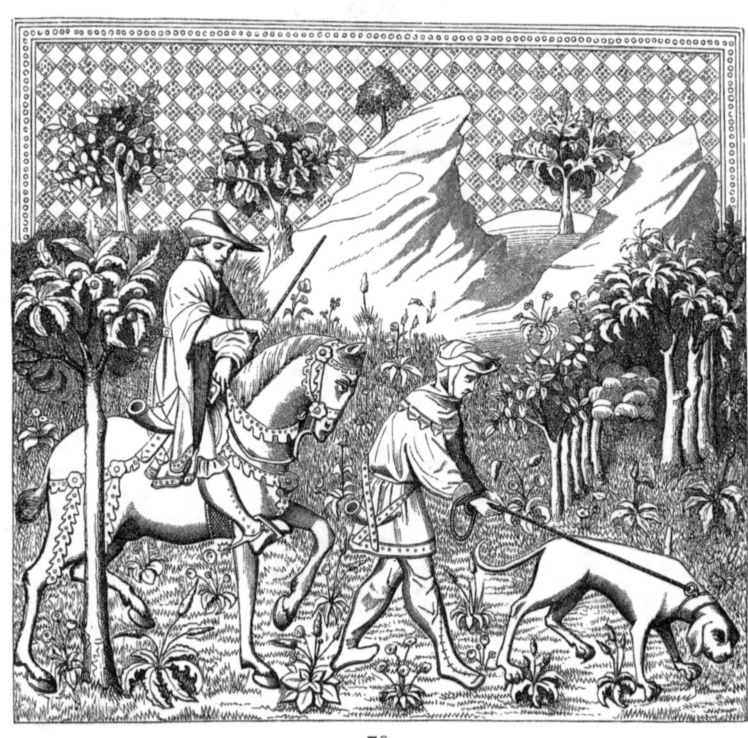

78

73. Tristan at the chase, from "The Romance of Tristan," 15th century. **74.** How to carry a cloth to approach beasts. **75.** Falconers dressing their birds. **76.** Judicial duel; combat of a knight with a dog, 13th century. **77.** German sportsman. **78.** Nobleman in hunting costume, preceded by his servant, trying to find the scent of a stag, 14th century.

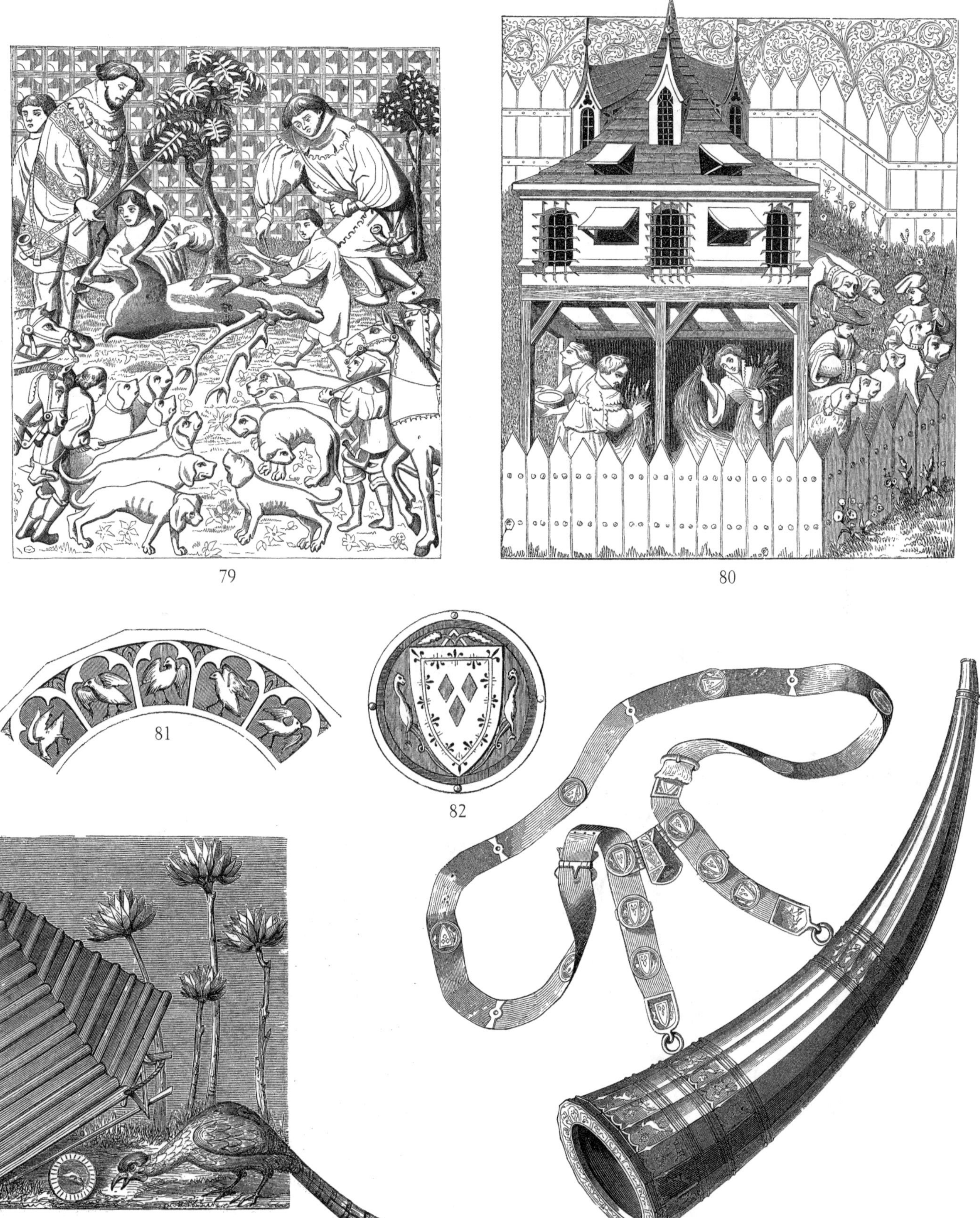

79. The way to skin and cut up a stag. **80.** "Kennel in which dogs should live, and how they should be kept," 15th century. **81.** Detail of hunting horn. **82.** Detail of hunting horn. **83.** Pheasant fowling. **84.** Olifant, or hunting horn.

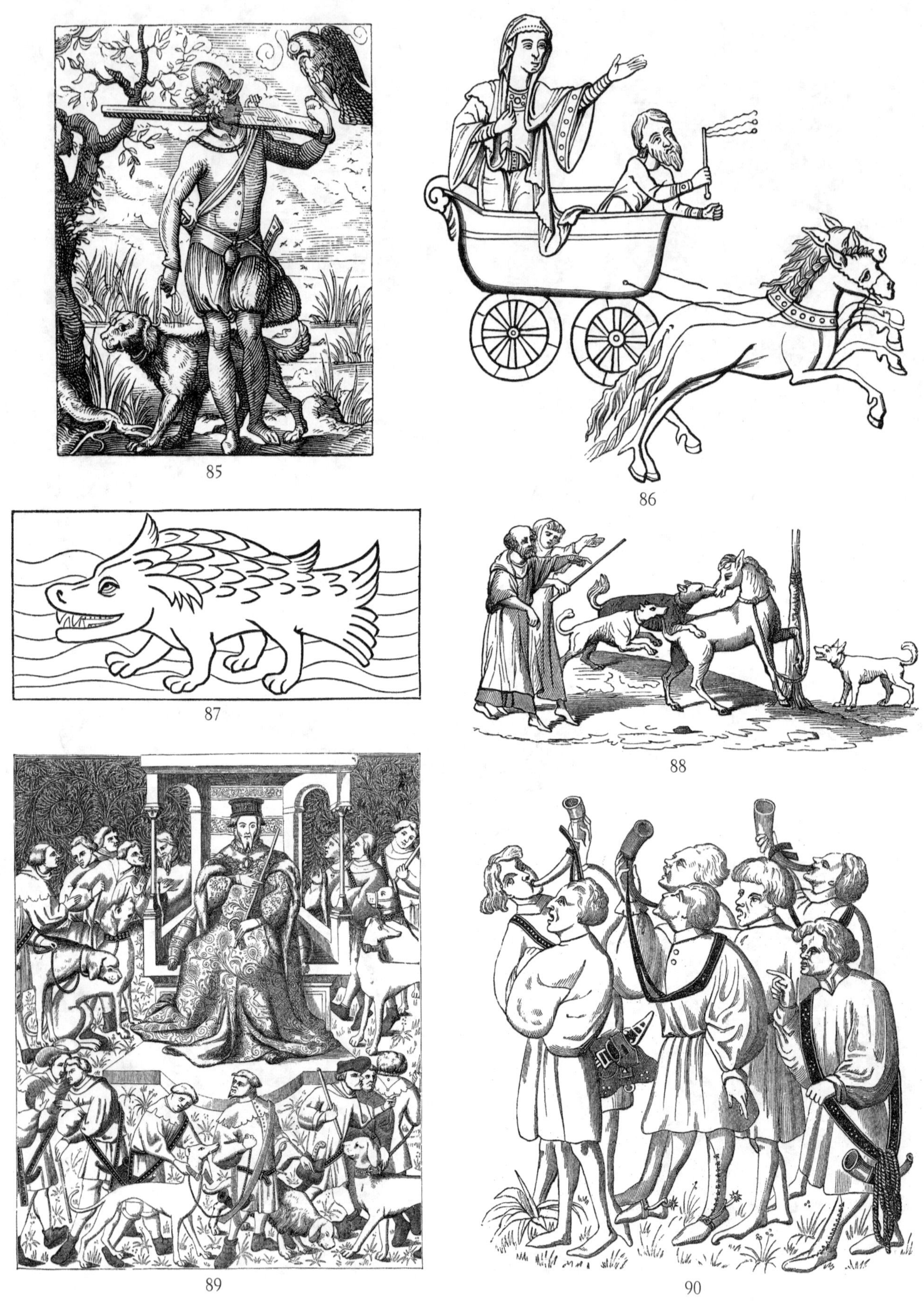

85. German falconer. **86.** The carucca, or pleasure-carriage, drawn by a pair of horses, 5th to 10th centuries. **87.** The sea-dog, 1482. **88.** Fight between a horse and dogs, 13th century. **89.** Gaston Phœbus teaching the art of venery, 15th century. **90.** How to shout and blow horns.

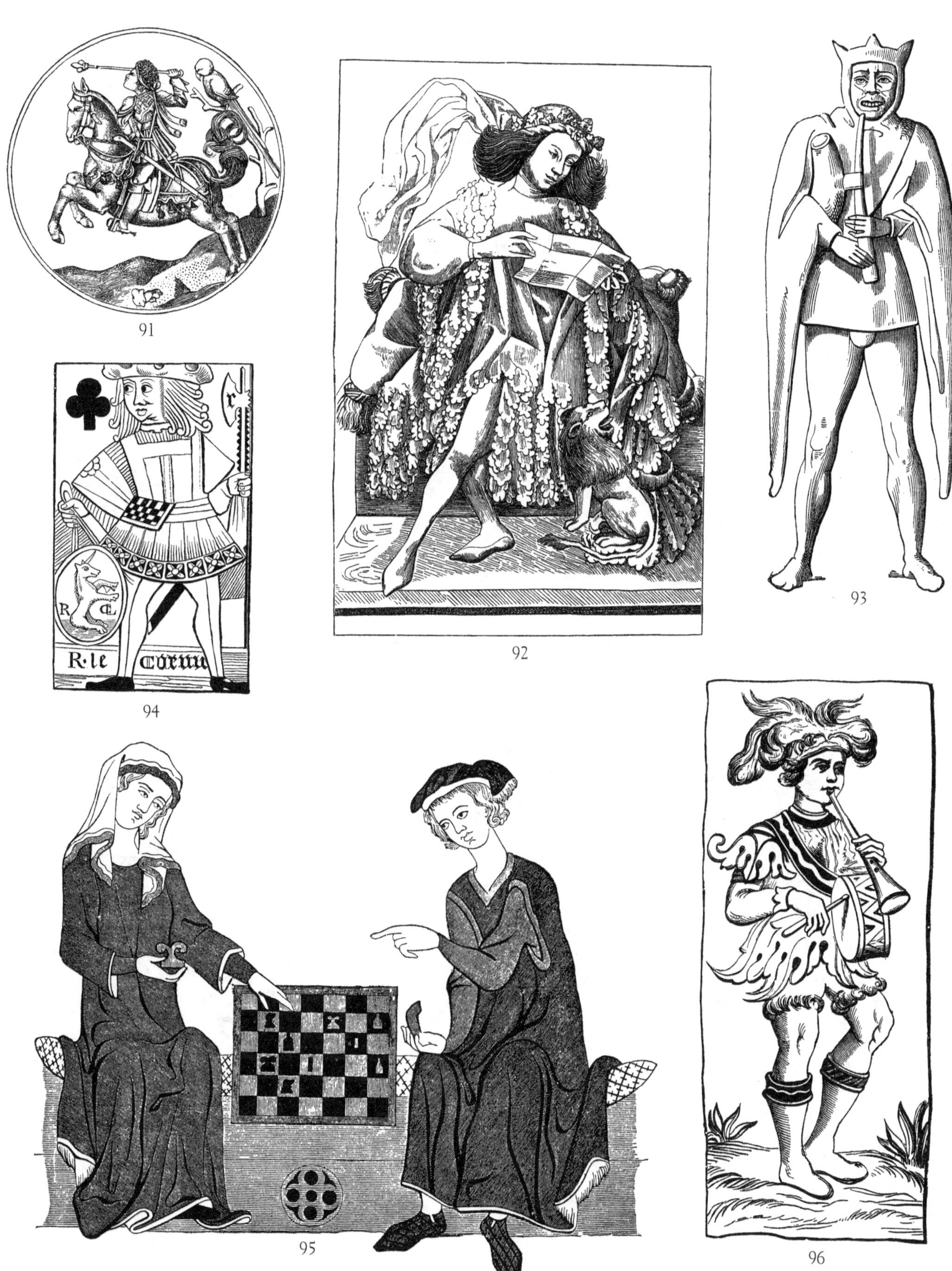

91. King of parrots. **92.** The knight, from a pack of cards engraved by "The Master of 1466." **93.** Buffoon playing the bagpipe. **94.** The "Knave of Clubs" in the packs of cards of R. Passerel and R. Le Cornu, 16th century. **95.** Chess players, 13th century. **96.** The buffoon, a card from a pack of *Tarots*.

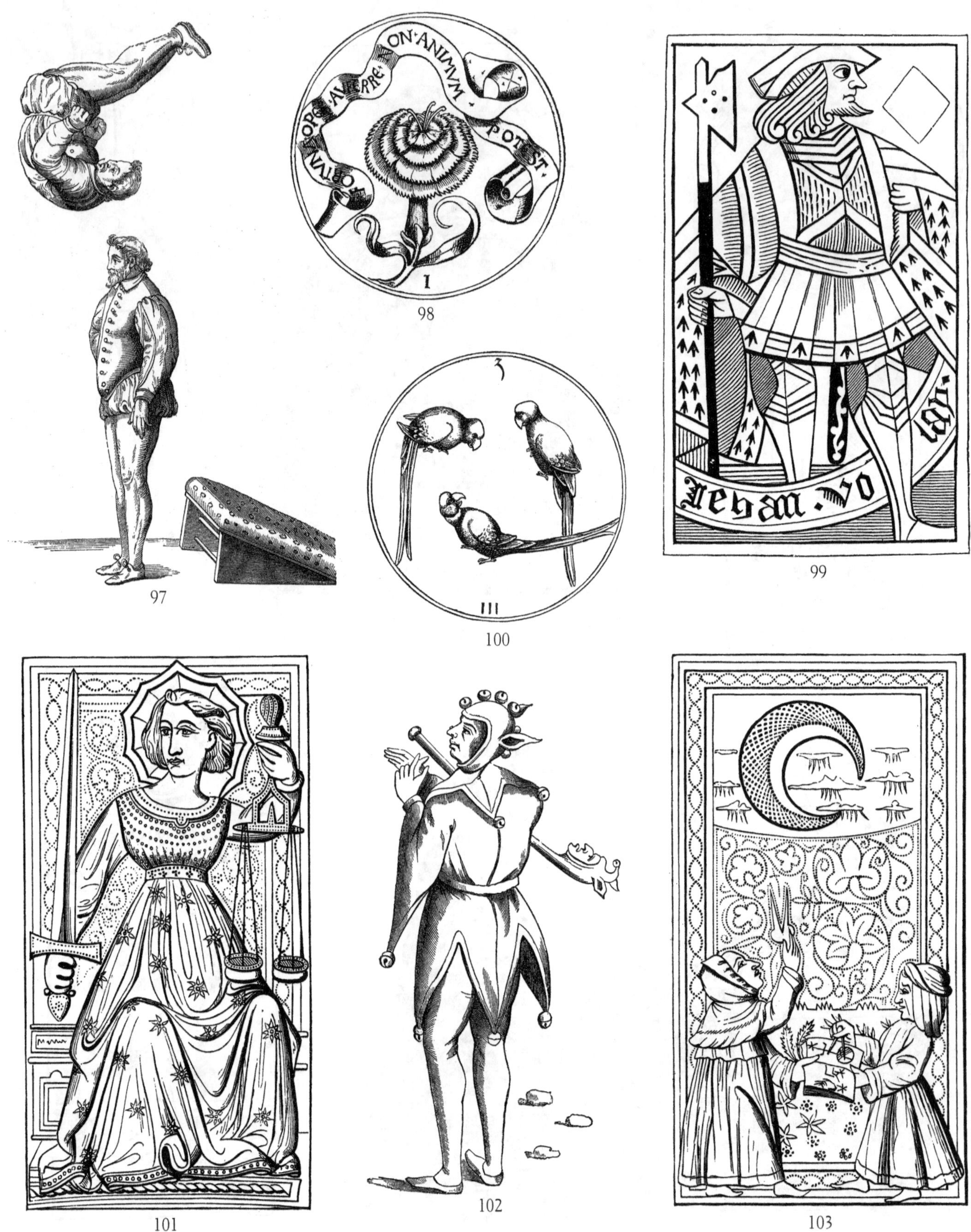

97. The spring-board, 1599. **98.** Ace of carnations. **99.** Ancient French card, 15th century. **100.** Three of parrots. **101.** Justice; card taken from the pack said to belong to Charles VI. **102.** Buffoon holding a bauble beneath his arm, 15th century. **103.** The moon, card taken from the pack said to belong to Charles VI.

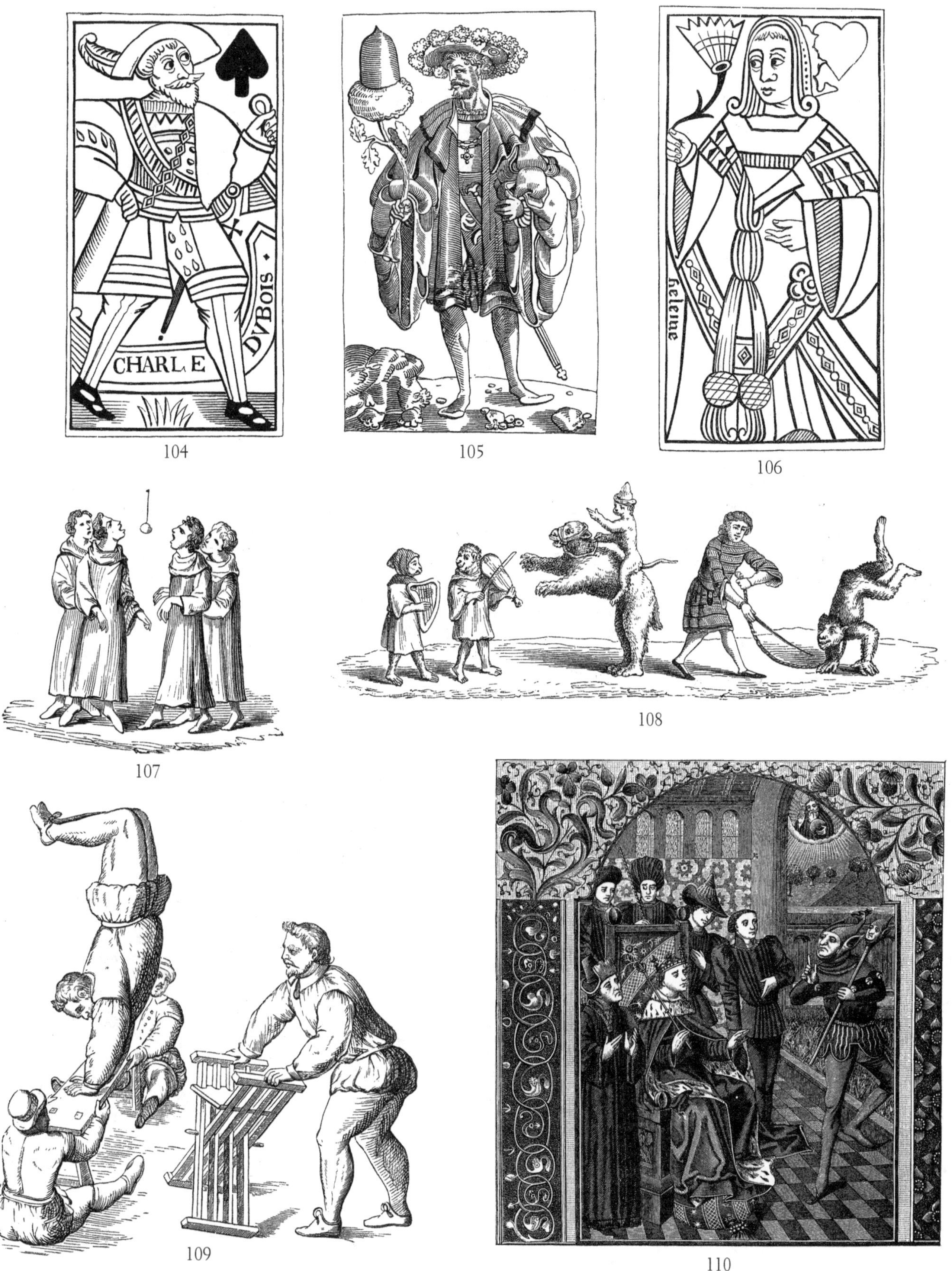

104. Specimen of a pack of cards, 16th century. **105.** King of acorns. **106.** French card for a game of piquet. **107.** The game of bob apple, or swinging apple, 14th century. **108.** Jugglers exhibiting monkeys and bears, 13th century. **109.** Somersaults, 1599. **110.** A court jester; miniature from a French bible, 15th century.

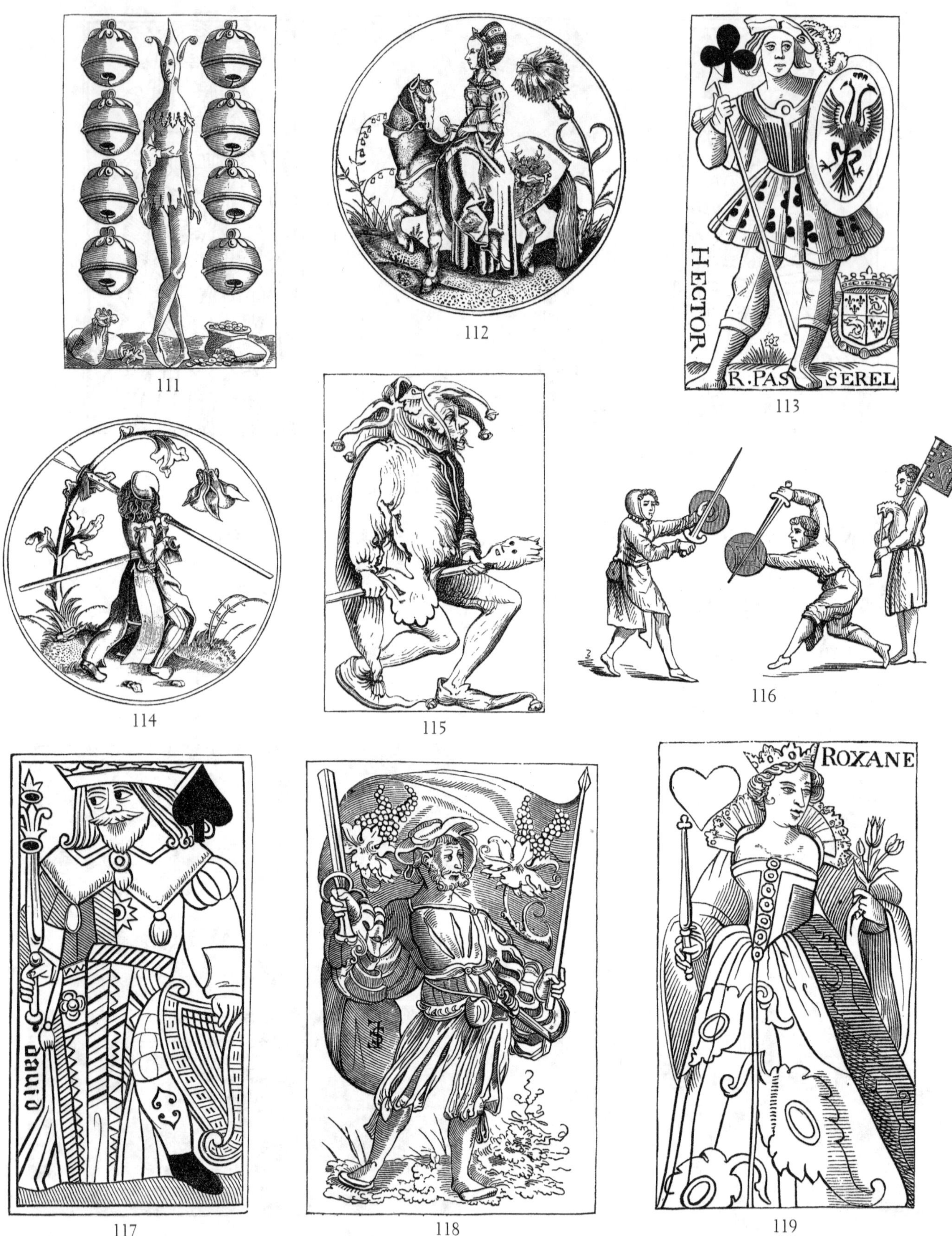

111. Eight of bells. **112.** Queen of carnations. **113.** The "Knave of Clubs" in the packs of cards of R. Passerel and R. Le Cornu, 16th century. **114.** Knave of Columbine. **115.** Court fool. **116.** Sword dance to the sound of the bagpipe. **117.** French card for a game of piquet. **118.** The "two" of a pack of German Lansquenet cards. **119.** Roxane, queen of hearts.

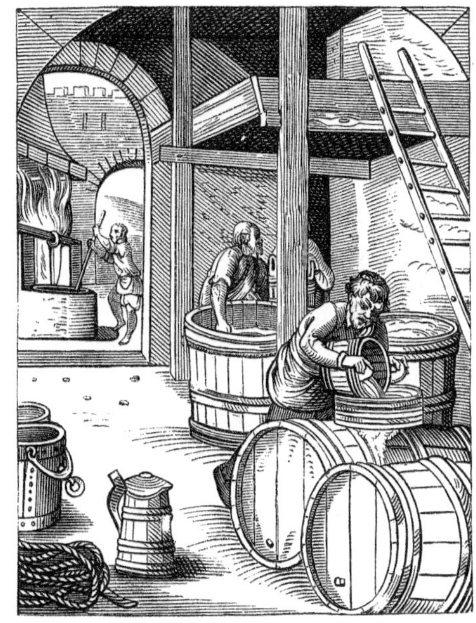

120

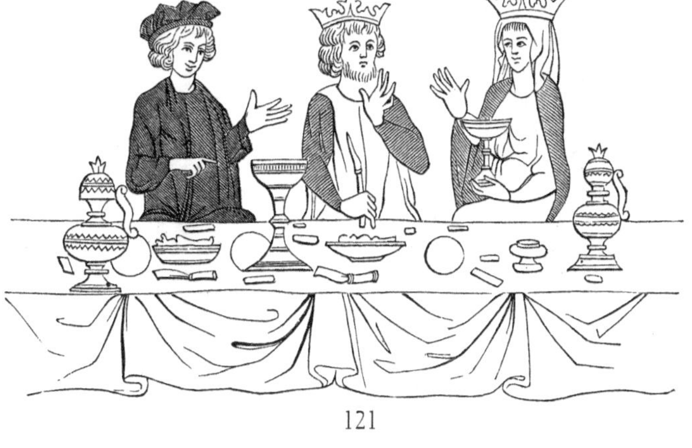

121

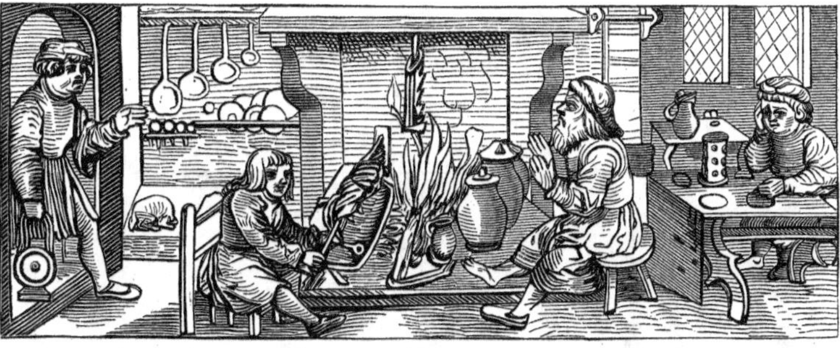

123

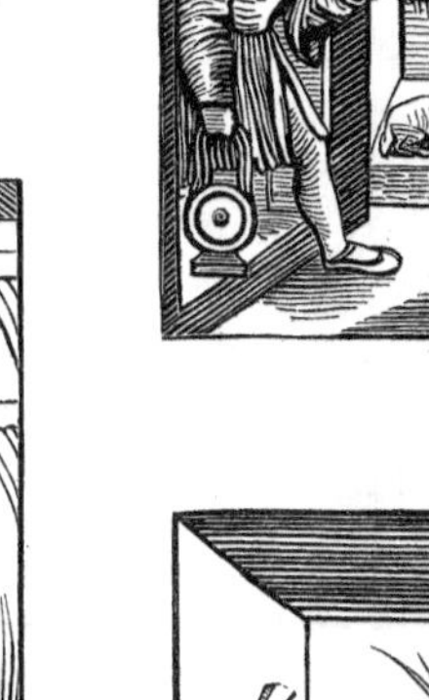

122

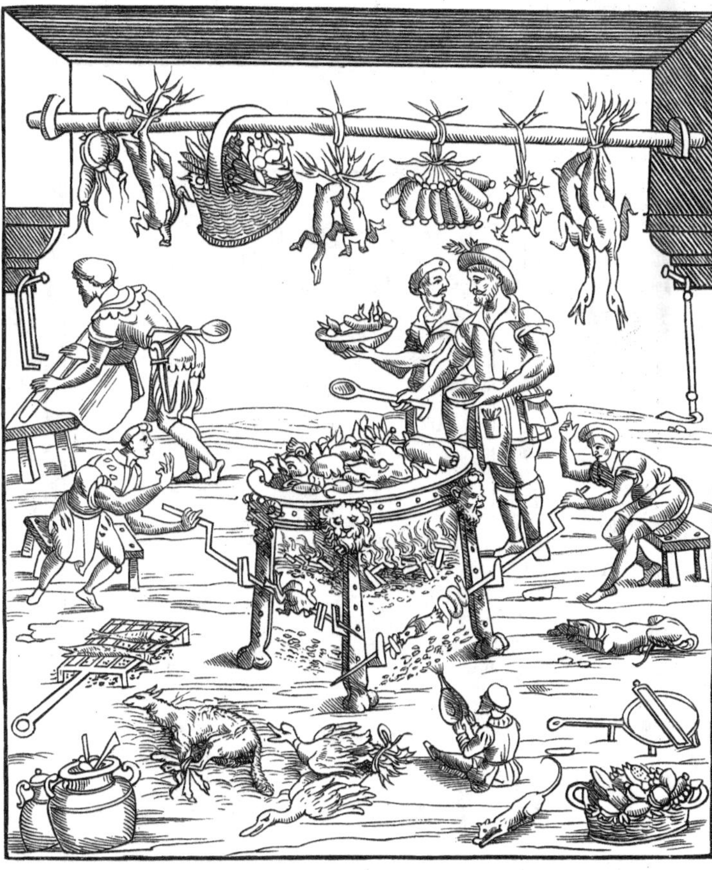

125

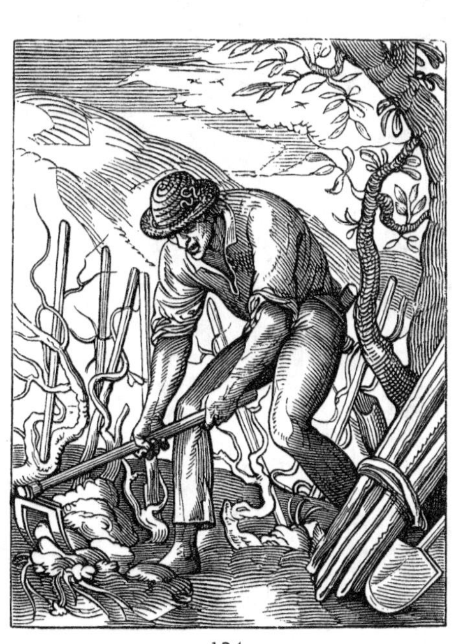

124

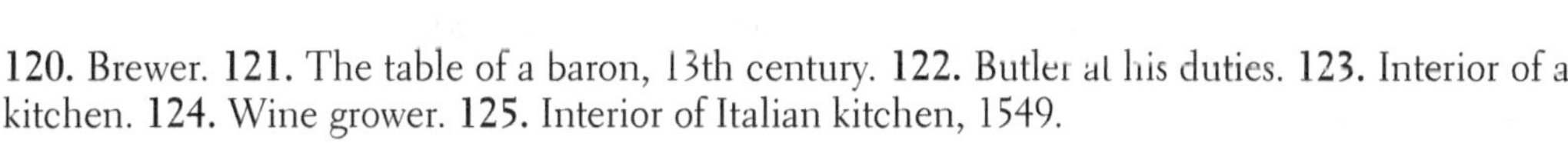

120. Brewer. **121.** The table of a baron, 13th century. **122.** Butler at his duties. **123.** Interior of a kitchen. **124.** Wine grower. **125.** Interior of Italian kitchen, 1549.

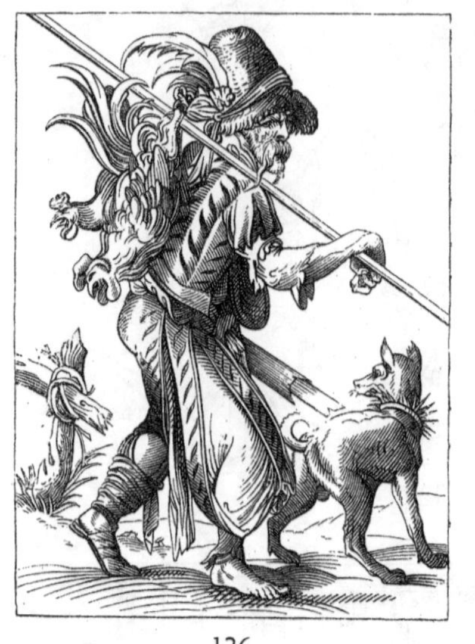

126

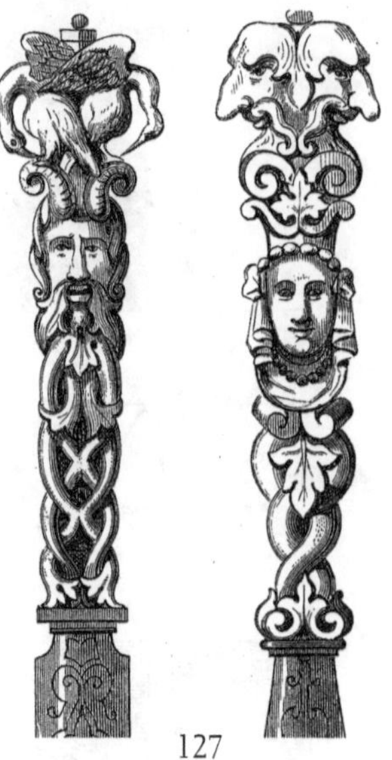

127

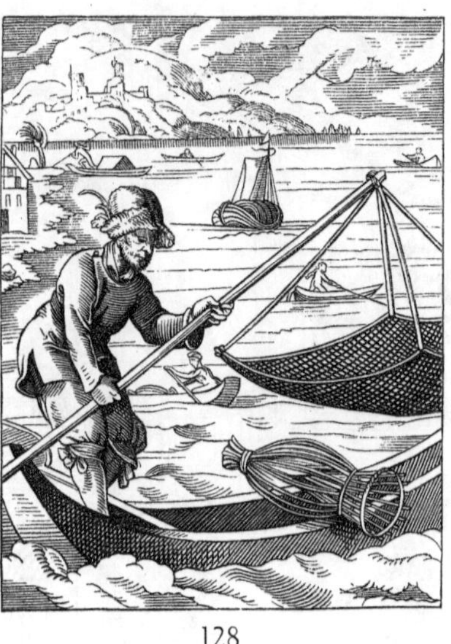

128

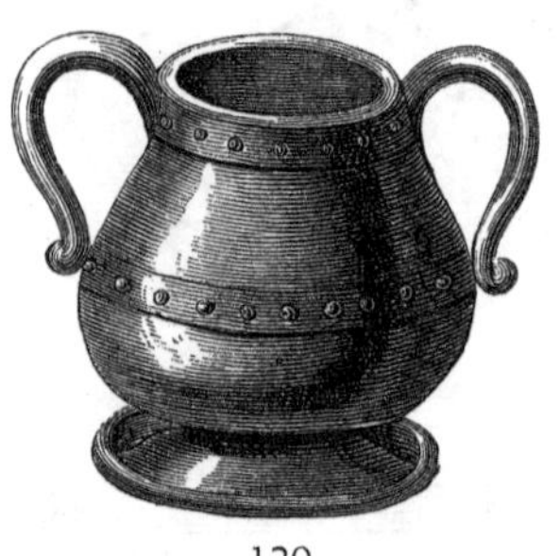

129

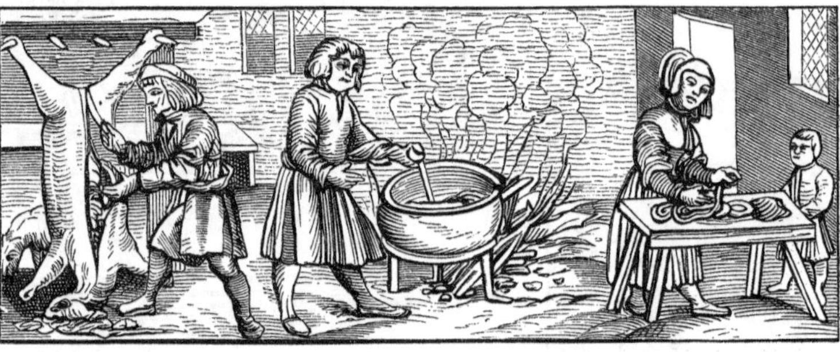

130

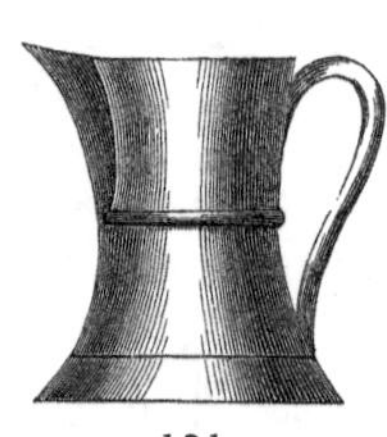

131

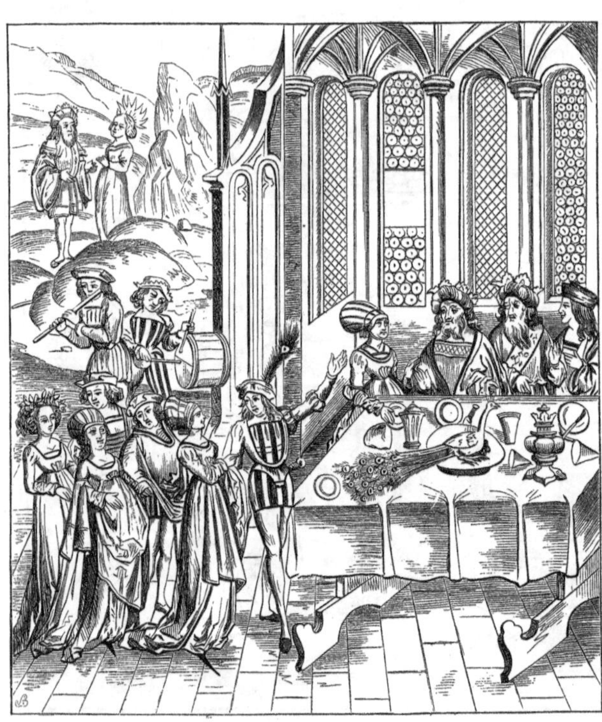

132

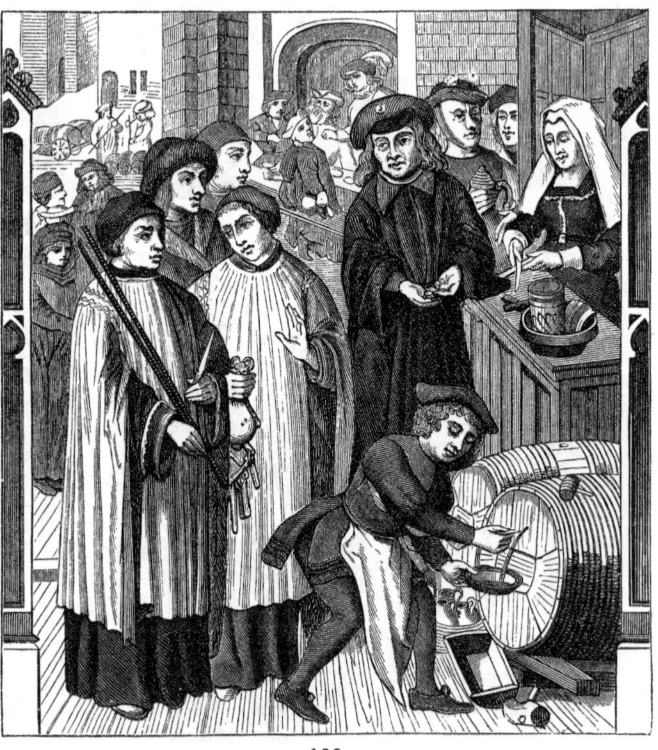

133

126. The poulterer, 16th century. **127.** Knife handles. **128.** River fisherman. **129.** Double-handled pot. **130.** Interior of a kitchen. **131.** Metal boiler, or tin pot. **132.** State banquet—serving the peacock, 1517. **133.** Dues on wines.

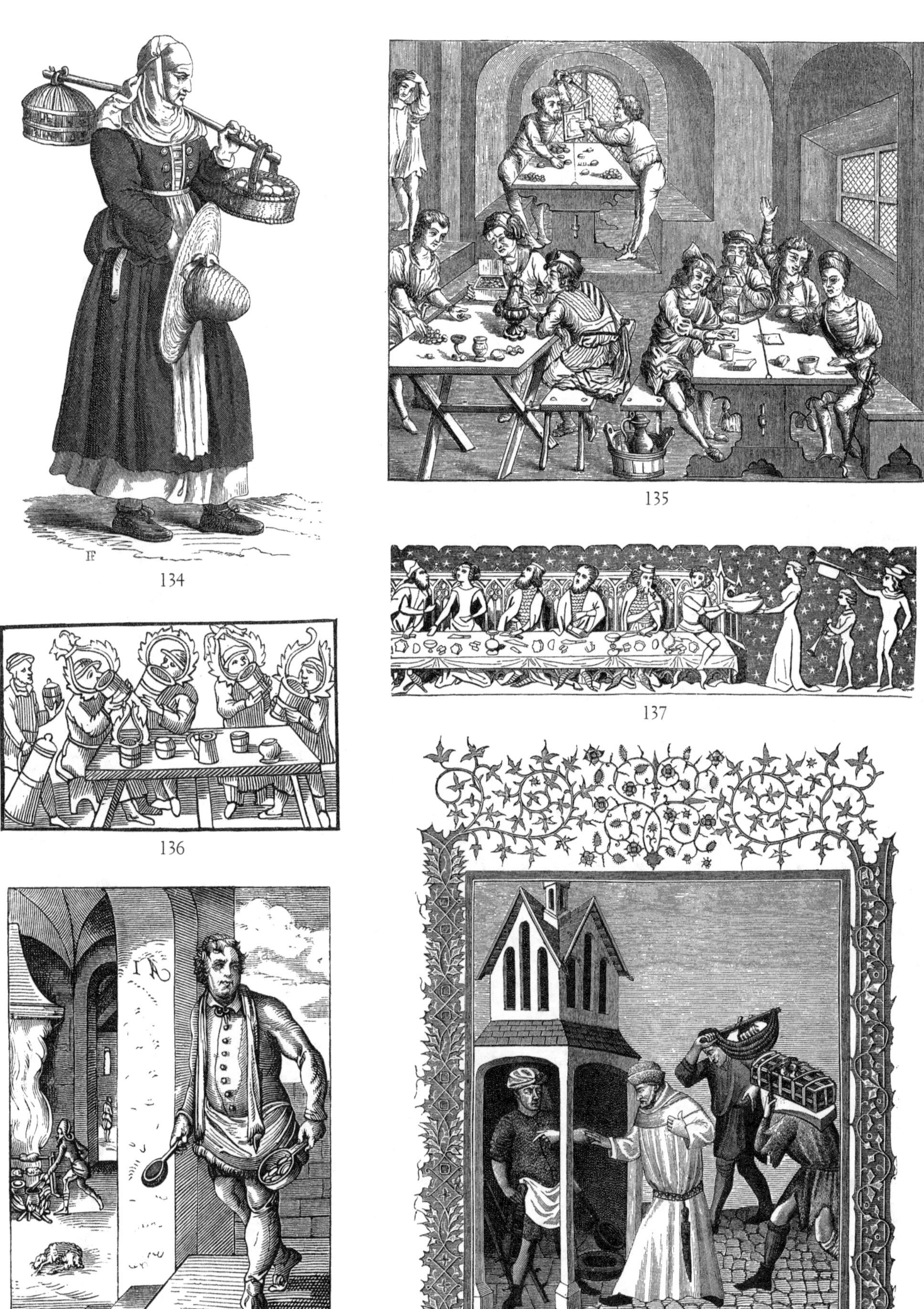

134
135
136
137
138
139

134. Dealer in eggs. **135.** Interior of a hostelry. **136.** Great drinkers of the north. **137.** State banquet. **138.** Cook. **139.** The cook, 15th century.

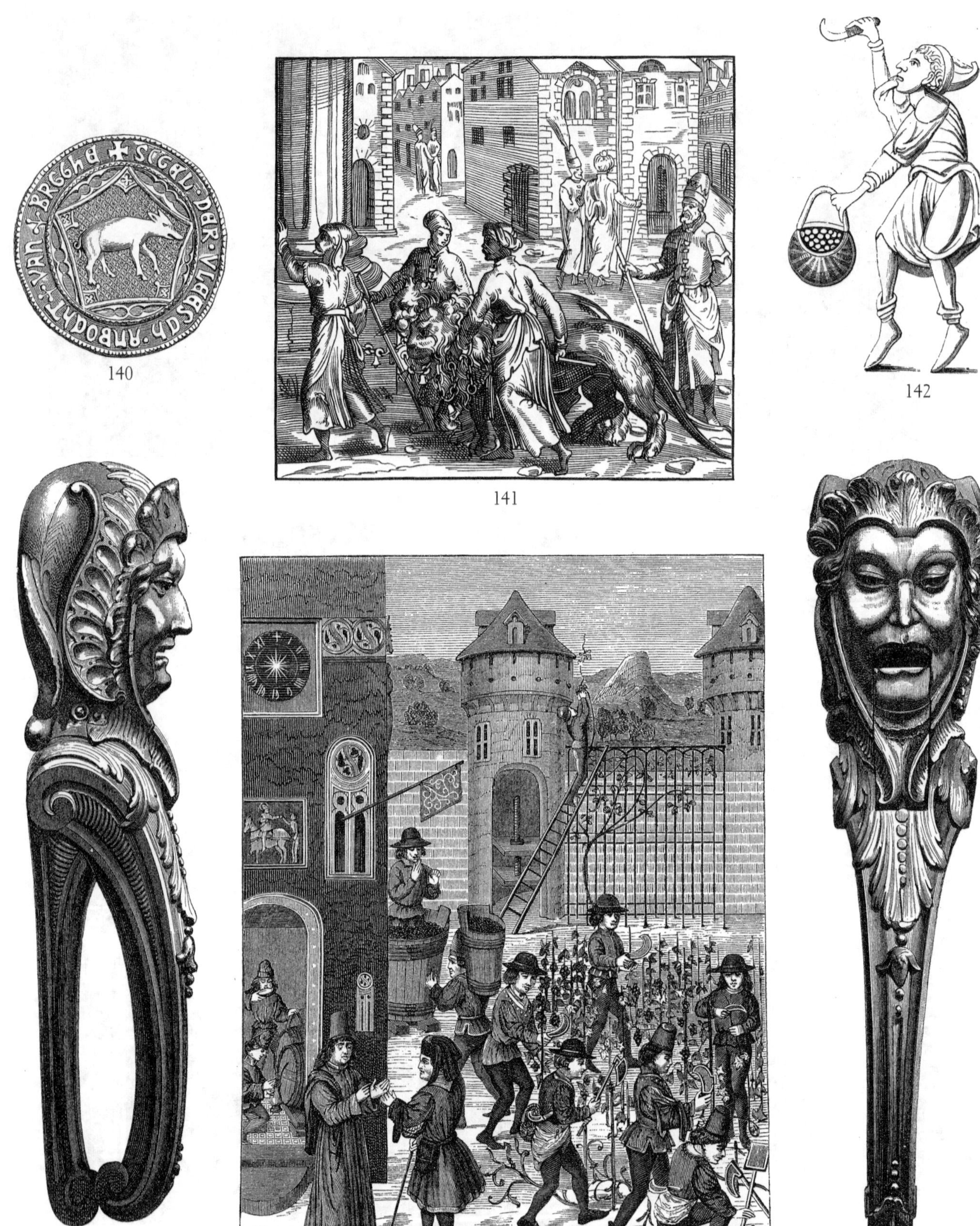

140. Counter seal of the butchers of Bruges. **141.** Merchants and lion-keepers, Constantinople, 1575. **142.** Vintager. **143.** Nutcracker. **144.** Cultivation of fruit. **145.** Nutcracker.

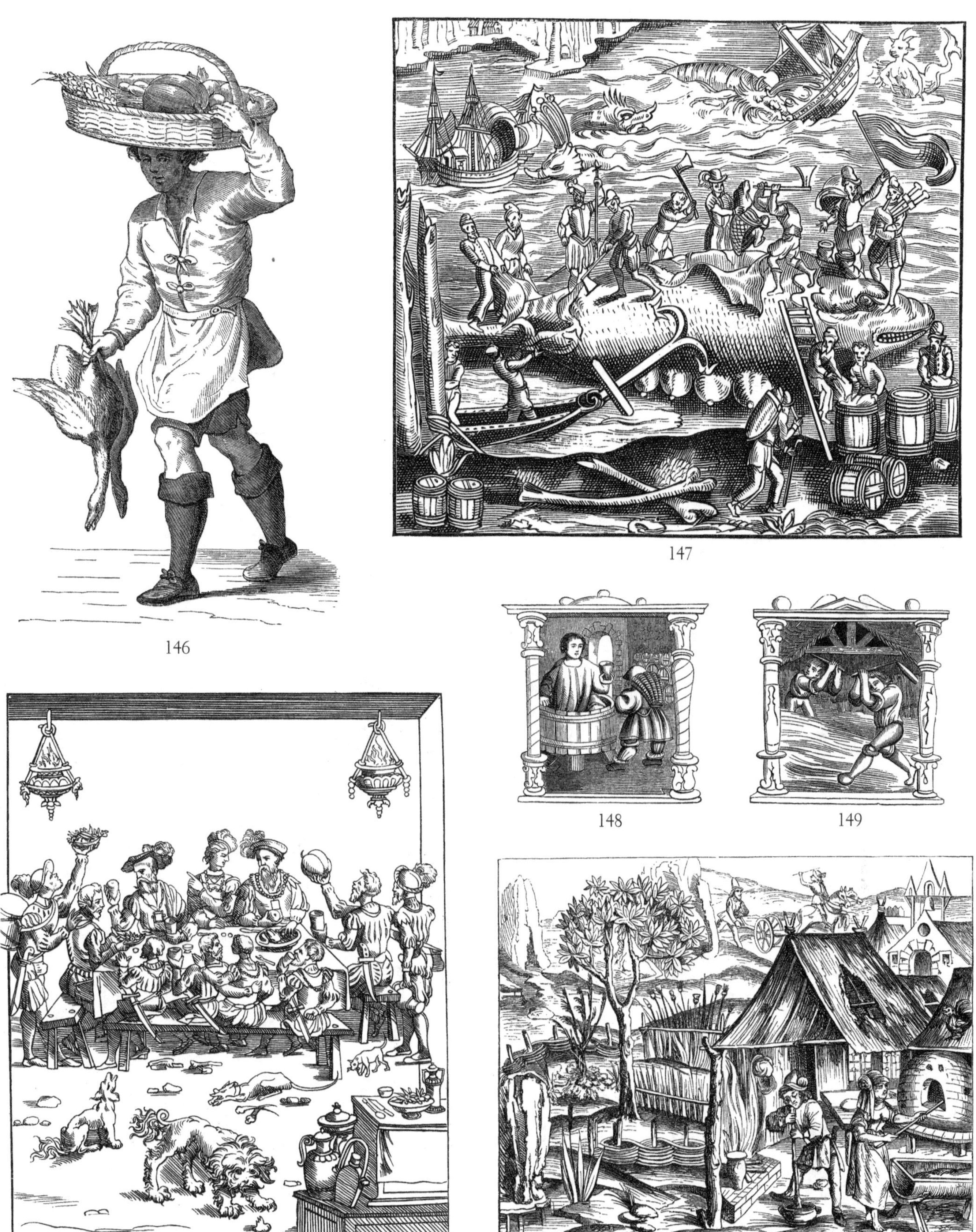

146. Poultry dealer. 147. Whale fishing. 148. Treading the grape. 149. Corn-threshing, from the calendar of a *Book of Hours,* 16th century. 150. The *Issue de Table,* 1549. 151. Cultivation of grain in use amongst the peasants, and the manufacture of barley and oat bread, 1517.

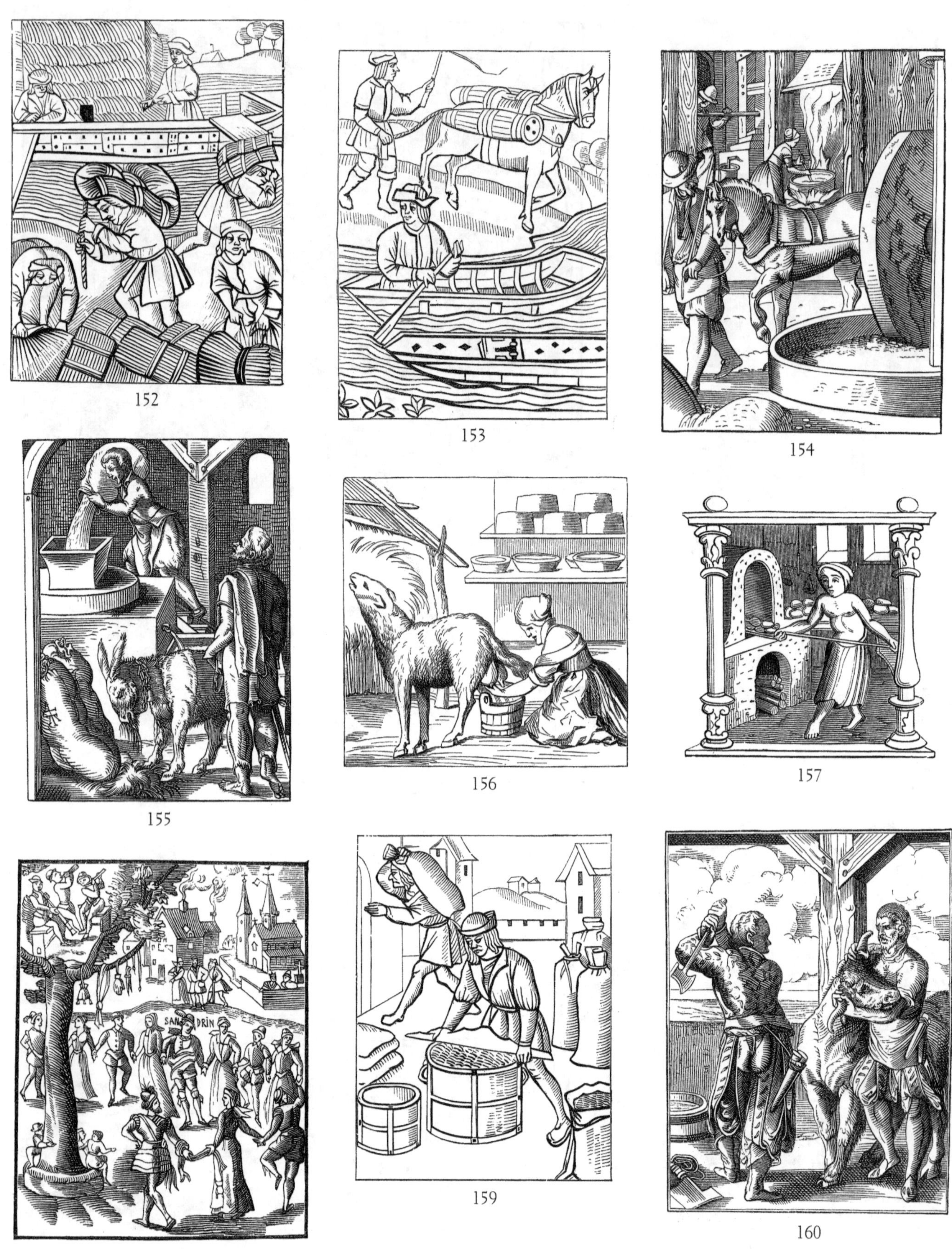

152. Hay carriers. **153.** Conveyance of fish by water and land. **154.** Manufacture of oil. **155.** Miller. **156.** Manufacture of cheeses in Switzerland. **157.** Bread-making, from the calendar of a *Book of Hours,* 16th century. **158.** Village feast. **159.** Measurers of corn. **160.** Butcher and his servant.

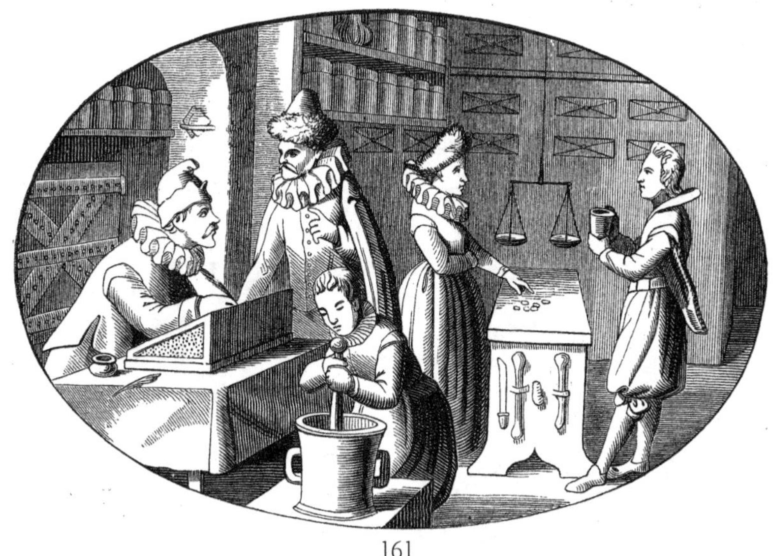

161

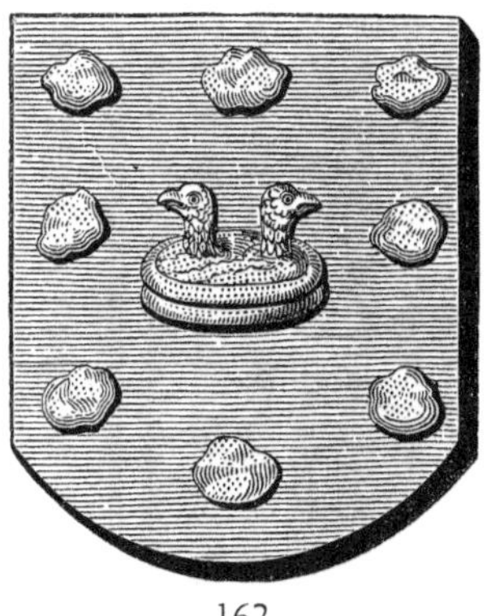

162

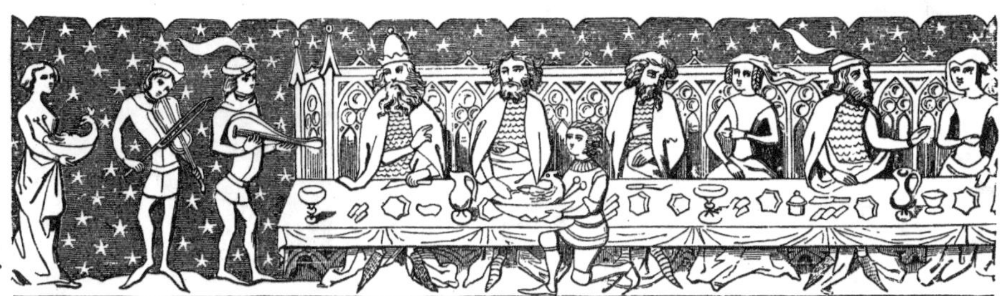

163

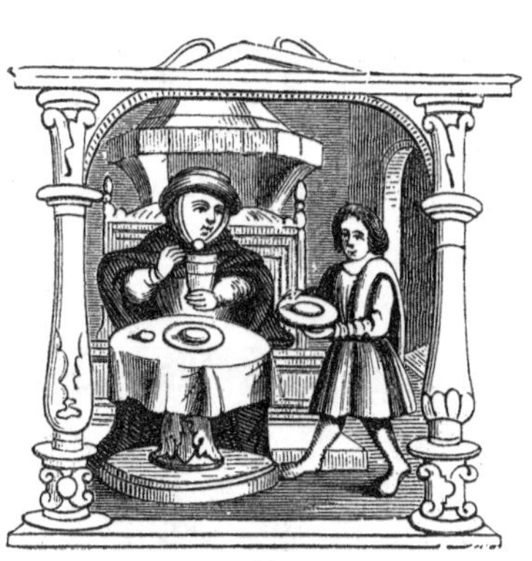

164

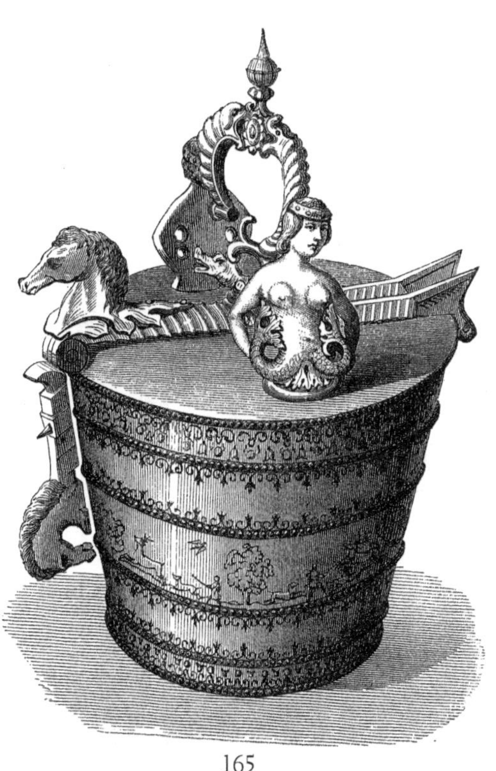

165

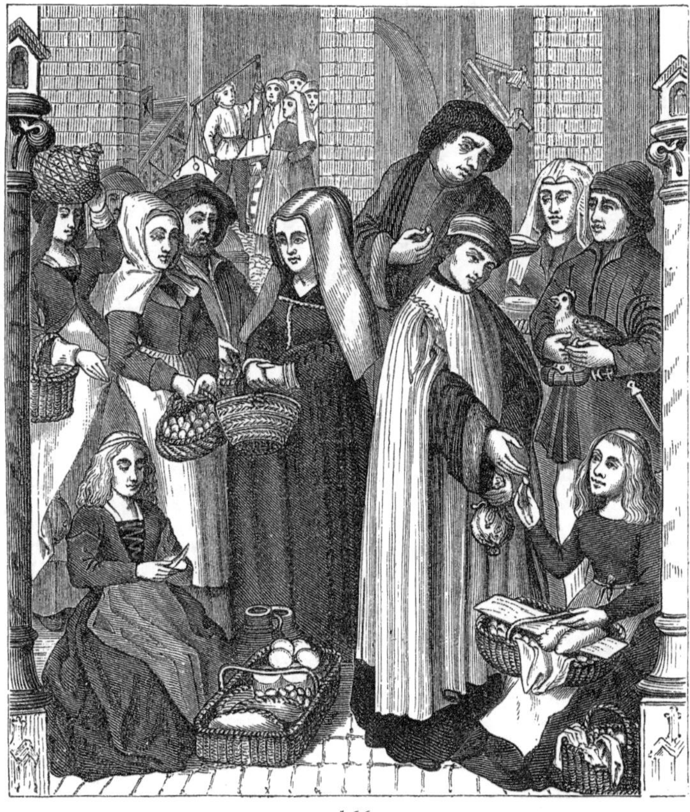

166

161. Shop of a grocer and druggist. **162.** Banner of the corporation of pastry cooks of Tonnerre. **163.** State banquet. **164.** Burgess at meals. **165.** Standard weight in brass of the fish market at Mans. **166.** Toll on markets levied by a cleric, 15th century.

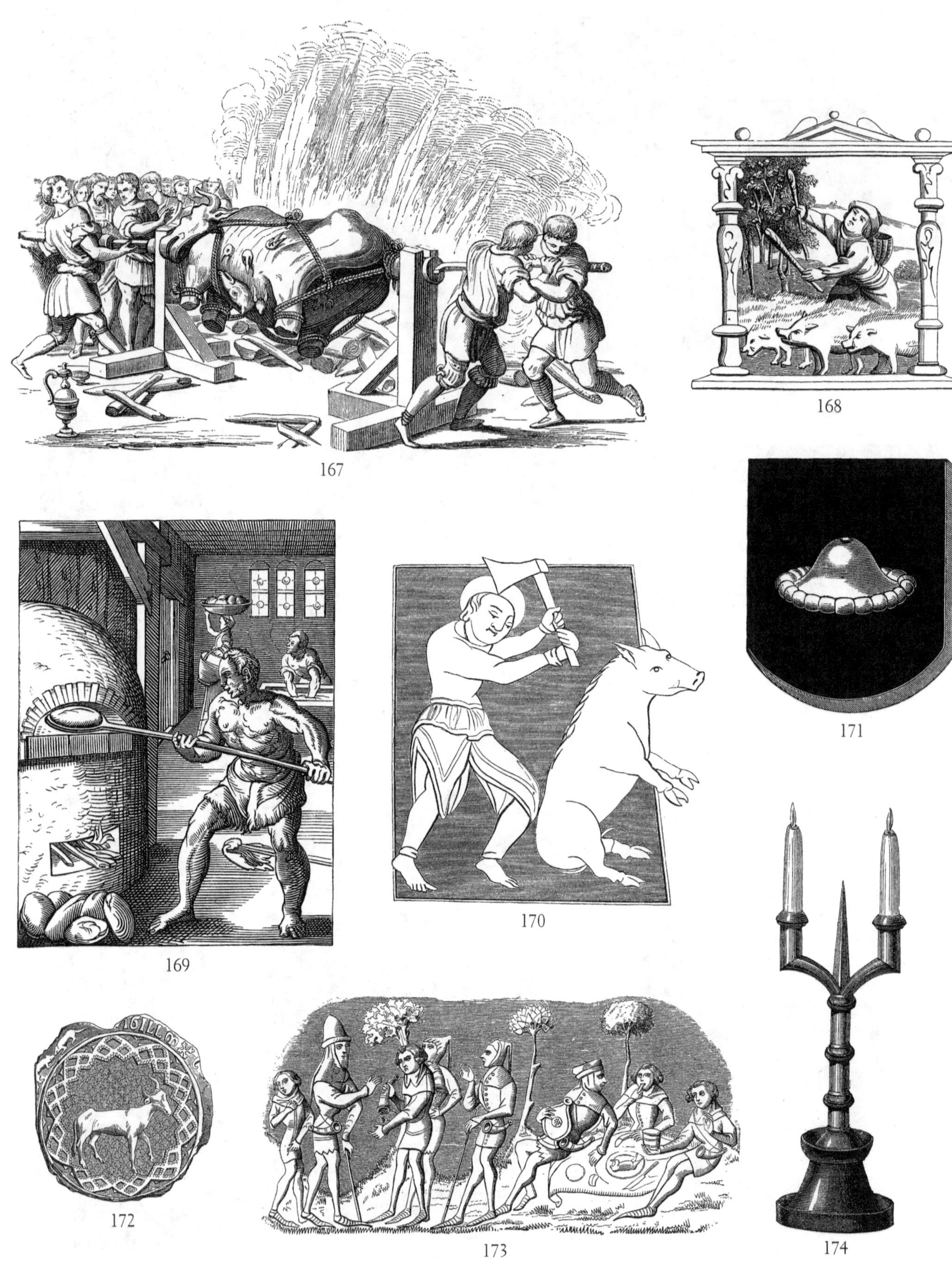

167. Free distribution of bread, meat, and wine to the people, 1530. **168.** Swineherd. **169.** Baker. **170.** The pork butcher, 14th century. **171.** Banner of the corporation of pastry cooks of Caen. **172.** Seal of the butchers of Bruges. **173.** Hunting meal. **174.** Two-branched candlestick.

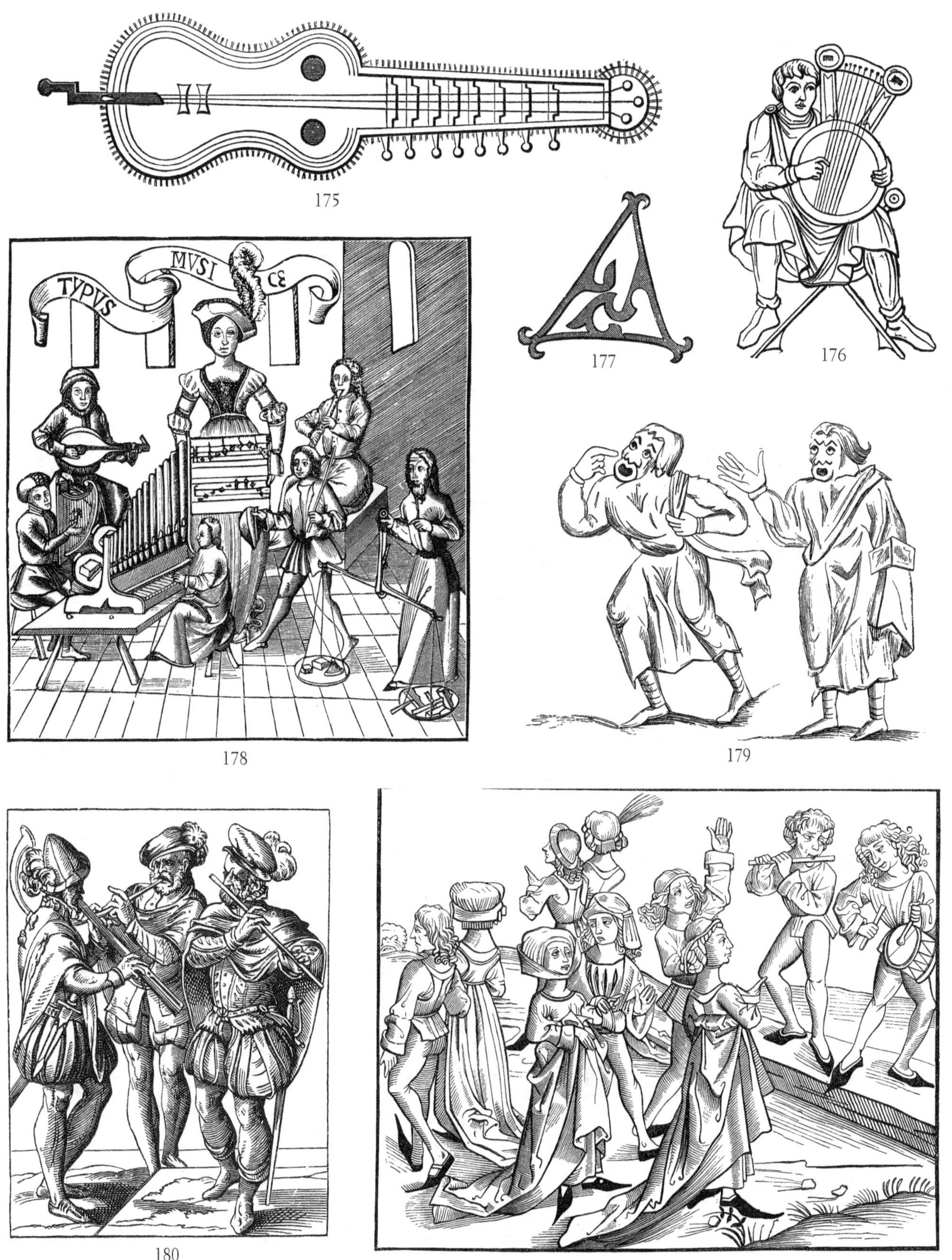

175. Organistrum, 9th century. 176. Psalterion, 12th century. 177. Triangle of the ninth century. 178. Personification of music. 179. The slave and the lawyer—representative characters of the ancient theatre, 10th century. 180. German musicians playing on the flute and goat's horn. 181. Dancers on Christmas night punished for their impiety.

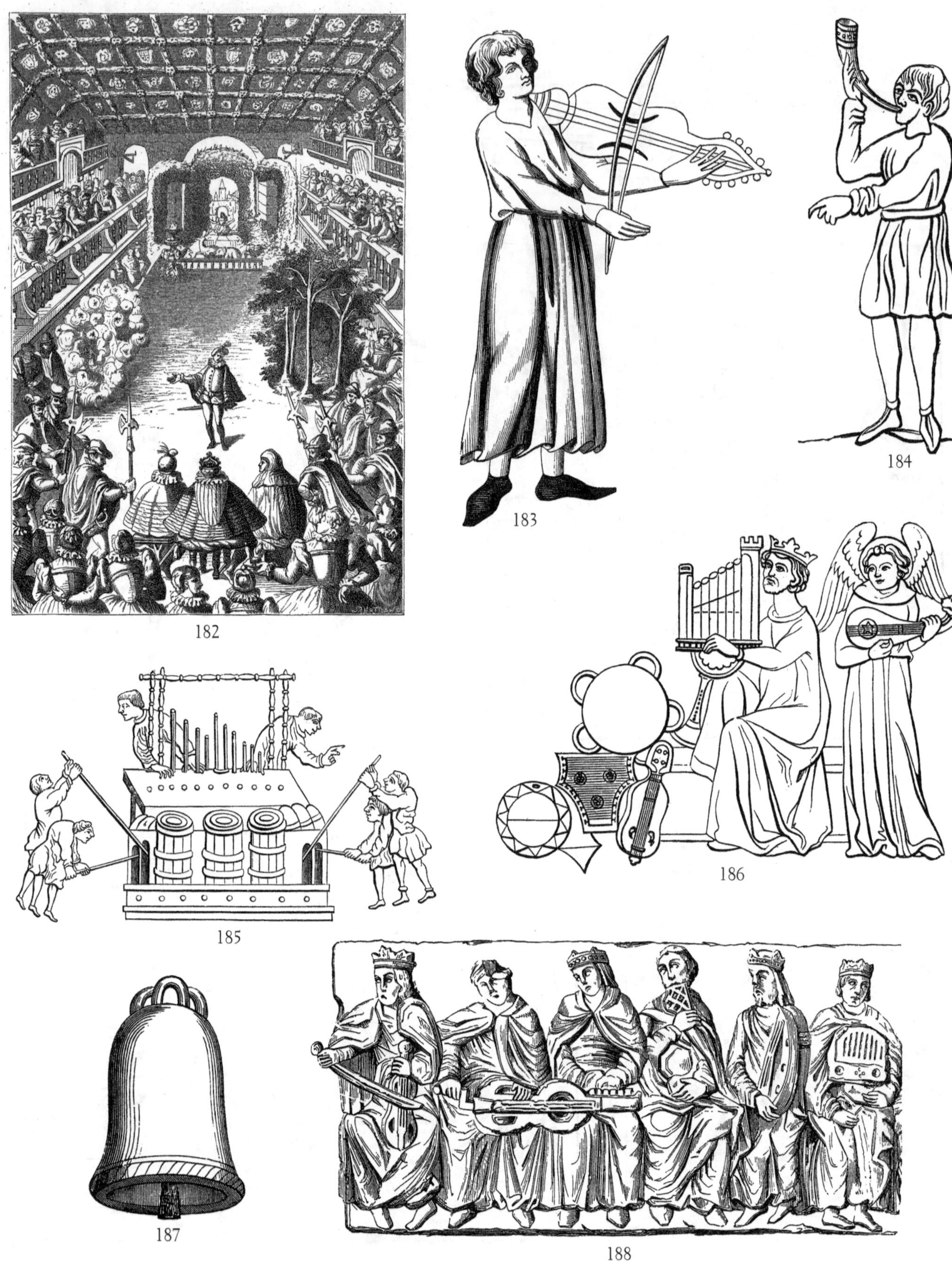

182. Representation of a ballet before Henry III and his court, in the gallery of the Louvre, 1582. **183.** Ballad singer accompanying himself upon the violin. **184.** Curved trumpet, 11th century. **185.** Great organ, with bellows and double keyboard. **186.** Concert and musical instruments, 13th century. **187.** *Tintinnabulum*, hand-bell of the ninth century. **188.** Concert; a bas-relief, 11th century.

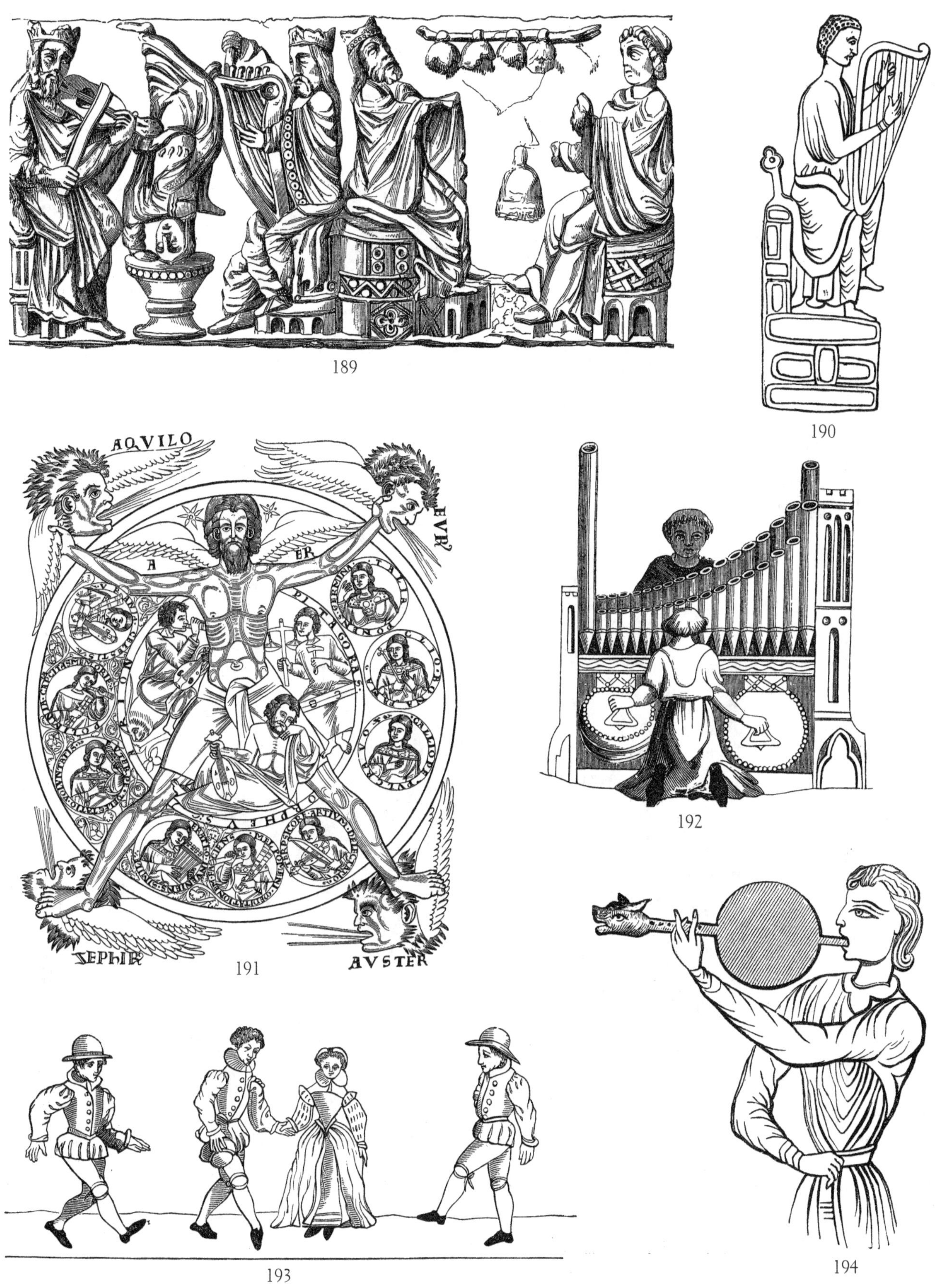

189. Concert; a bas-relief, 11th century. **190.** Harp-player, 15th century. **191.** Poetry and music, miniature, 13th century. **192.** Organ with single keyboard, 14th century. **193.** Dance called La Gaillarde. **194.** Chorus with single bell-end with holes, 9th century.

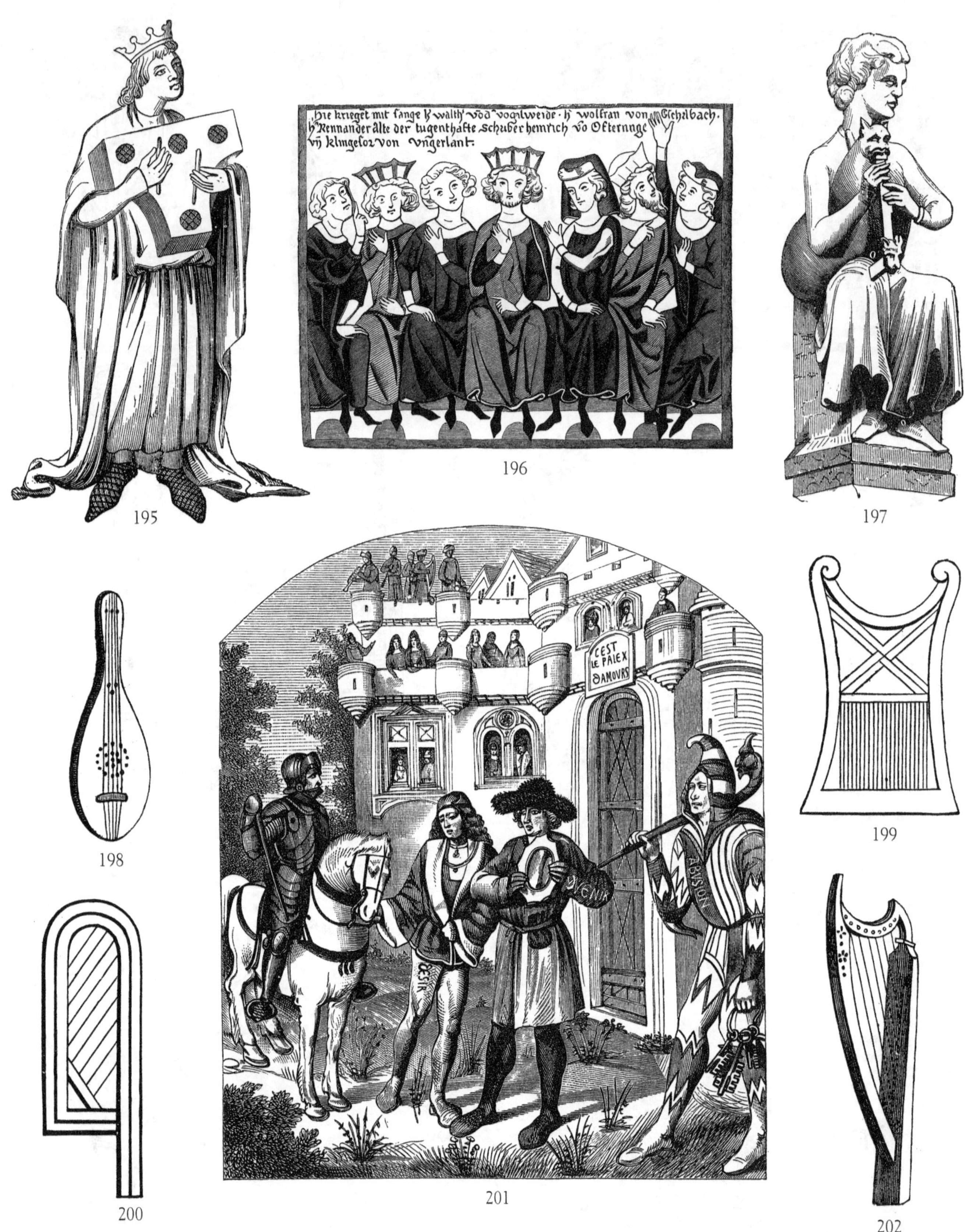

195. Performer on the *Psalterion,* 14th century. **196.** Poetical and musical congress at Wartburg, 1207; 14th century. **197.** Bagpiper, 13th century. **198.** Five-stringed lute, 13th century. **199.** Buckler-shaped psaltery with many strings, 9th century. **200.** Choron, 9th century. **201.** "How the actor lost his way, and arrived in front of the Palace of Love, into which Desire bid him enter, while Remembrance held him back," miniature, 15th century. **202.** Minstrel's harp, 15th century.

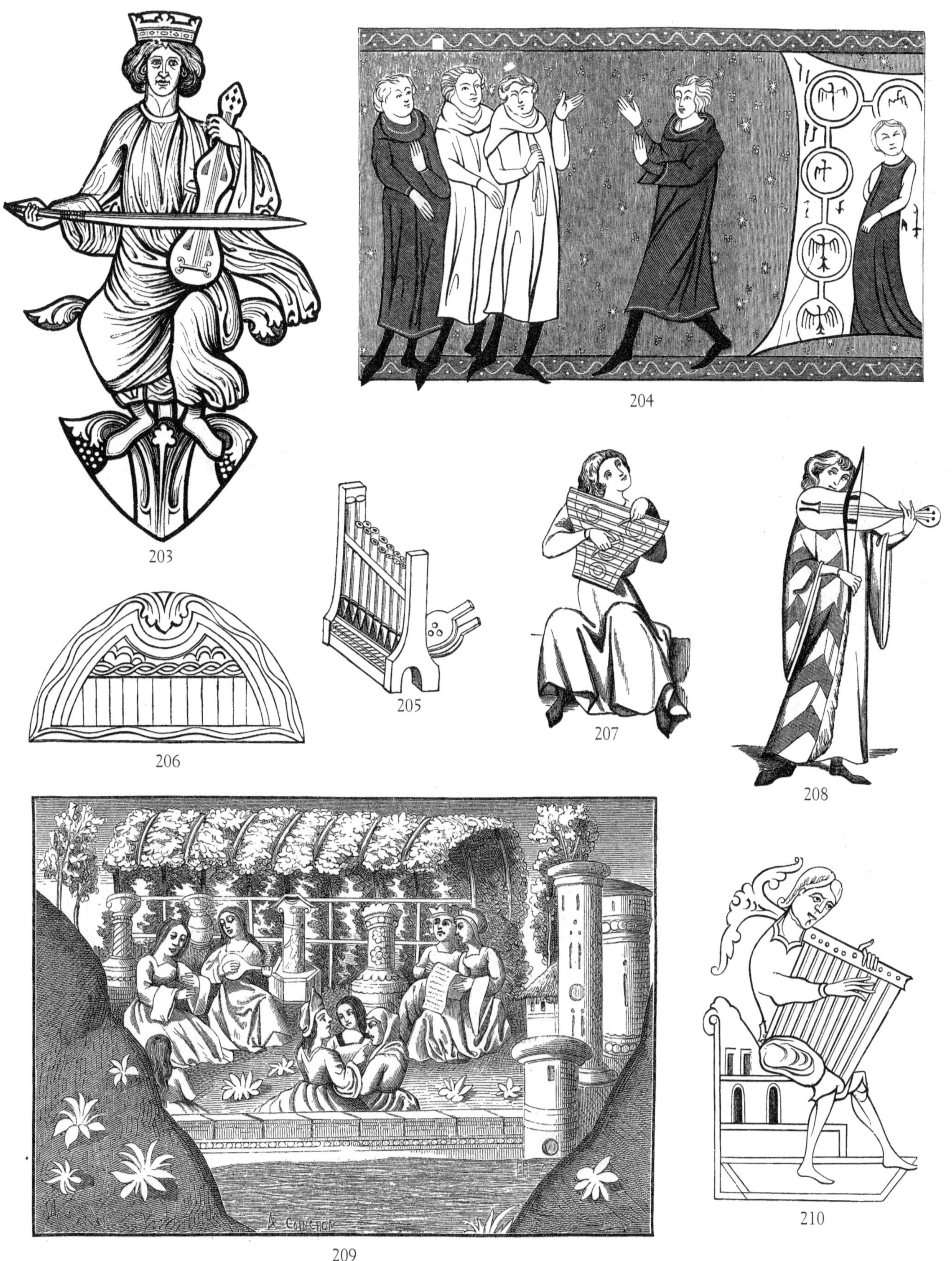

203. King David playing on a rote. **204.** Jugglers performing in public. **205.** Portable organ, 15th century. **206.** Nabulum, 9th century. **207.** Minnesingers, 14th century. **208.** Minnesingers, 14th century. **209.** Castle of Alamond and its enchantments. **210.** Psaltery to produce a prolonged sound.

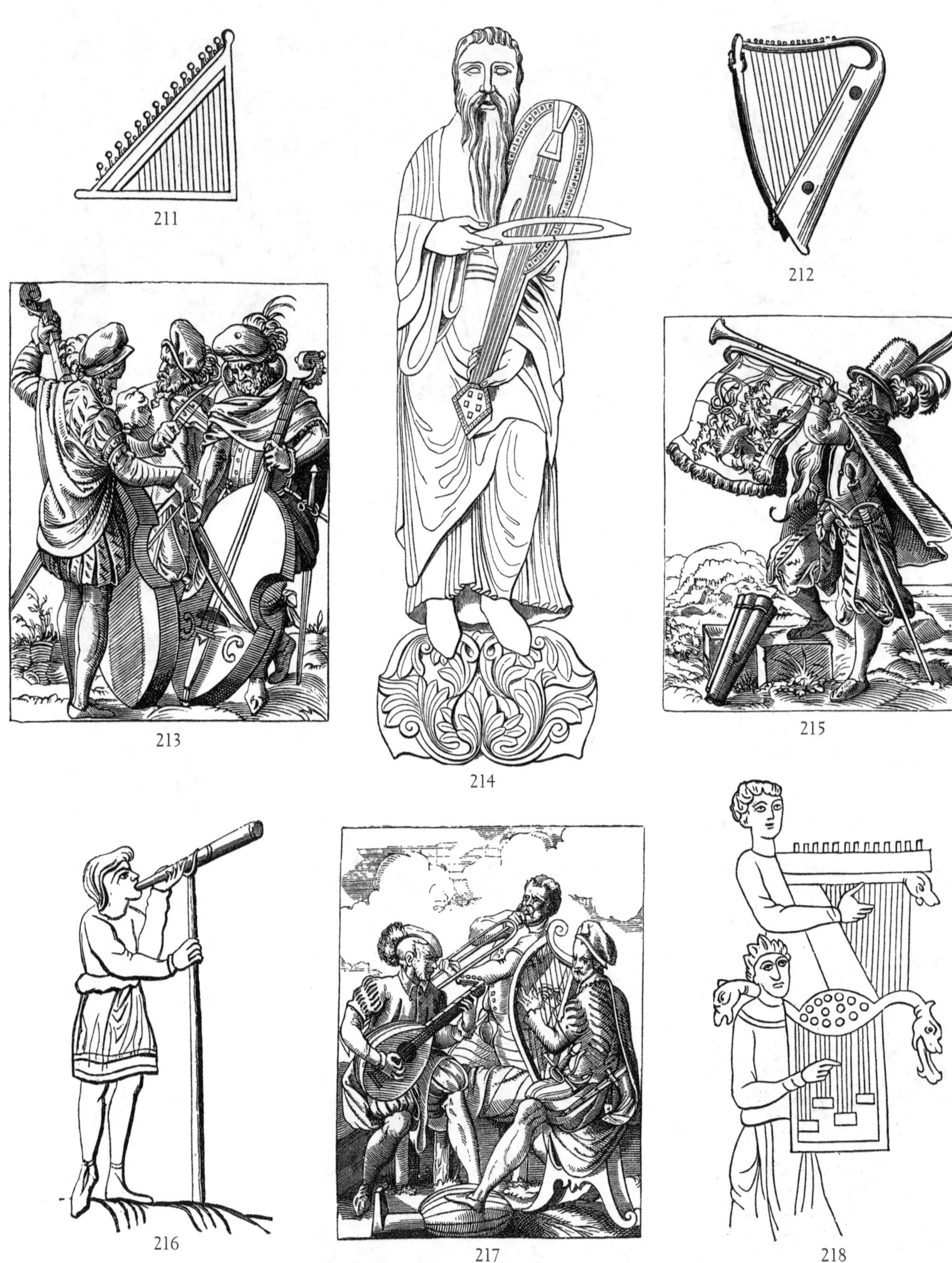

211. Triangular Saxon harp, 9th century. **212.** Fifteen-stringed harp, 12th century. **213.** German musicians playing on the flute and goat's horn. **214.** Trouveur accompanying himself upon the violin. **215.** German musician sounding the military trumpet. **216.** Straight trumpet with stand, 11th century. **217.** German musicians playing the lute and the guitar, 16th century. **218.** Harpists, 12th century.

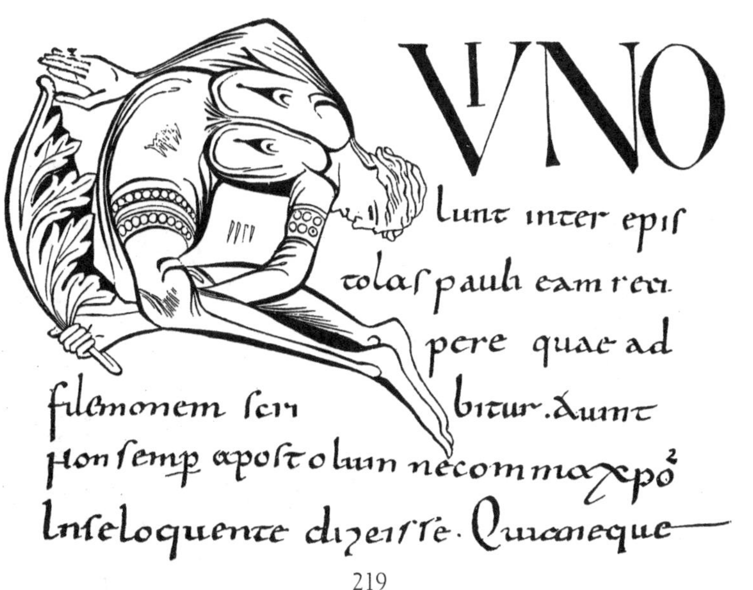

219

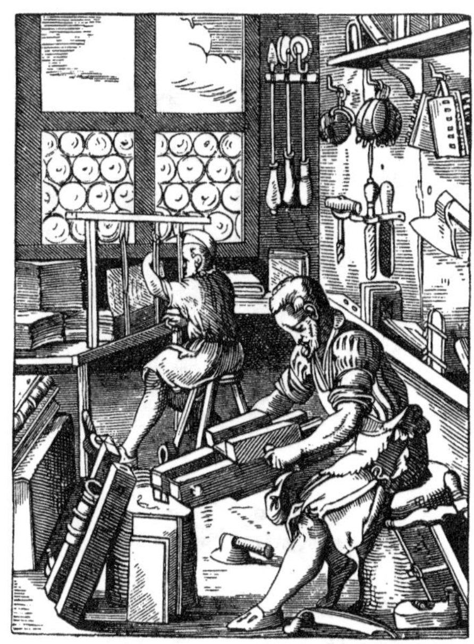

220

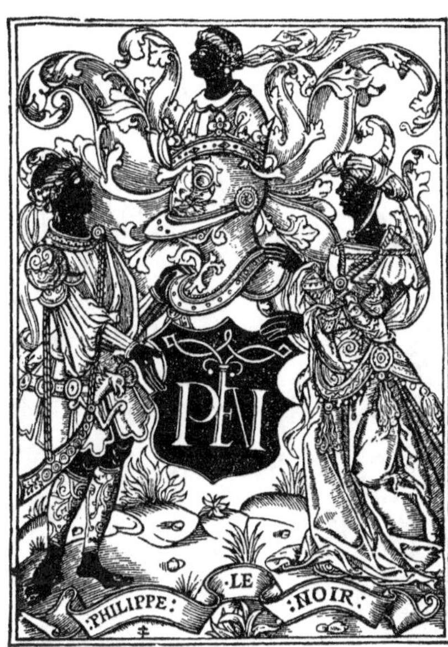

222

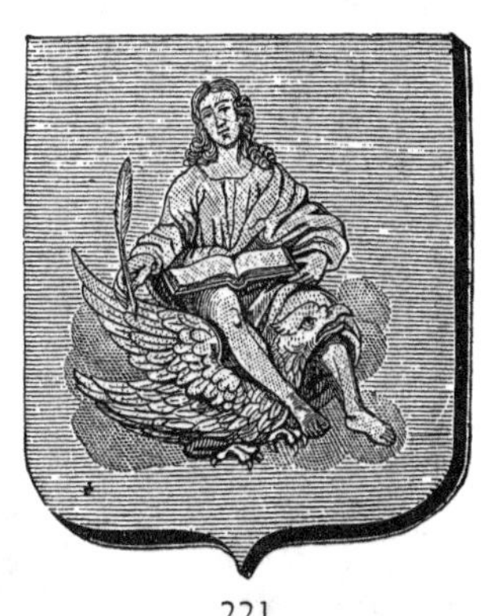

221

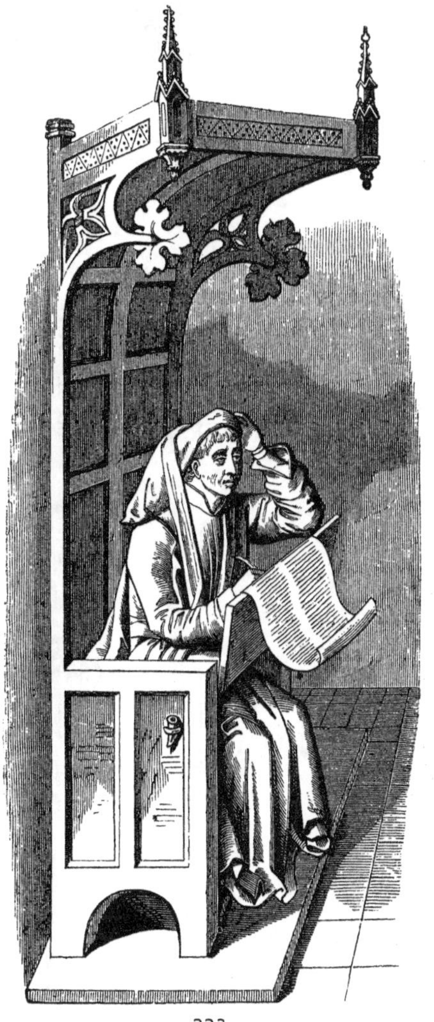

223

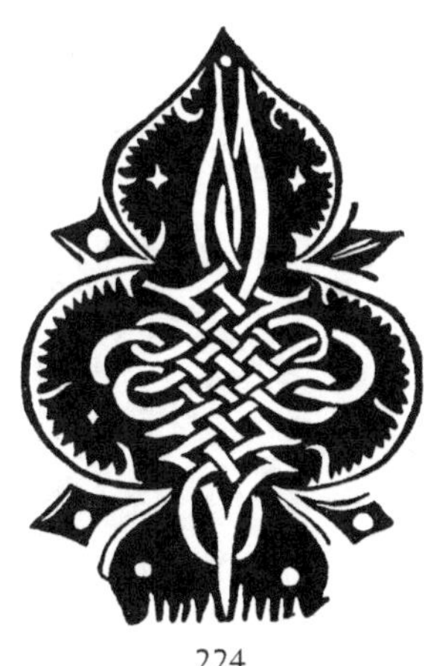

224

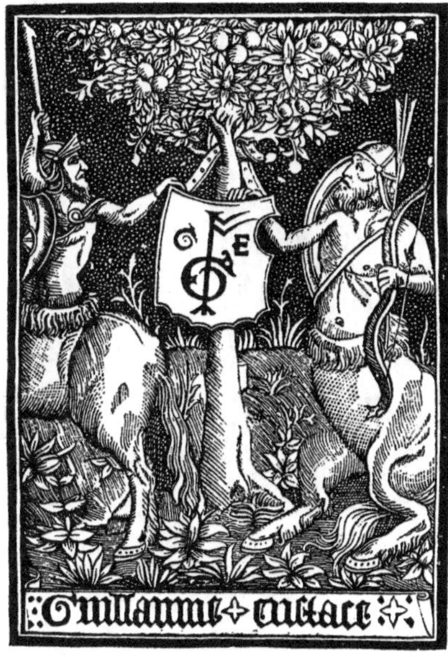

225

219. Writing of the tenth century. **220.** Bookbinder's work room. **221.** Banner of the corporation of printers-booksellers of Autun. **222.** Mark of Philippe le Noir, printer, bookseller, and bookbinder at Paris, 1536. **223.** A compiler, 15th century. **224.** Mark of Arnold de Keyser, printer at Ghent, 1480. **225.** Mark of William Eustace, bookseller and binder, Paris, 1512.

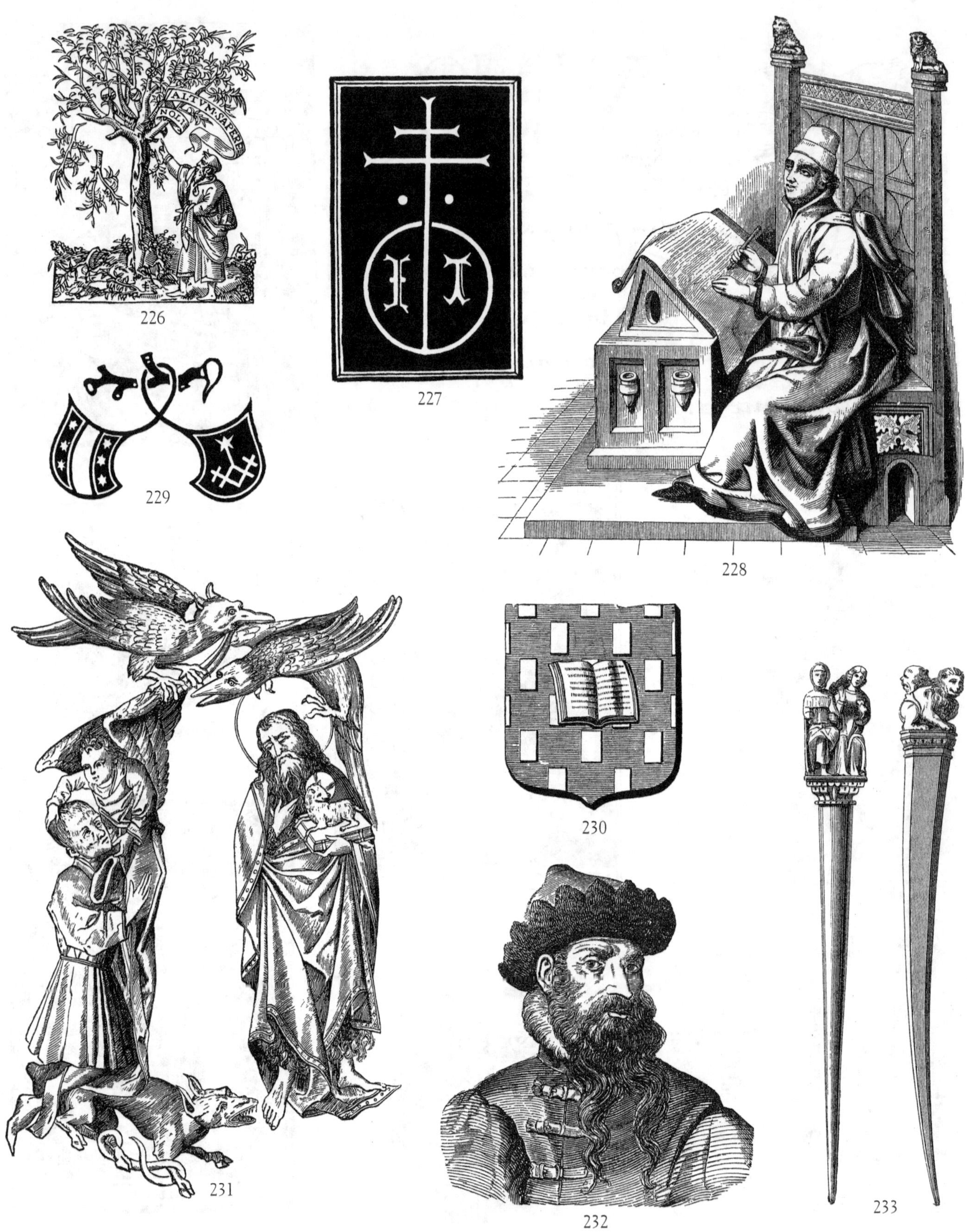

226. Mark of Charles Estienne, printer at Paris. **227.** Mark of Trechsel, printer at Lyons, 1489. **228.** Copyist writing upon a sheet of vellum, 15th century. **229.** Mark of Fust and Schoeffer, Printers, 15th century. **230.** Banner of the papermakers of Paris. **231.** Facsimile of the letter N from the "Grotesque Alphabet," 1466. **232.** Portrait of Gutenberg, 16th century. **233.** Styli used in writing, 14th century.

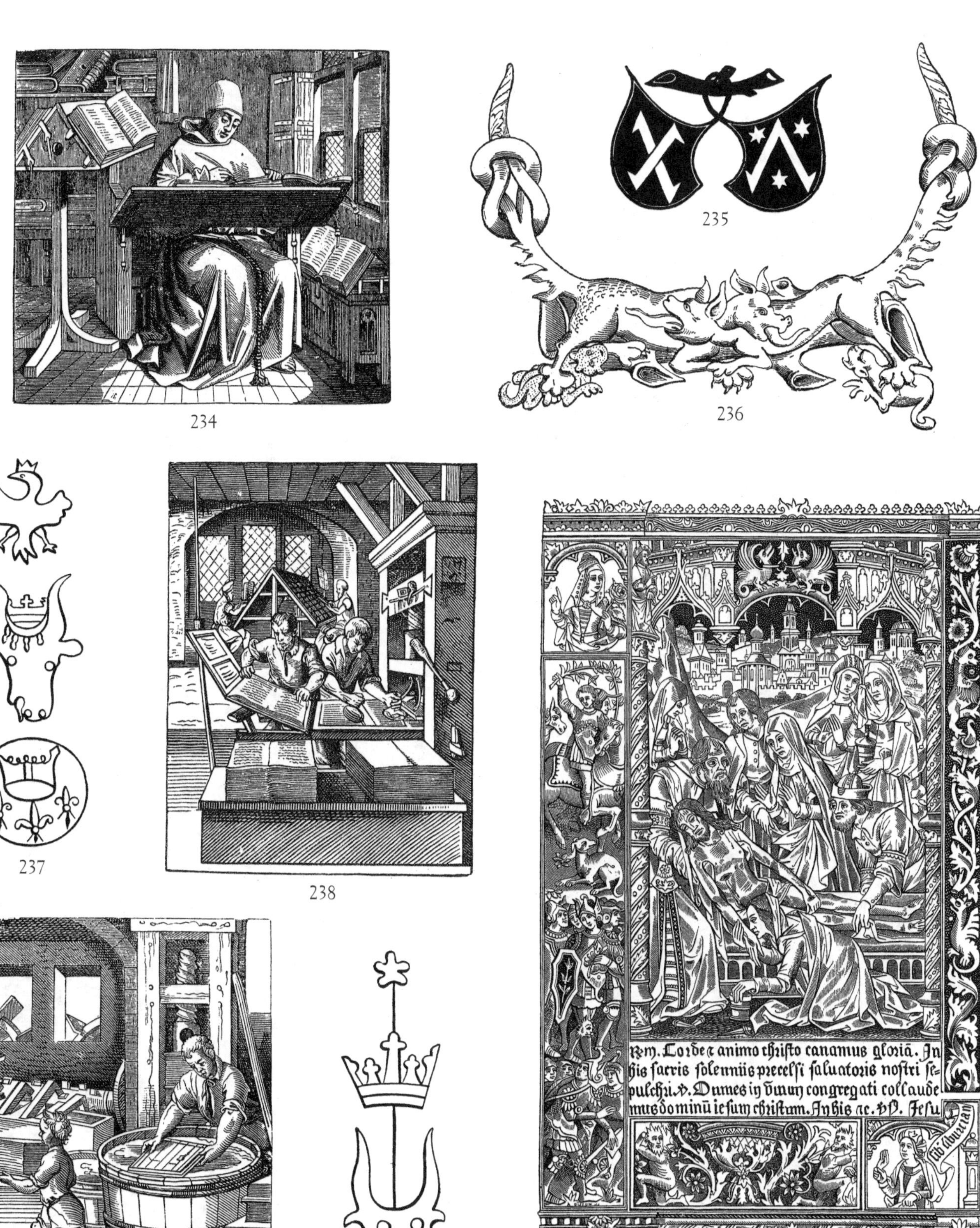

234. Scribe or copyist in his workroom, 15th century. **235.** Mark of Gérard Lecu, printer at Gouwe, 1482. **236.** Calligraphic ornament from a charter of the University of Paris, 15th century. **237.** Three water-marks on paper, 14th to 15th centuries. **238.** Interior of a printing office, 16th century. **239.** Paper maker. **240.** Water-mark on paper, 14th or 15th century. **241.** Facsimile of a page of a *Livre d'Heures*, Paris, 1512.

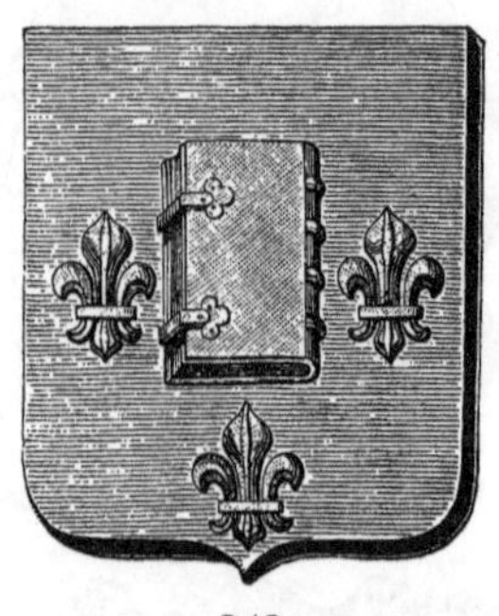

242

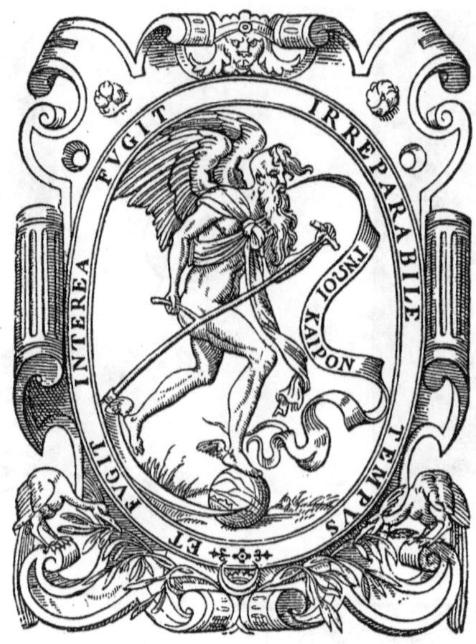

243

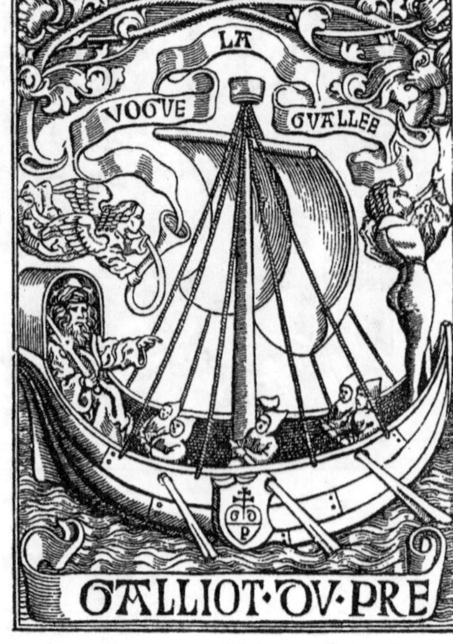

244

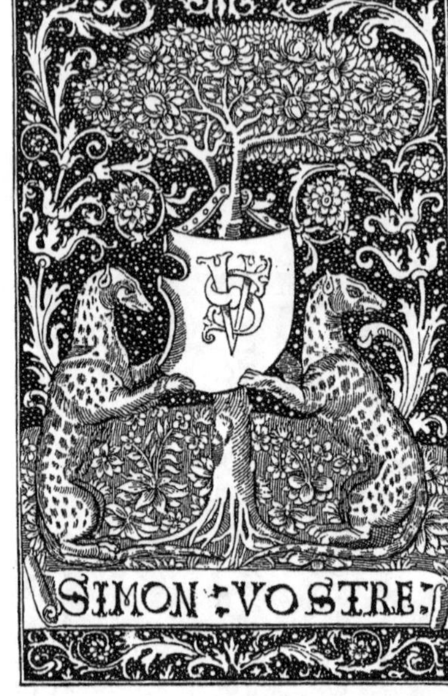

245

Fait et imprime
a Bruges par colard
mansion lan et jour
dessusdis

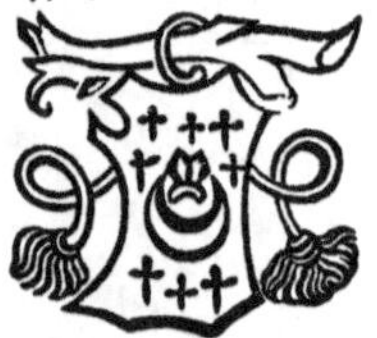

246

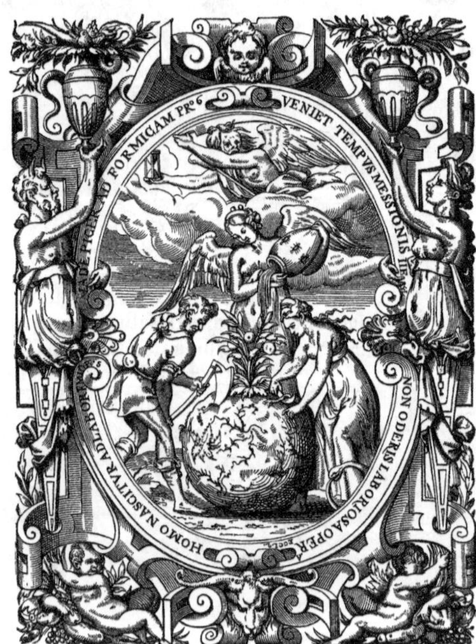

247

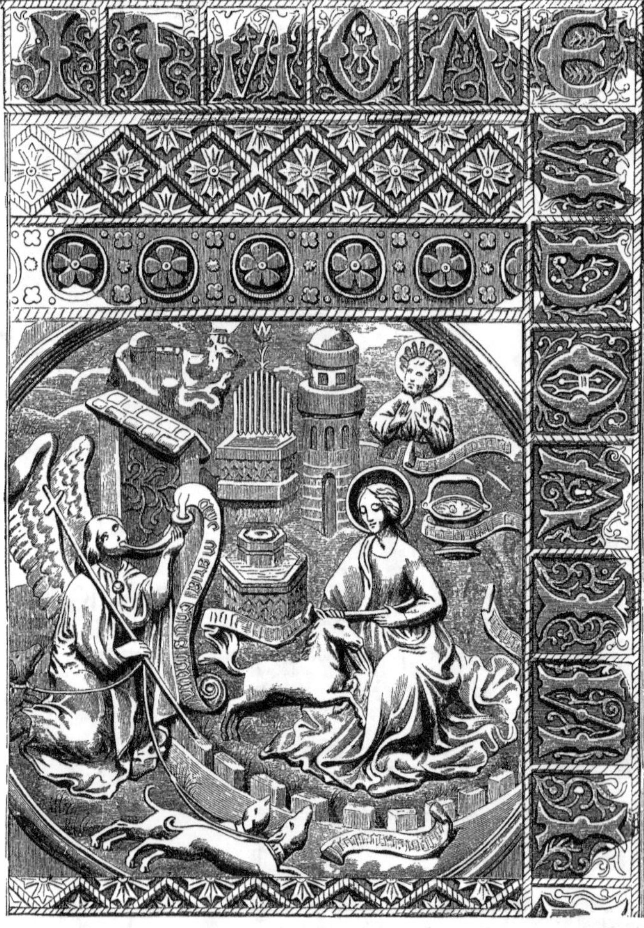

248

242. Banner of the corporation of printers-booksellers of Angers. **243.** Mark of Temporal, printer at Lyons, 1550–1559. **244.** Mark of Galliot du Pré, bookseller at Paris. **245.** Mark of Simon Vostre, printer at Paris, 1531. **246.** Mark of Colard Mansion, printer at Bruges, 1477. **247.** The vegetable kingdom, mark of Guillaume Merlin, bookseller at Paris, 16th century. **248.** Fragment of an engraved and stamped binding, 15th century.

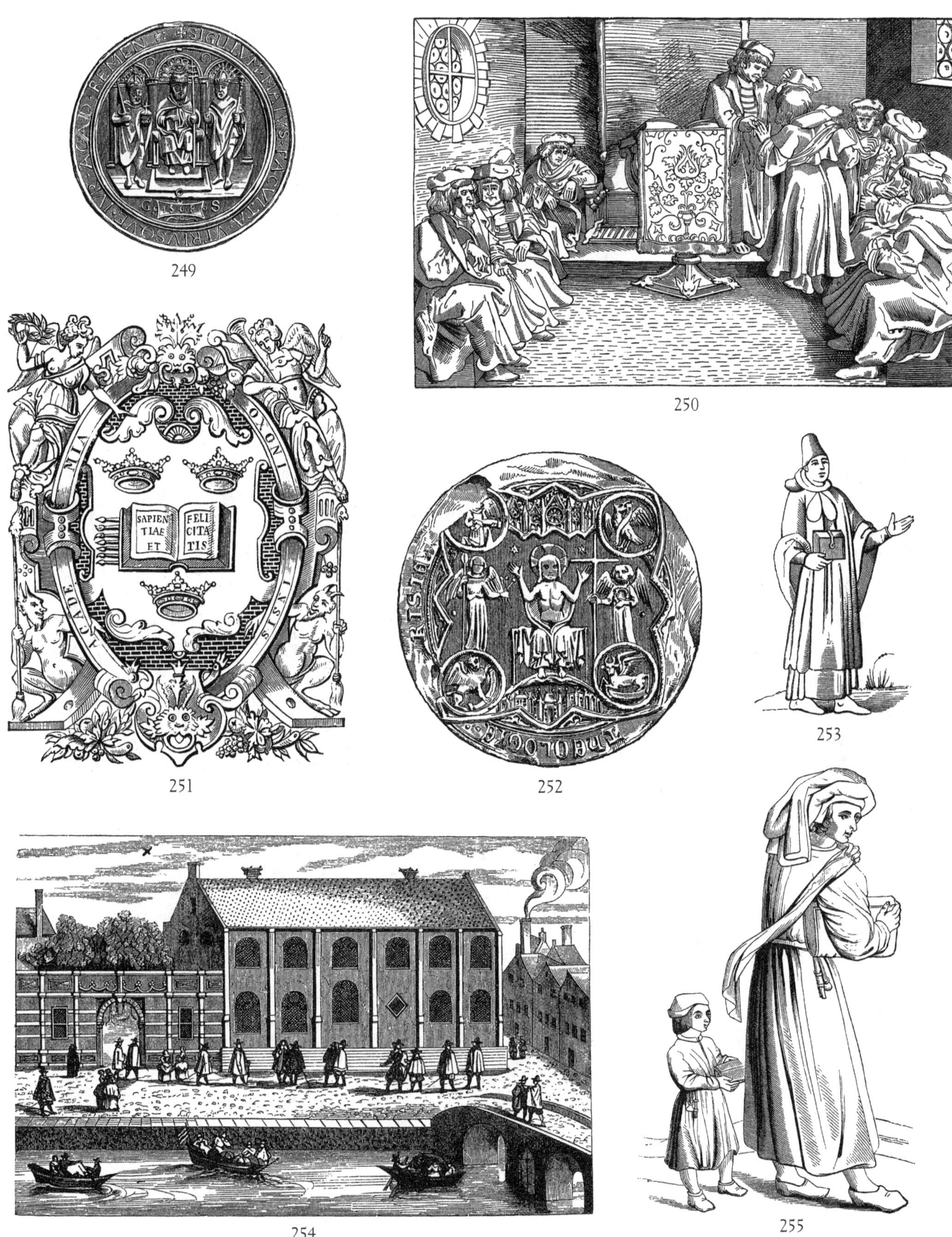

249. Seal of the Rheims University, 1568. **250.** Reception of a doctor, facsimile of a wood engraving, 14th century. **251.** Seal of the University of Oxford. **252.** Seal of the Faculty of Theology of Paris, 14th century. **253.** Master Jean de Vandeuil, Proctor of the Picardy nation, 15th century. **254.** External view of Leyden University, 1614. **255.** The schoolmaster, from the *Danse macabre*, 1490.

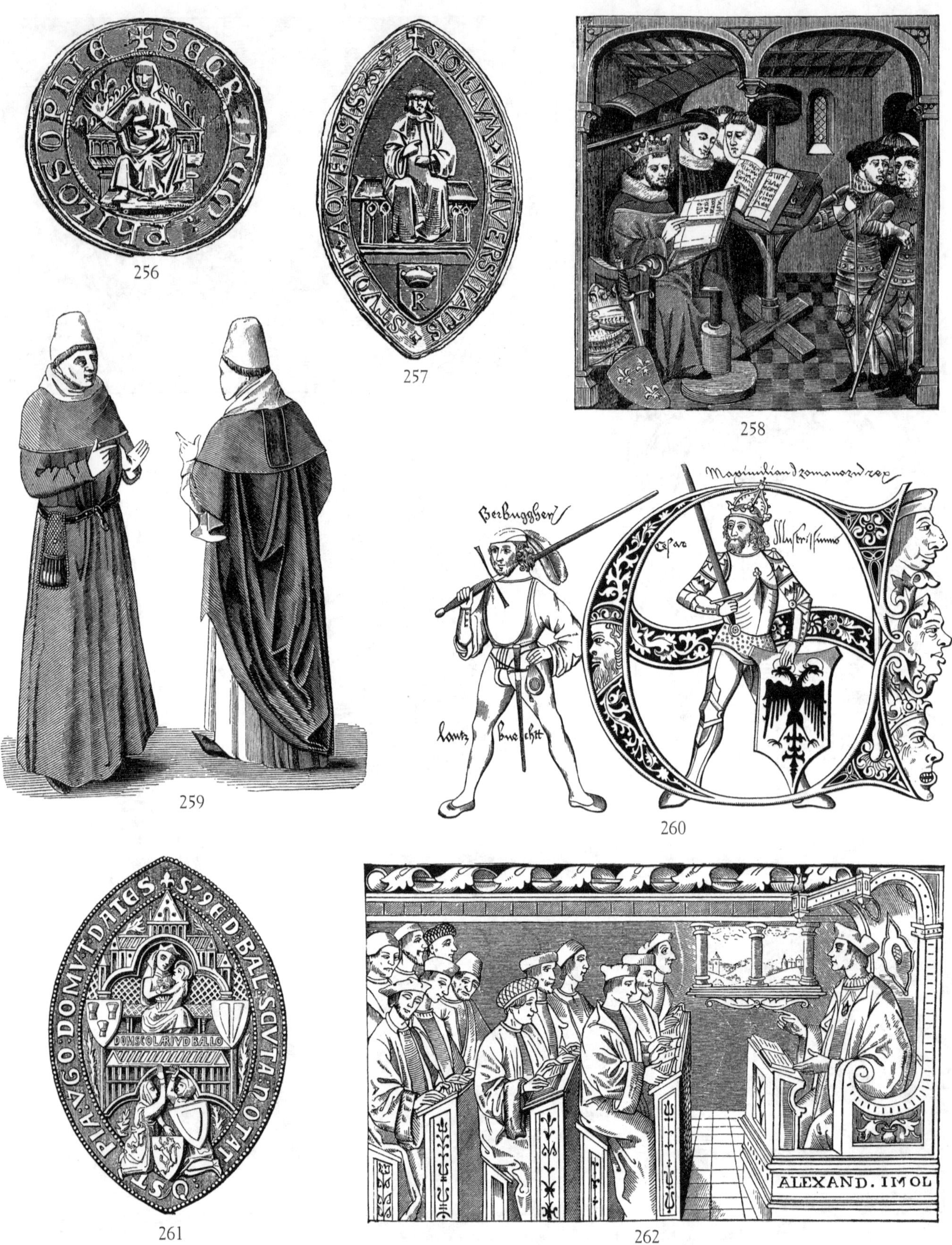

256. Counter-seal of the University of Paris, 14th century. **257.** Seal of the Aix University, Provence, 16th century. **258.** King Robert, son of Hugh Capet, composing sequences and responses in Latin, 14th century. **259.** Rector and doctor of the University of Paris, 15th century. **260.** Grand initial, representing types of students, 15th century. **261.** Seal of Balliol College (founded 1269), Oxford. **262.** Interior of a school, 16th century.

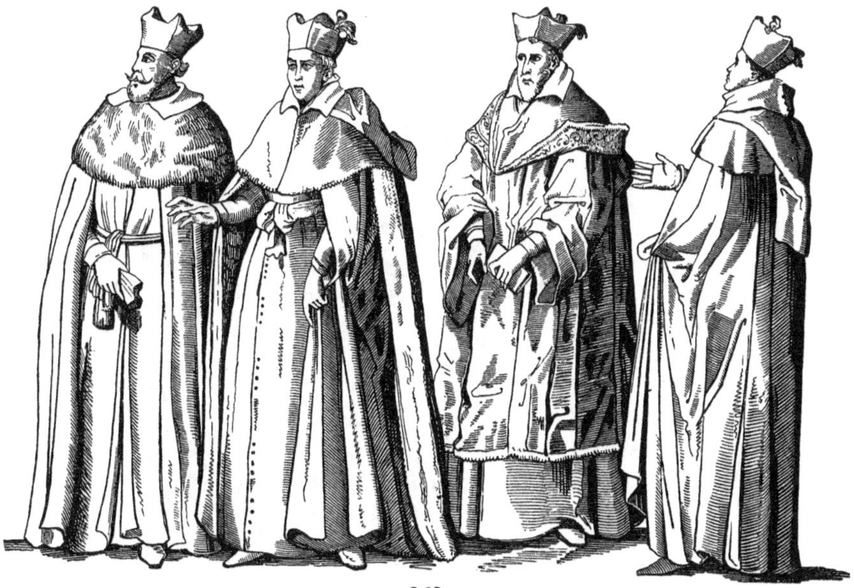

263

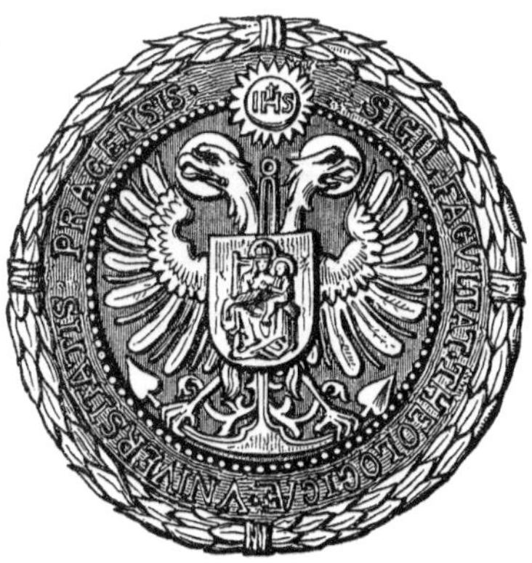

264

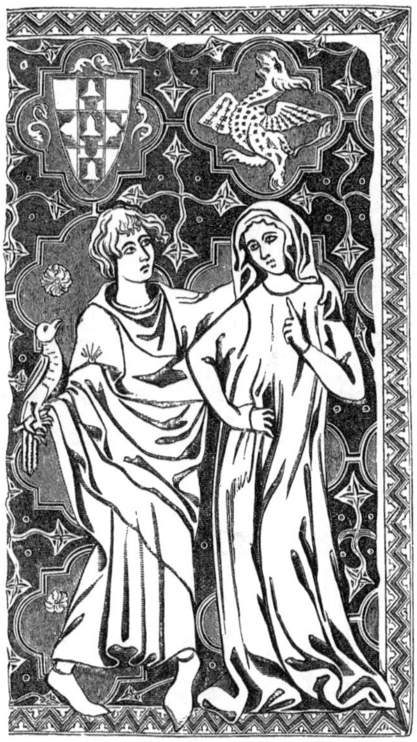

266

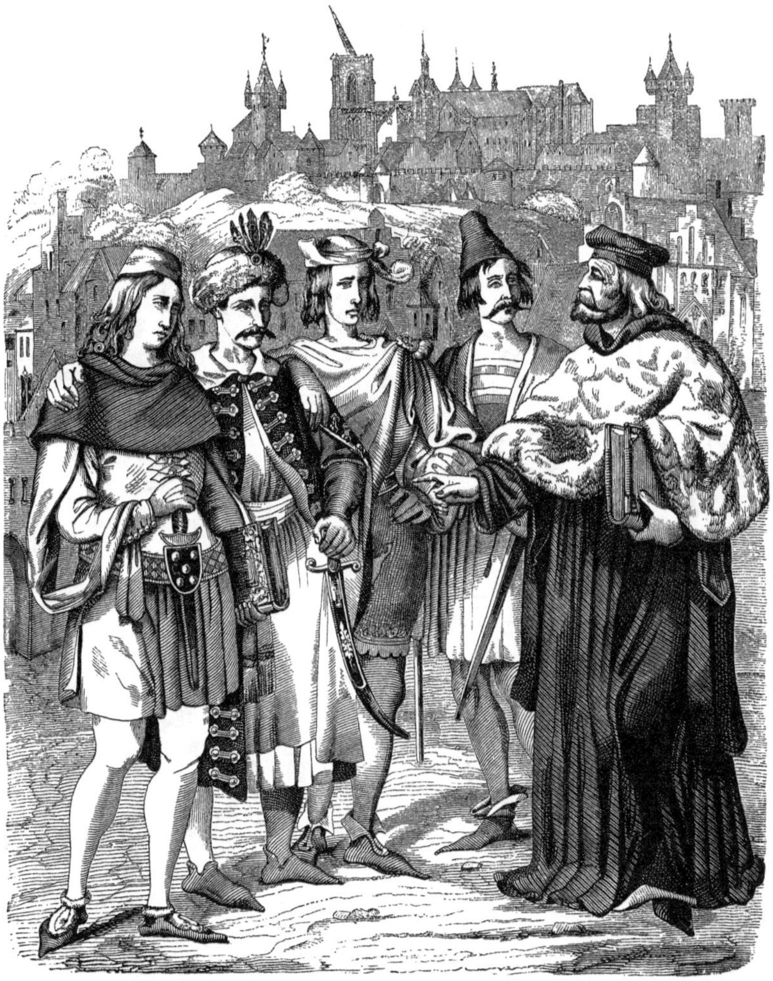

265

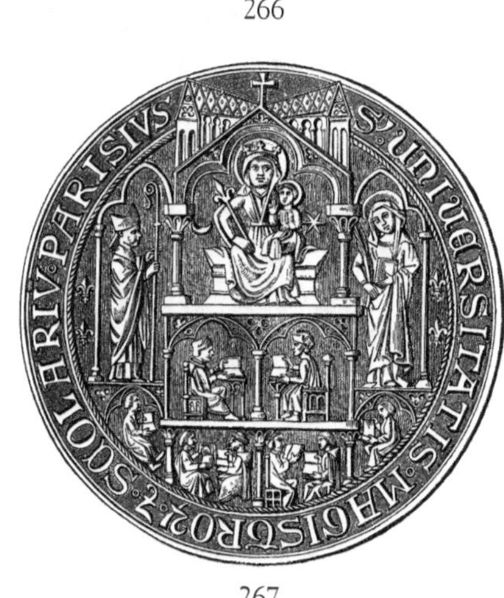

267

263. Bachelors of the faculty of theology, and professors of the faculties of theology, jurisprudence, and medicine at the University of Pont-à-Mousson. **264.** Seal of the faculty of theology, Prague. **265.** Rector of the Prague University and scholars. **266.** The Enchanter Merlin, fragment of the binding of a book, Limoges. **267.** Seal of the University of Paris, 14th century.

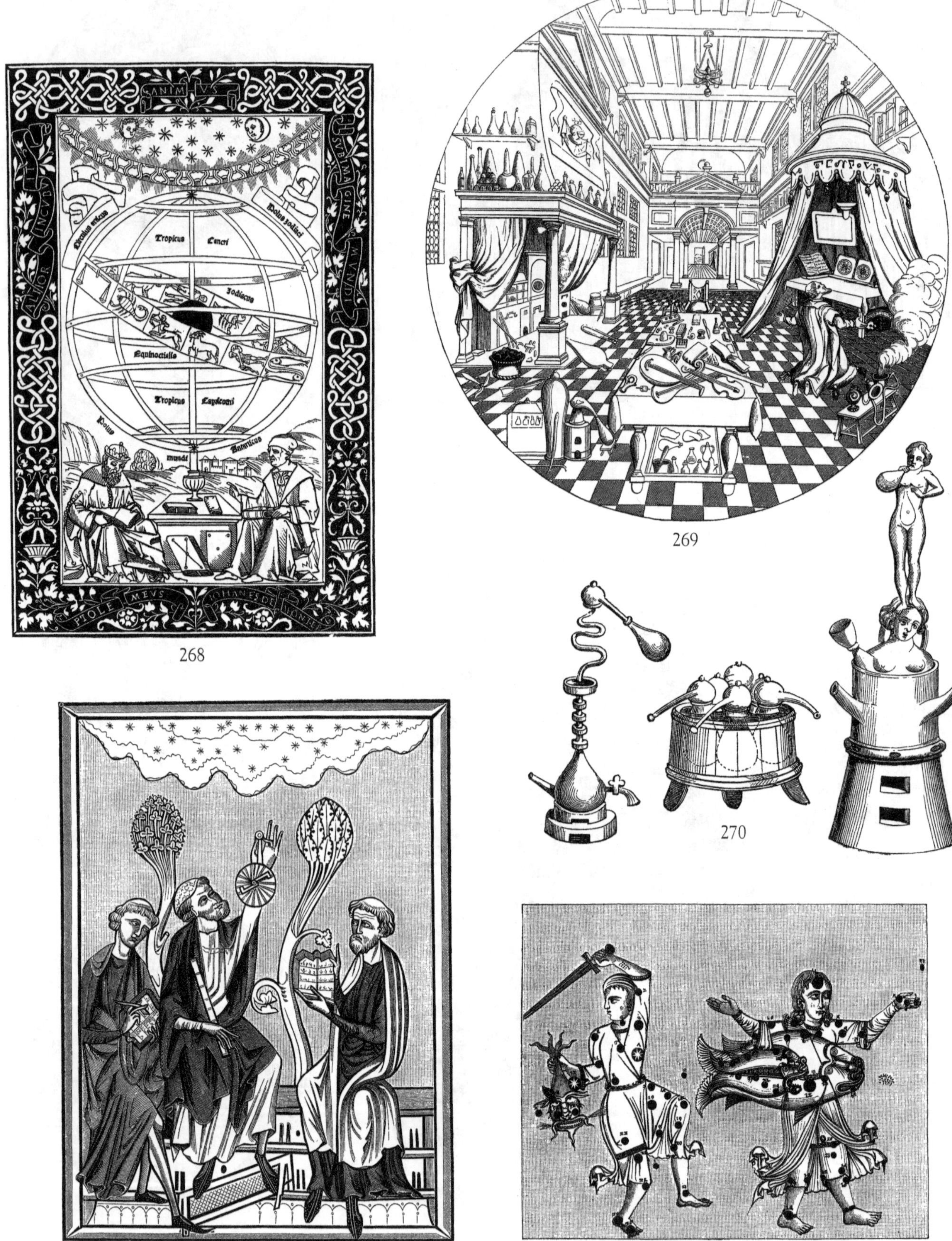

268. Ptolemy's System, facsimile of a wood engraving, 1543. **269.** The alchemist. **270.** Furnace, retorts, and stills as used by chemists and alchemists, 16th century. **271.** A lesson in astronomy, 13th century. **272.** Perseus and Andromeda.

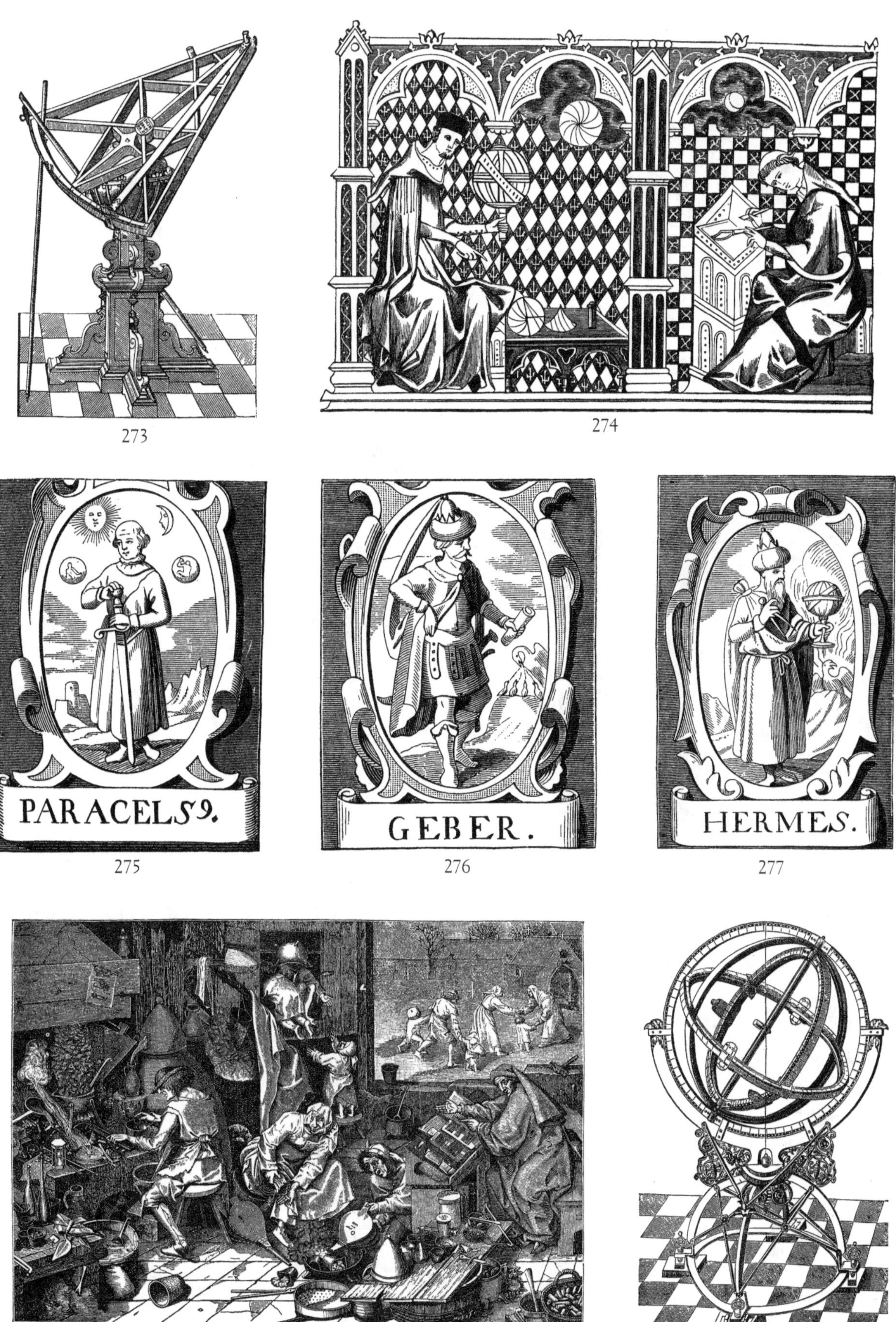

273 274 275 276 277 278 279

273. Astronomical sextant for measuring distances. **274.** Mathematician monks, 13th century. **275.** The alchemist Paracelsus. **276.** The alchemist Geber. **277.** The alchemist Hermes. **278.** The alchemist's laboratory, 16th century. **279.** Equatorial rings or circles.

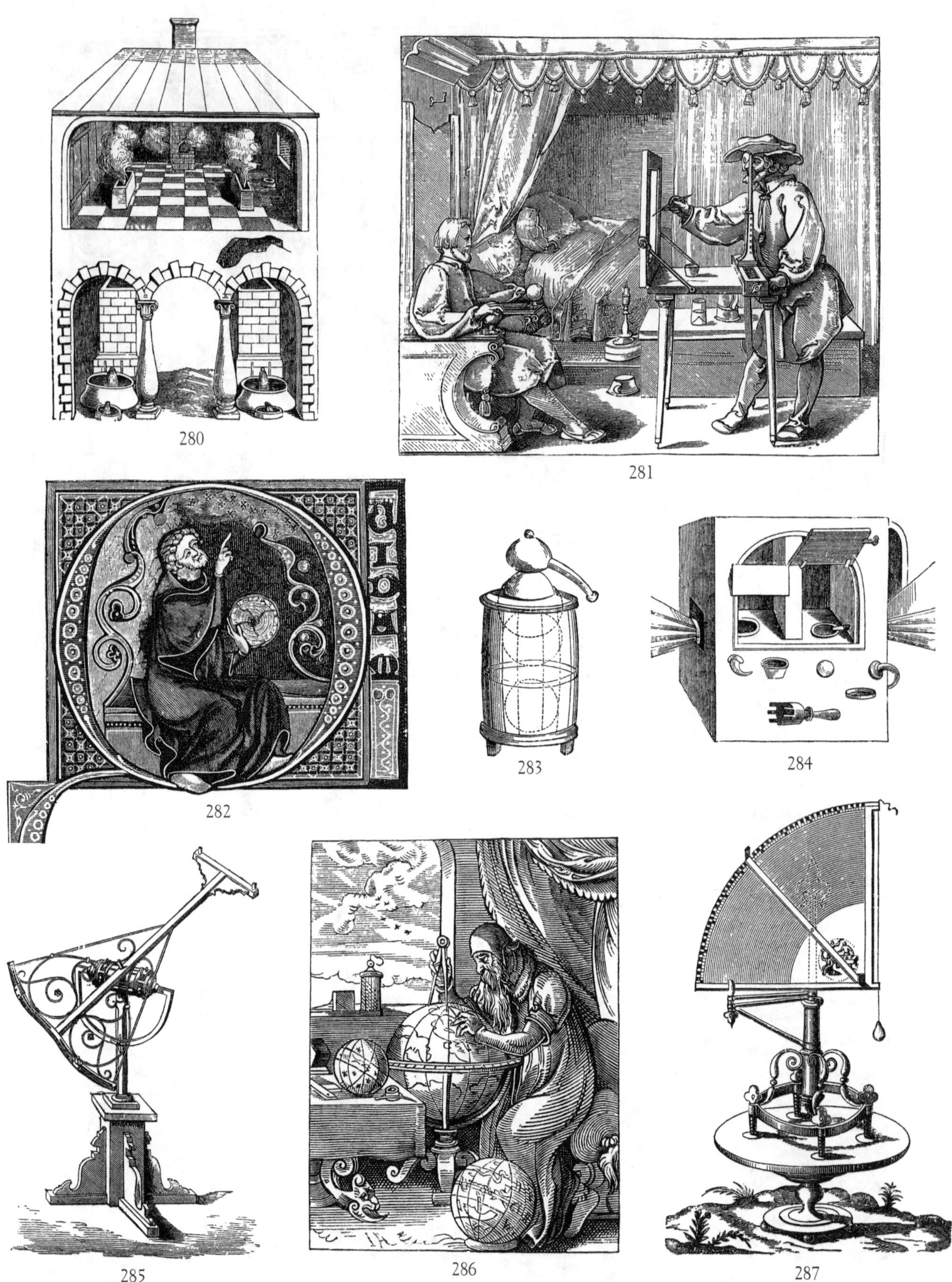

280, 283, 284. Furnaces and various apparatus of the Middle Ages. 281. Instruments of mathematical precision for executing portraits. 282. Astronomer accused of sorcery, 13th century. 285. Arc with double compartment for measuring the shortest distances of the stars, 1602. 286. German astronomer and cosmographist, 16th century. 287. Small quadrant, or quarter of a circle, 1602.

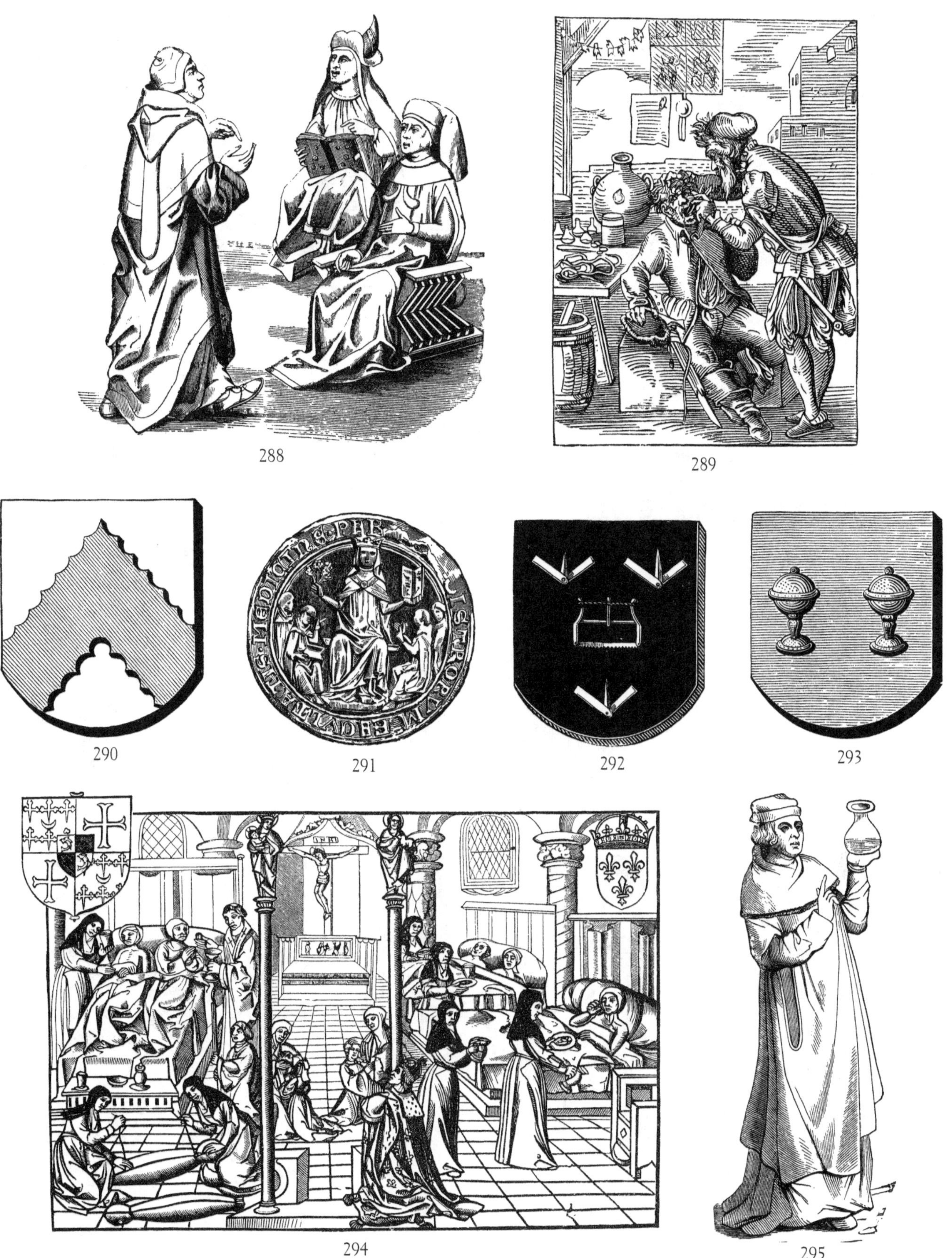

288. Italian doctors, 15th century. **289.** An operator. **290.** Banner of the corporation of the physicians at Amiens. **291.** Seal of the faculty of medicine, Paris, 14th century. **292.** Banner of the corporation of surgeons at Le Mans. **293.** Banner of the corporation of physicians in the Mayenne. **294.** A ward in the Hôtel-Dieu, Paris, 16th century. **295.** Physician, from the *Danse Macabre*, 1490.

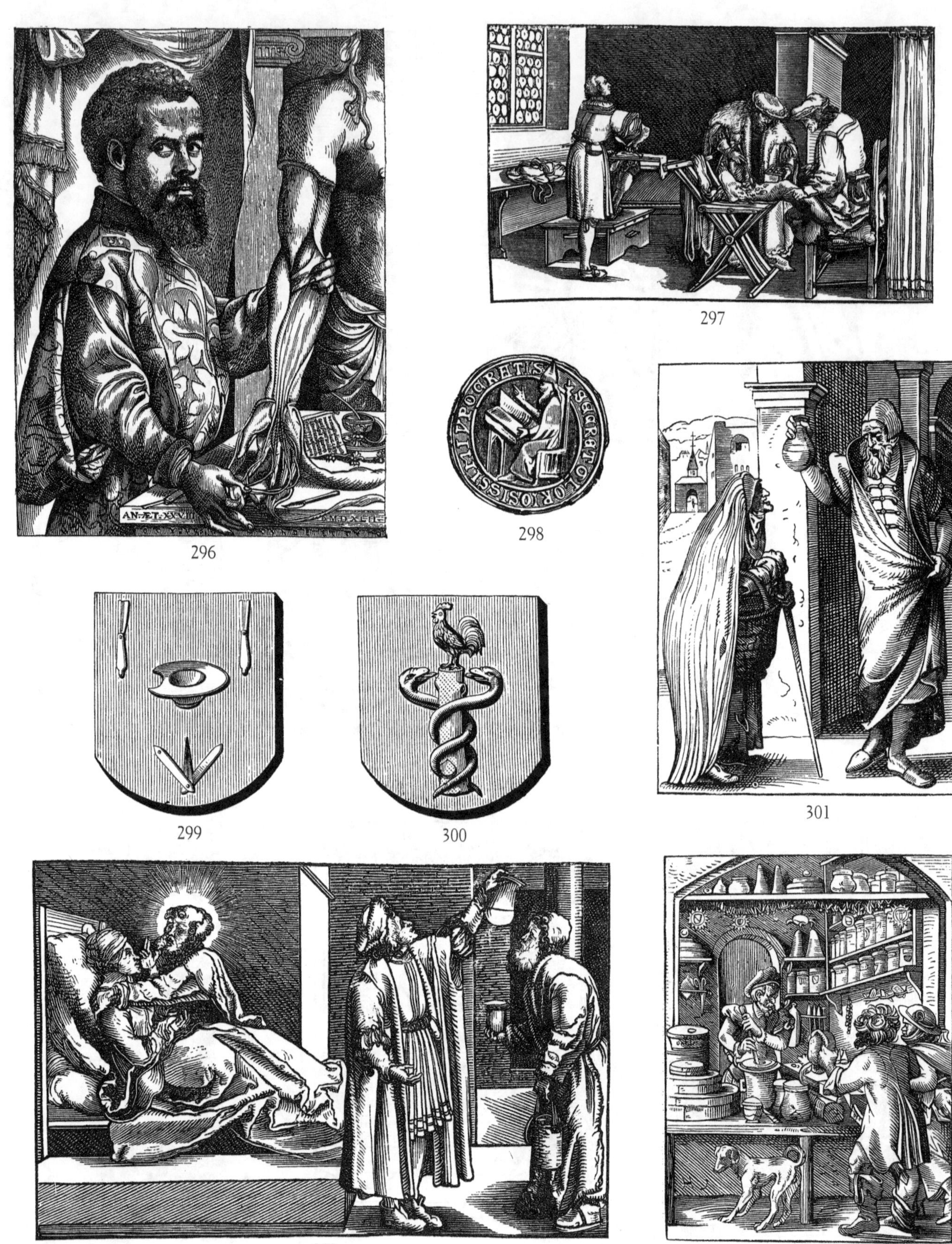

296. Andrew Vesalius. **297.** A German surgeon, 1537. **298.** Counter-seal of the faculty of medicine, Paris, 14th century. **299.** Banner of the corporation of surgeons at Saintes. **300.** Banner of the corporation of physicians at Vire. **301.** The physician, 16th century. **302.** Cure through the intercession of a healing saint, 1537. **303.** Druggist.

304. From Book of the Gospels. **305.** Ornament of a dish, Italian ware. **306.** From missal of Pope Paul V. **307, 308.** Border of a manuscript page, 15th century. **309.** Border from a prayer book belonging to Louis of France, 14th century.

310

311

312

313

314

315

316

310. Border from a book of the Gospels, 8th century. **311.** Fragment of a binding, 14th century. **312.** From the cathedral of Metz. **313.** Framework of first page of manuscript, "Douze dames de Rhétorique," 16th century. **314, 315.** Decorative borders. **316.** Border taken from a Gospel in Latin, 13th century.

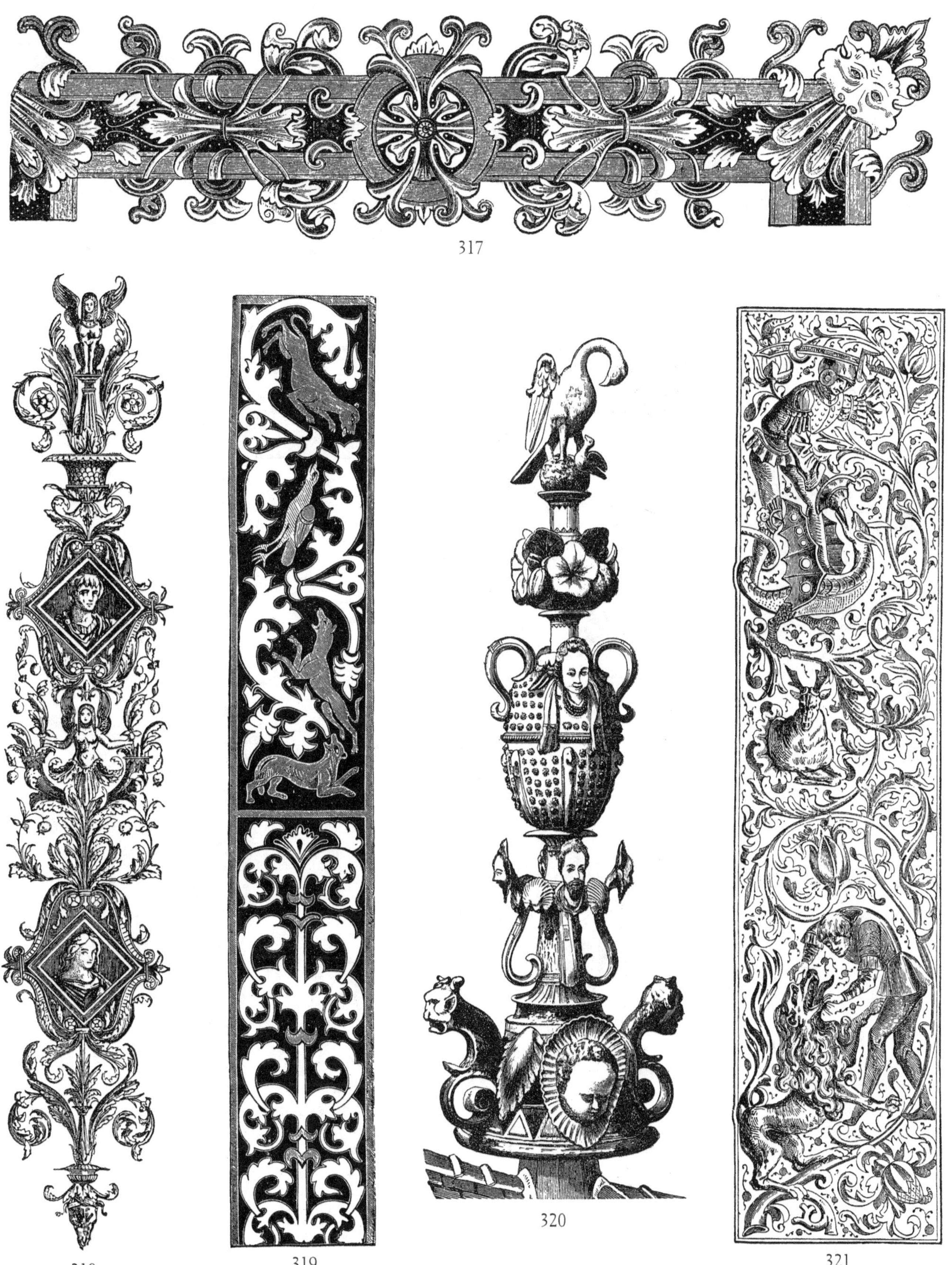

317. Border taken from the Sacramentary of Aethelgar. **318.** From an ovid. **319.** From bible of St. Martial of Limoges. **320.** Table ornament from the palace of the Bishop of Lisieux, 16th century. **321.** From Froissart's *Chronicles*.

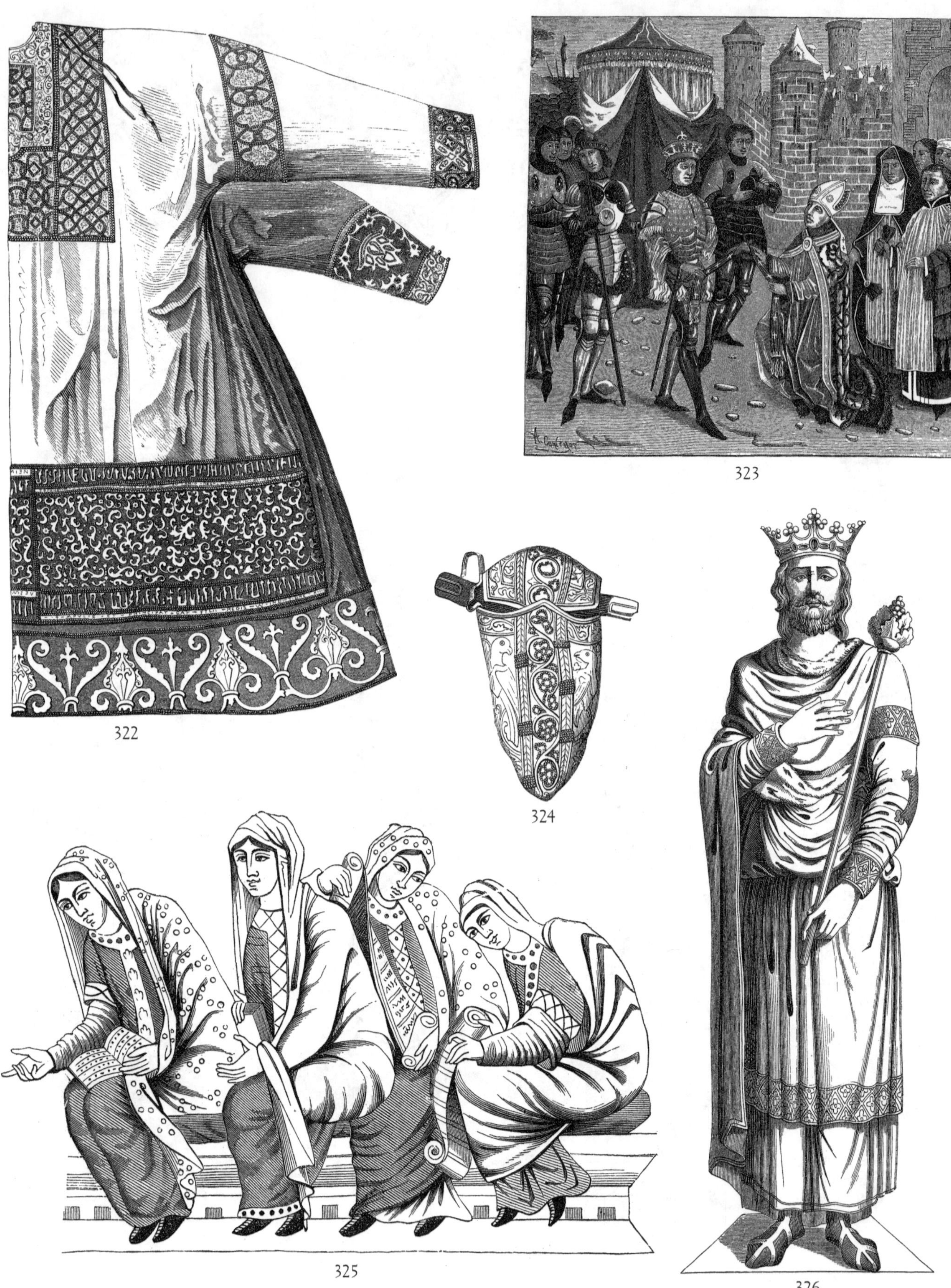

322. Dalmatica of Charlemagne. 323. St. Remy, Bishop of Rheims, 15th century. 324. Sandals of Charlemagne. 325. Ladies of the nobility. 326. Costume of King Louis le Jeune, 16th century.

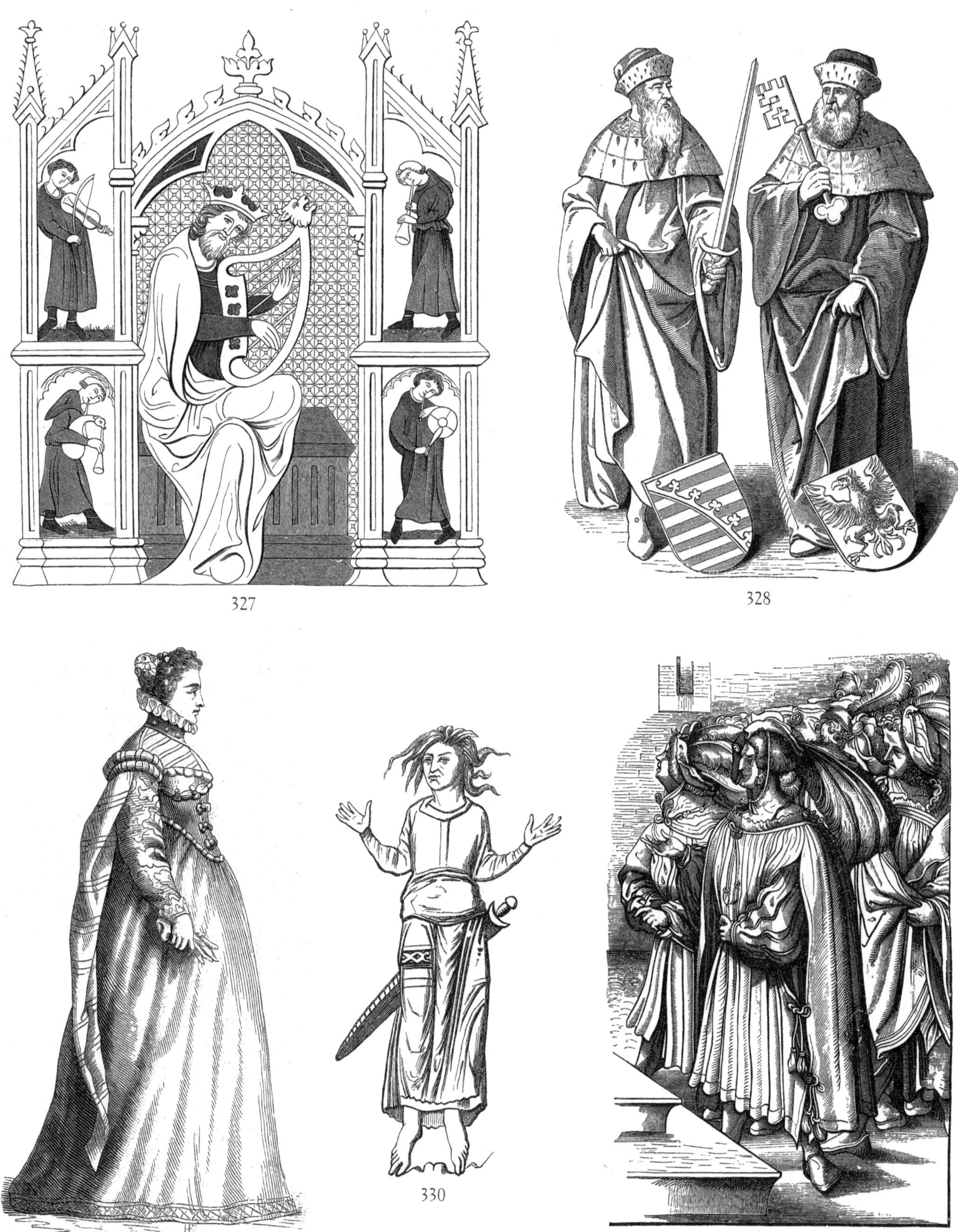

327 328 329 330 331

327. King David playing on the lyre, surrounded by four musicians, 13th century. **328.** The Duke of Saxony and the Marquis of Brandenburg. **329.** Lady of the court of Catherine de Medicis. **330.** Costume of the Franks, 4th to 8th centuries. **331.** The archdukes and high barons of Germany assisting, in state costume, at the coronation of the Emperor Maximilian, 16th century.

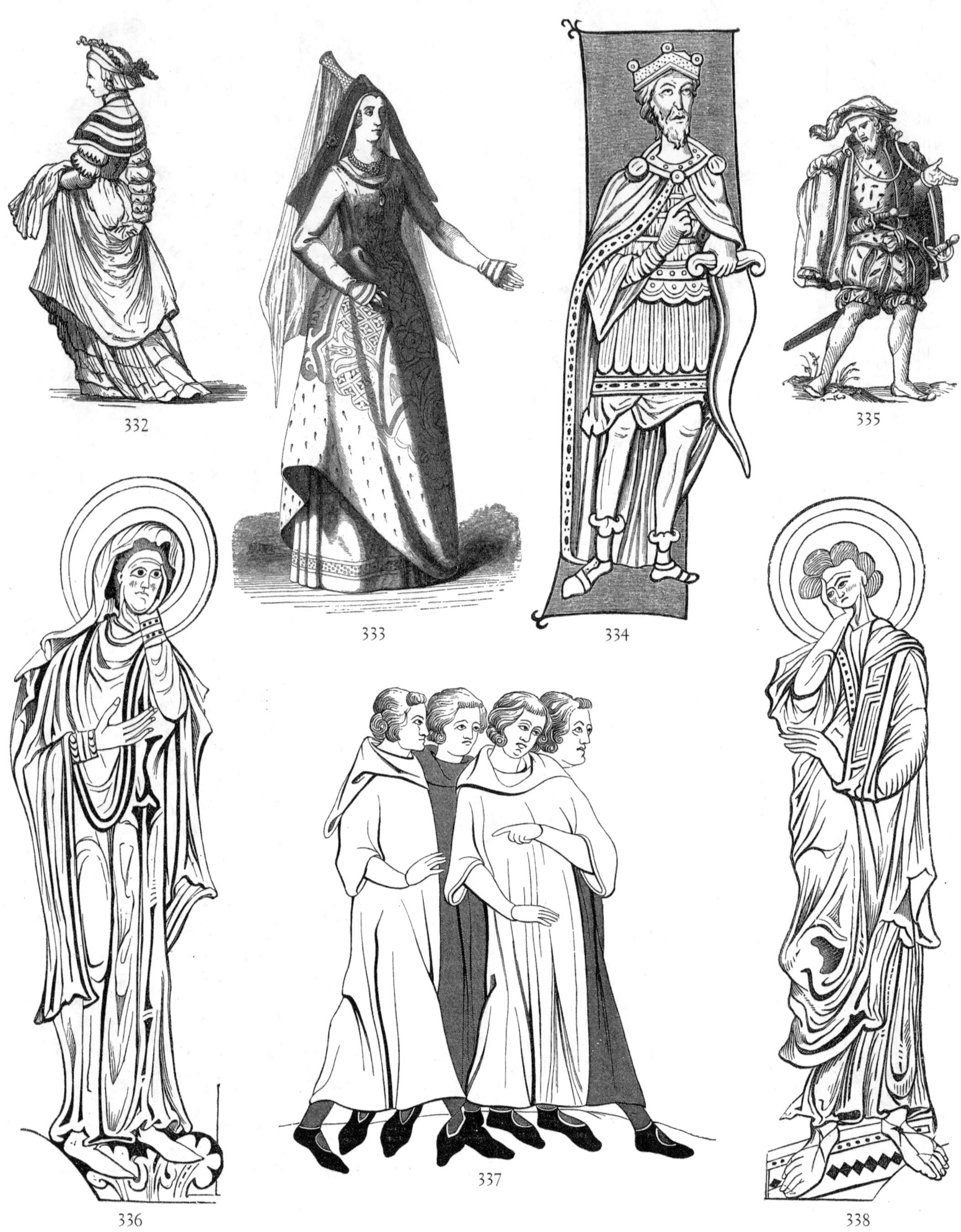

332. German bourgeoisie. **333.** Mary of Burgundy. **334.** King or chief of Franks armed with the scramasax. **335.** German bourgeoisie. **336.** Costume of the Prelates from the 8th to the 10th centuries, "Missal of St. Gregory." **337.** Bourgeois, end of 13th century. **338.** Costume of the Prelates.

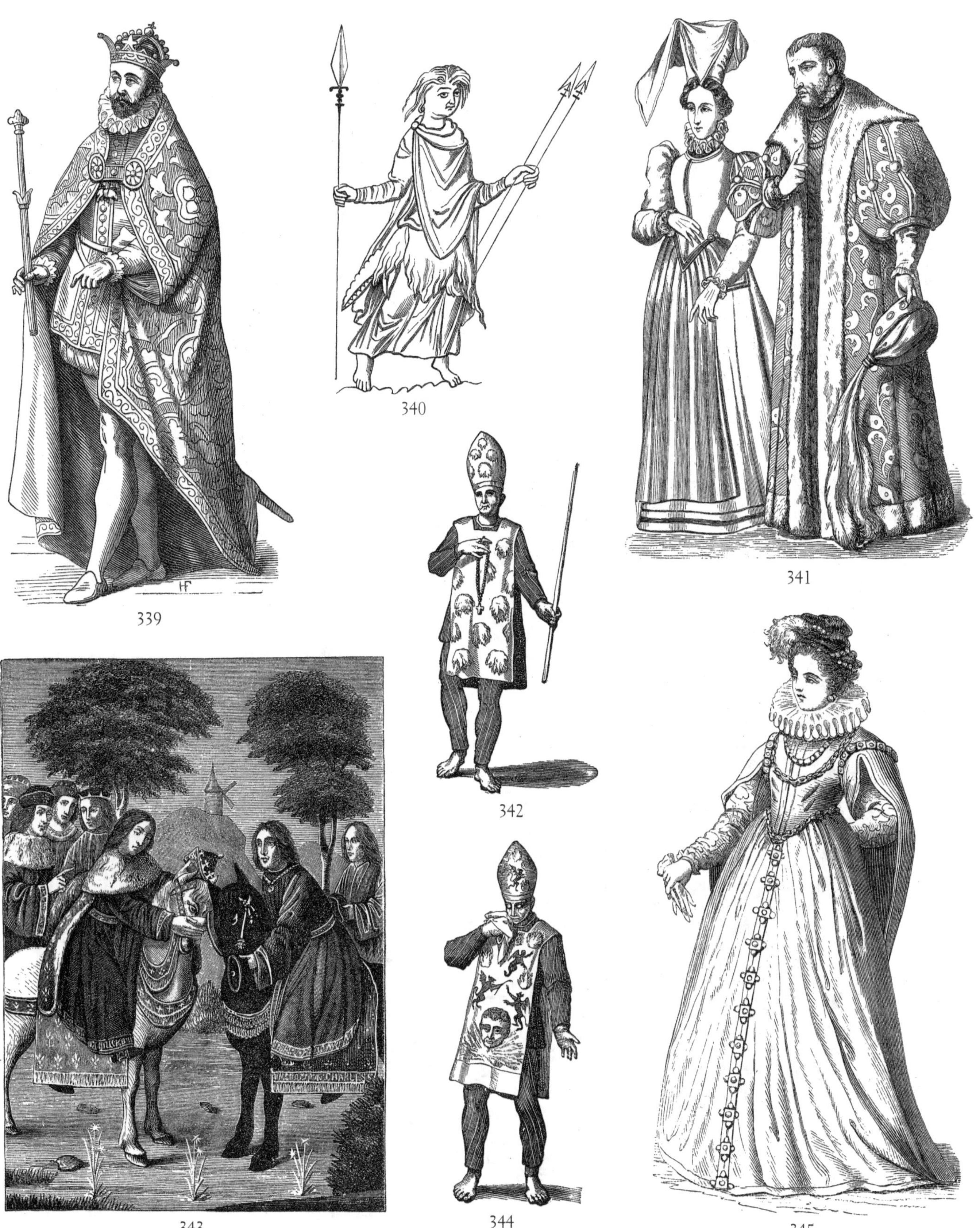

339. 340. 341. 342. 343. 344. 345.

339. Philip II, King of Spain, 1590. **340.** Costume of the Franks, 4th to 8th centuries. **341.** Rich bourgeoisie and a noble or person of distinction. **342.** *Fuego revolto*, garment worn by those who escaped being burnt alive by making a confession after they had been condemned. **343.** Interview of King Charles V with the Emperor Charles IV in Paris, 1378. **344.** *Samarra*, garment worn by those who, refusing to confess, were about to be burnt. **345.** Costume of the ladies and damsels of the court of Catherine de Medicis.

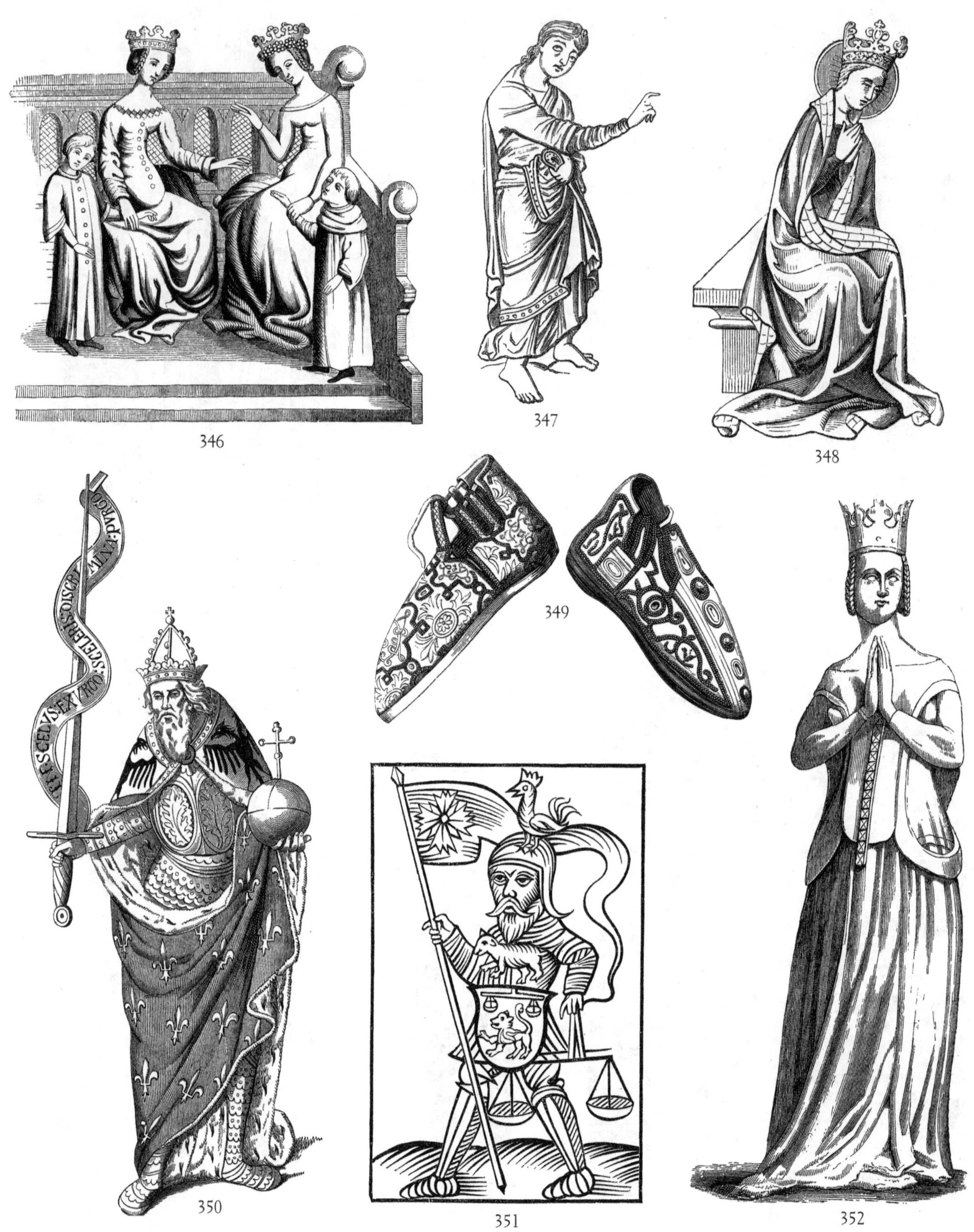

346. Noble ladies and children. **347.** Costume of the nobility, 7th to 9th centuries. **348.** Costume of a princess dressed in cloak lined with fur, 13th century. **349.** Sandal and buskin of Charlemagne. **350.** Emperor Charlemagne holding the globe and the sword. **351.** Hermensul or Irmensul, idol of the ancient Saxons, 1656. **352.** Costume of Jeanne de Bourbon, wife of Charles V.

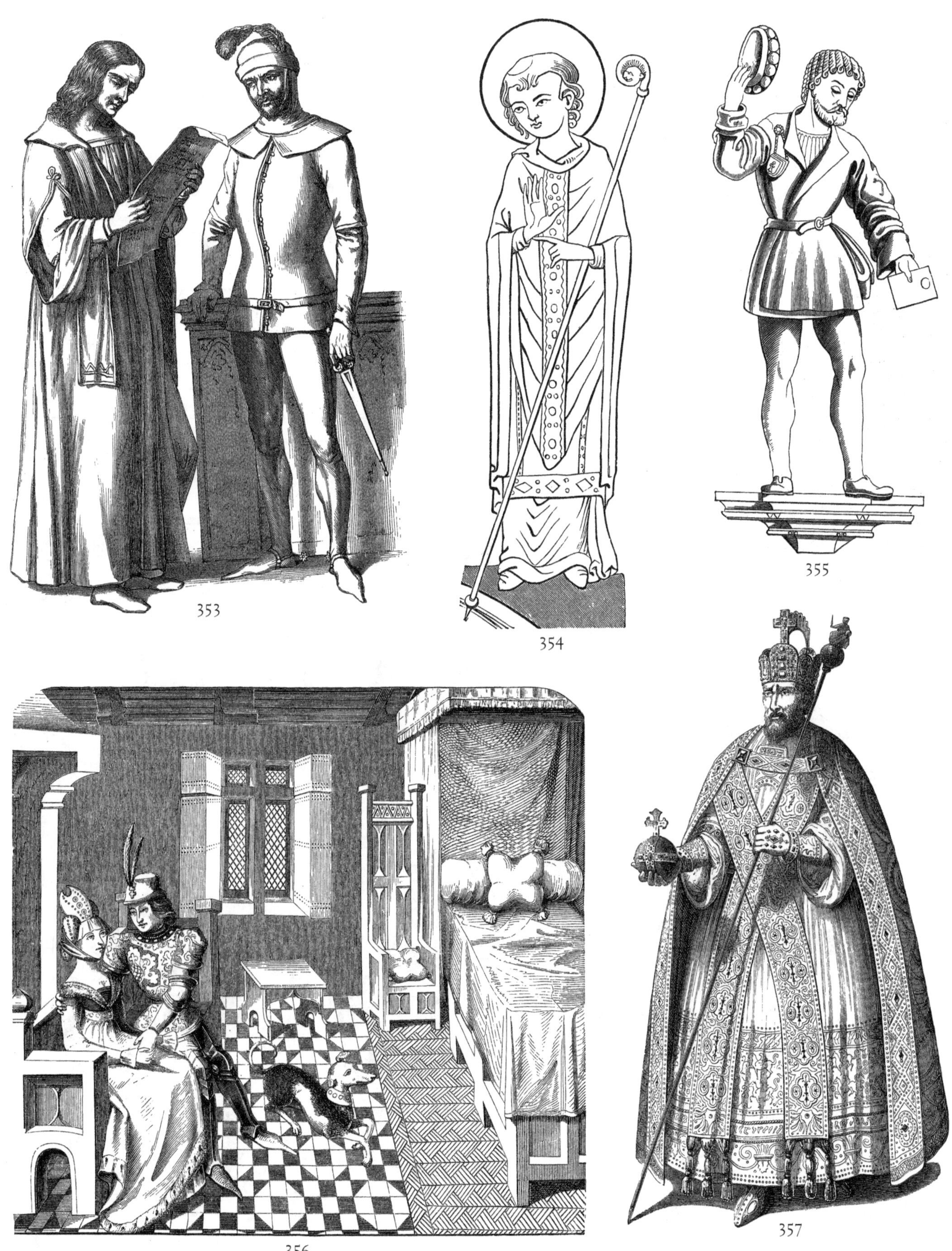

353. Italian costumes, notary and sbirro, 15th century. **354.** Costume of a bishop or abbot, 9th century. **355.** Swiss courier, 15th century. **356.** Knight and his lady. **357.** Emperor at coronation.

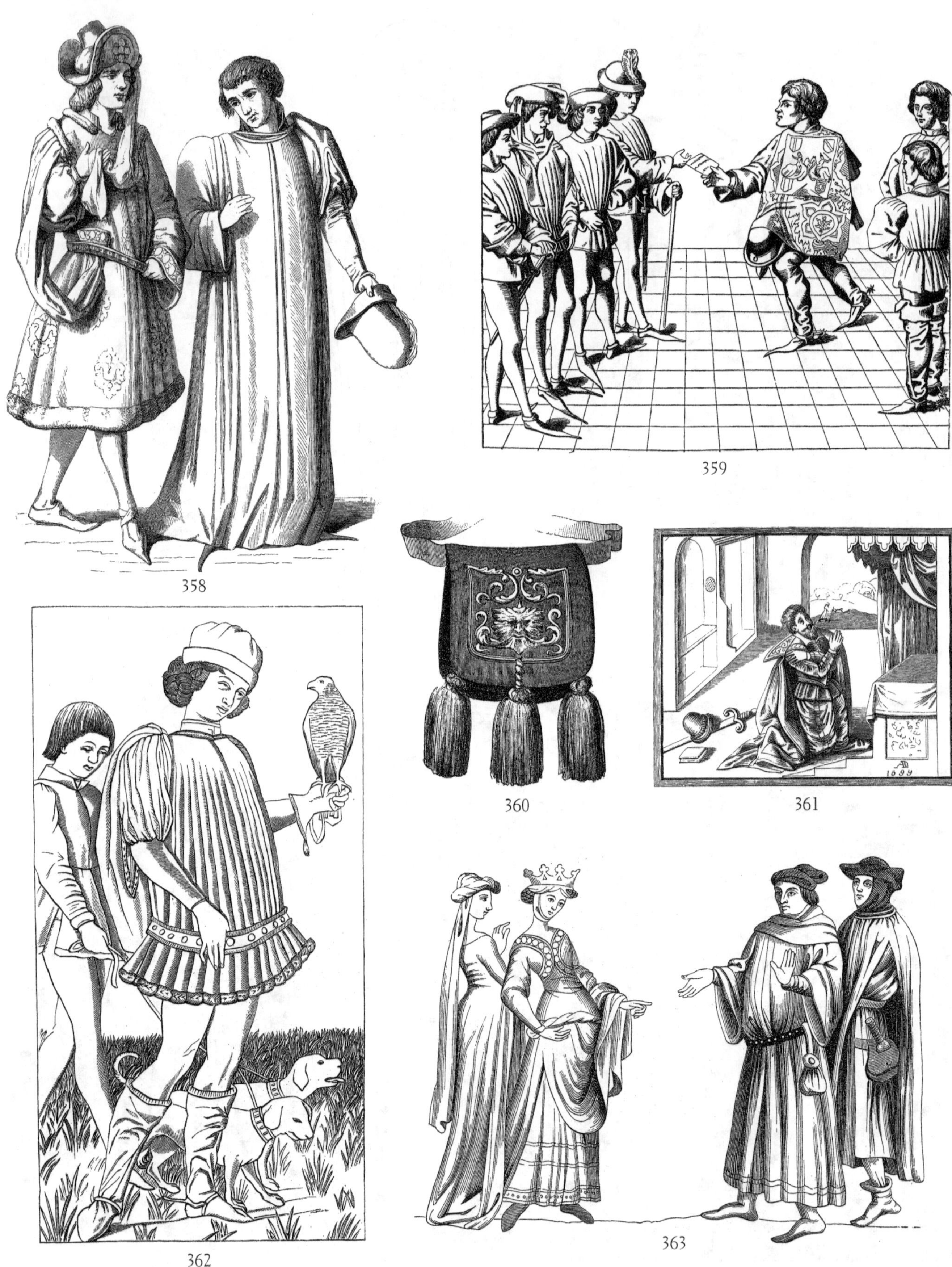

358. 359. 360. 361. 362. 363.

358. Young nobleman and a bourgeois. **359.** Fashion and manner, king of arms, judges, plaintiff and defendant, 15th century. **360.** Alms bag. **361.** Gentleman of the French court. **362.** Italian nobleman, 15th century. **363.** Noble lady and a maid of honor; two burgesses with hoods.

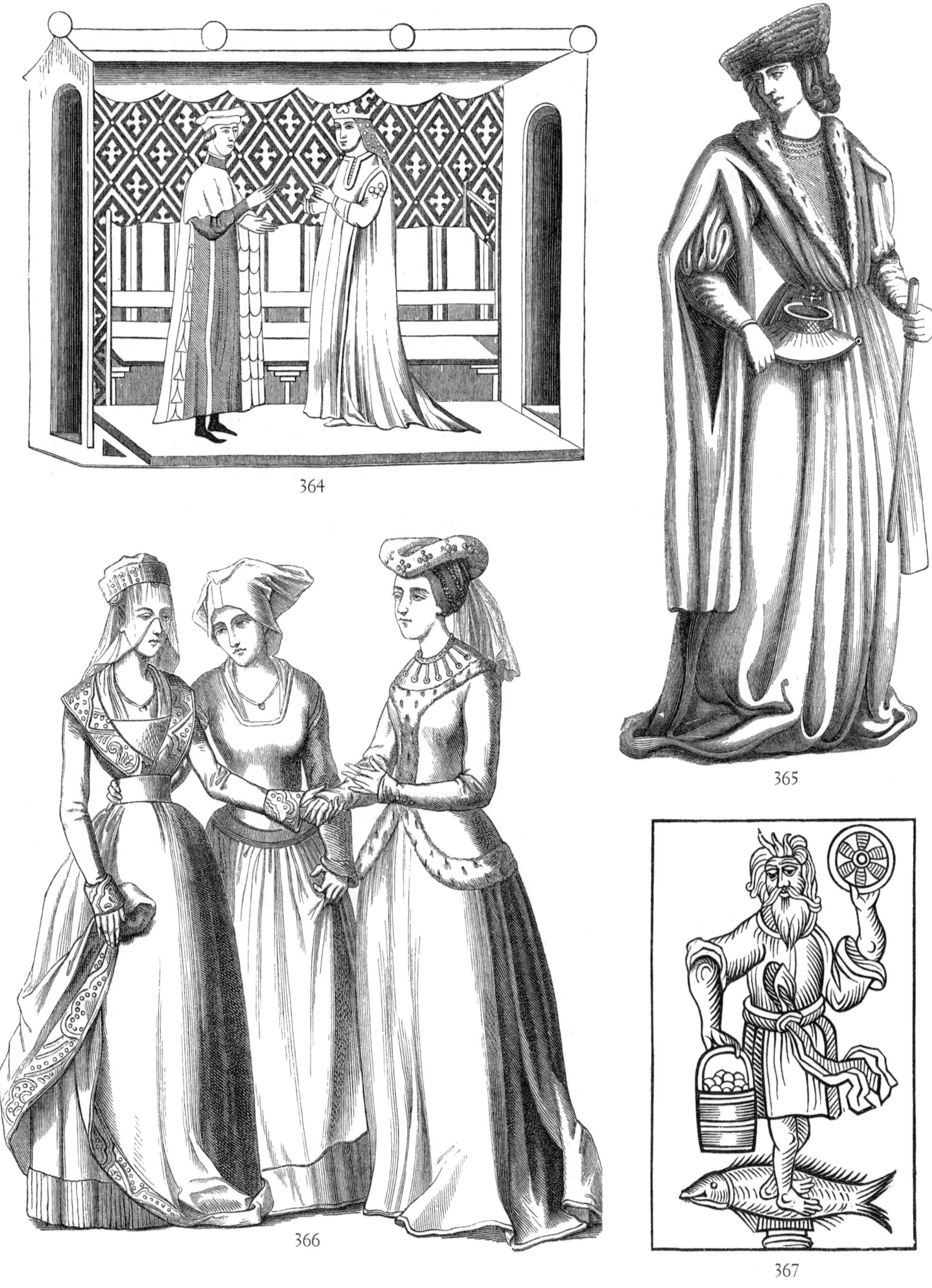

364. Costumes, Tristan and the beautiful Yseult, 14th century. **365.** Young noble of the court of Charles VIII. **366.** Rich bourgeoise, a peasant woman, and a lady of the nobility. **367.** Crodon, idol of the ancient Saxons, 1656.

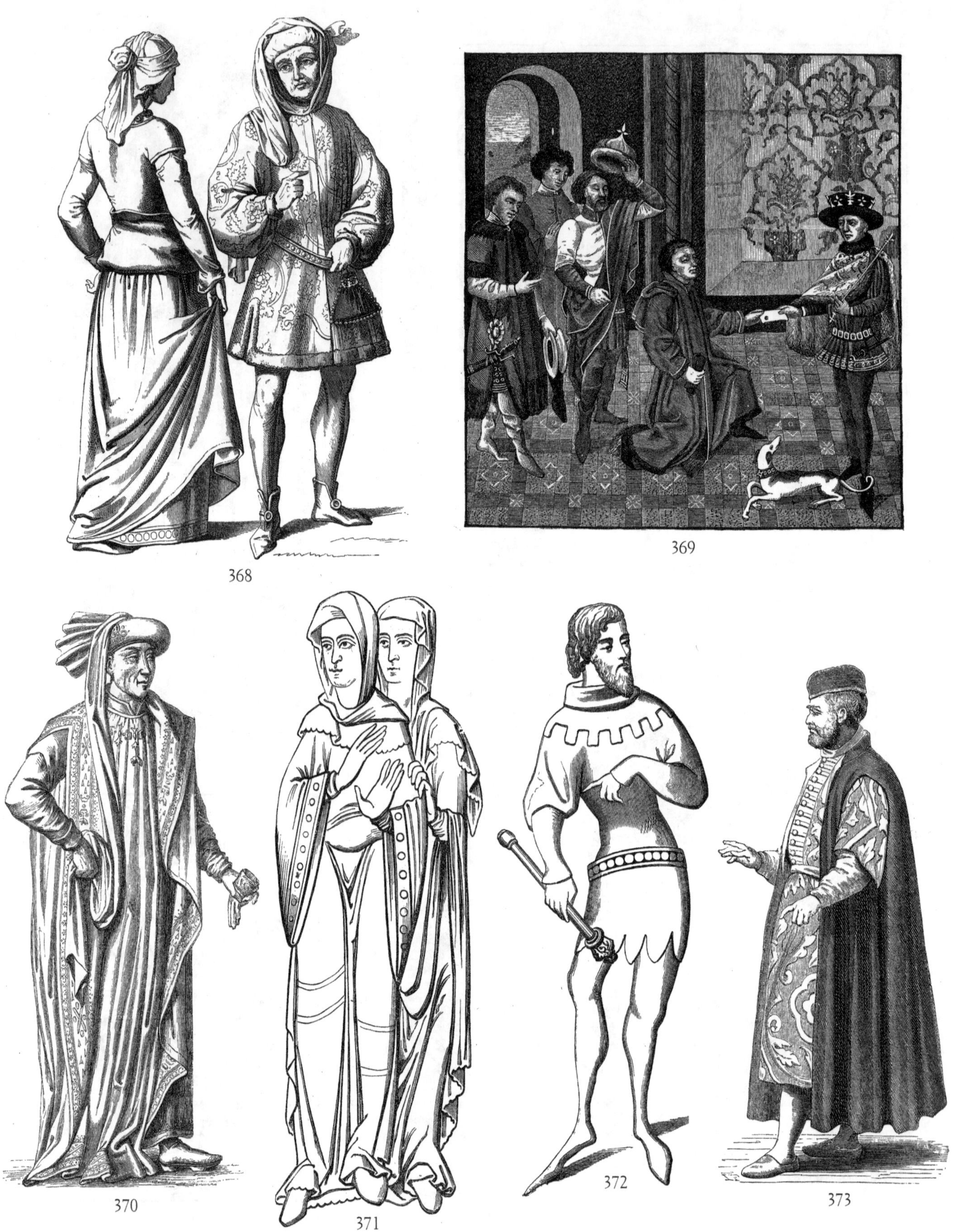

368. Mechanic's wife and a rich bourgeois. **369.** Charles, eldest son of King Pepin, 15th century. **370.** Philip the Good, with hood and cockade. **371.** Women of the court. **372.** Herald. **373.** Chief of Sbirri.

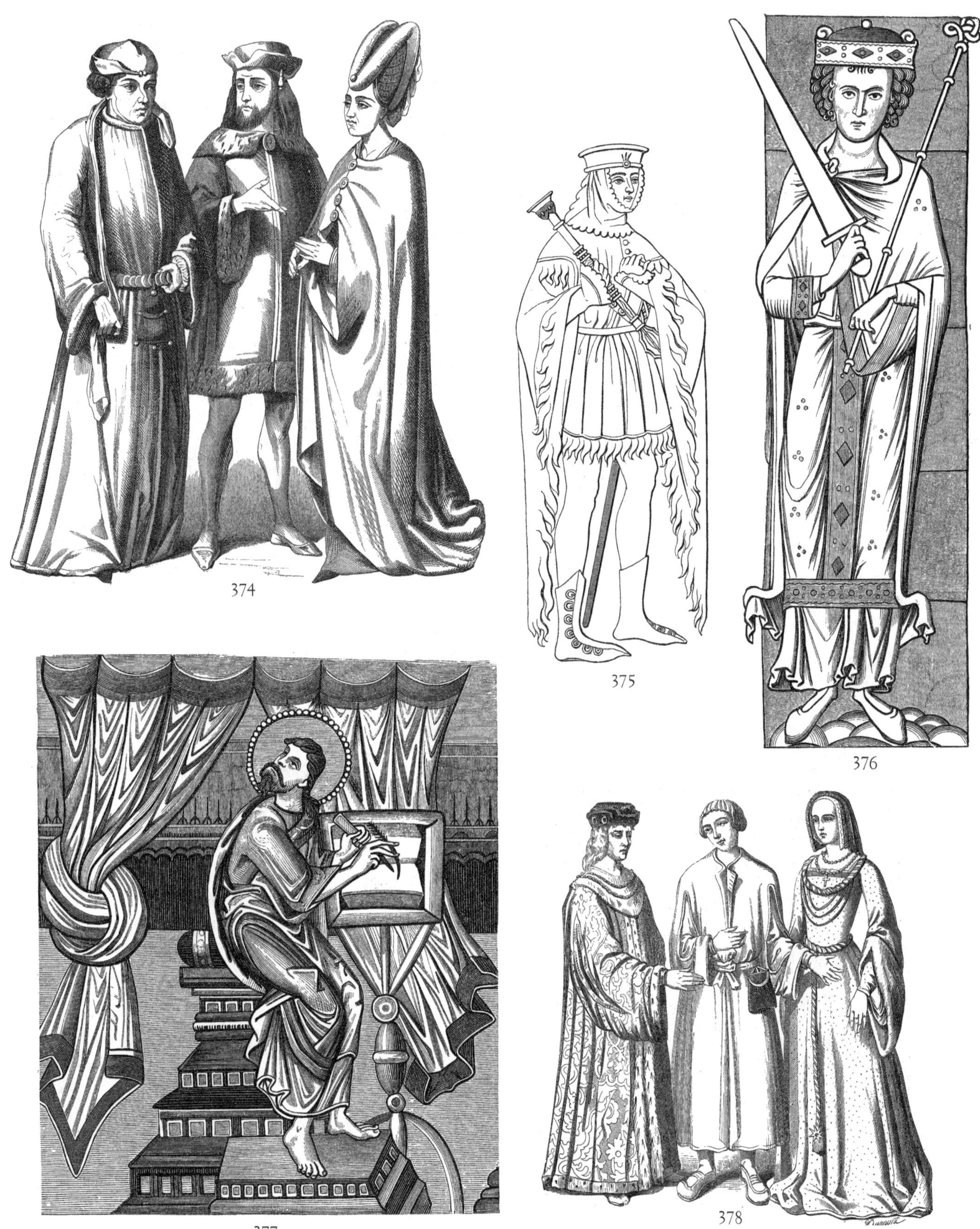

374. Bourgeois or merchant, a nobleman, and a lady of the court or rich bourgeoise. 375. Sergeant-at-arms, 14th century. 376. Royal costume. 377. Costume of a scholar, Carlovingian period. 378. Nobleman or a very rich bourgeois, a bourgeois or merchant, and a noble lady or rich bourgeoise.

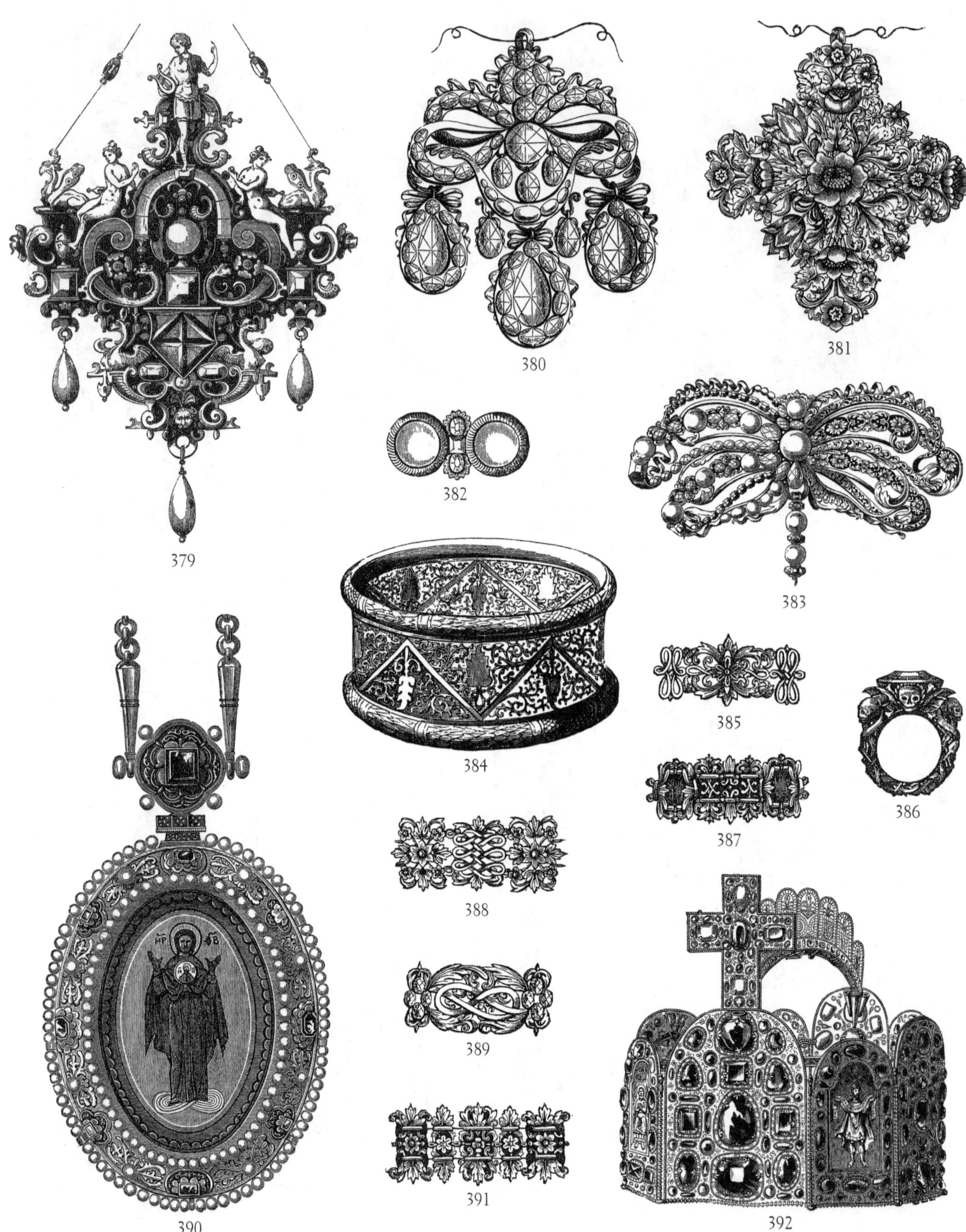

379. Pendant. **380.** Pendant. **381.** Gold cross. **382.** Chain. **383.** Chased and enameled brooch with pearls and diamonds, 17th century. **384.** Gallic bracelet, 9th century. **385.** Chain. **386.** Ring. **387.** Chain. **388.** Chain. **389.** Chain. **390.** Greek *Panagia,* or image of the Holy Virgin, 13th century. **391.** Chain. **392.** Diadem of Charlemagne.

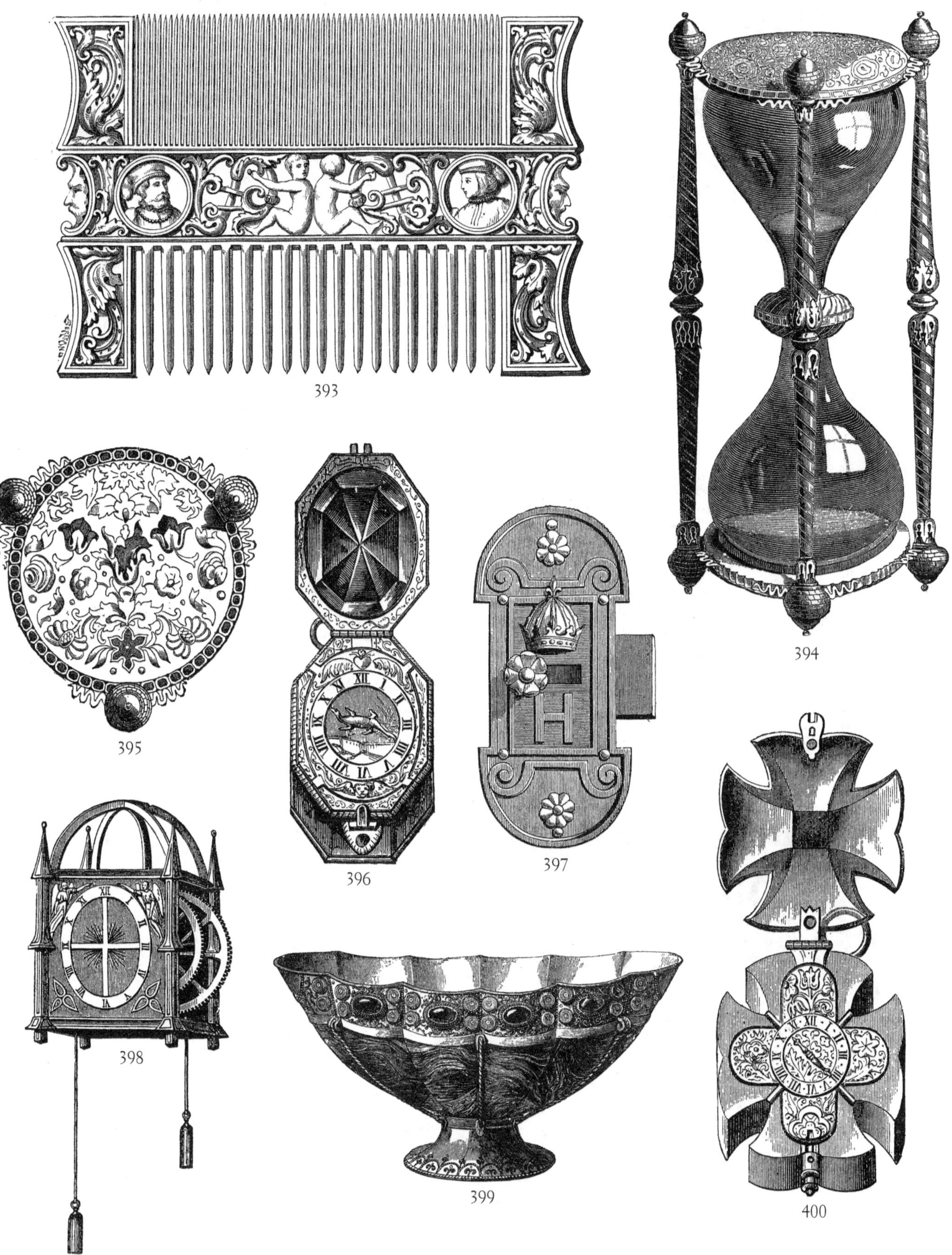

393. Sculptured comb. 394. Hour-glass. 395. Top of an hour-glass, 16th century. 396. Watch of the Valois epoch. 397. Bolt with initial of Henry II, 16th century. 398. Clock with wheels and weights, 15th century. 399. Drinking cup *(Gondole)*. 400. Banner of the Bordeaux upholsterers.

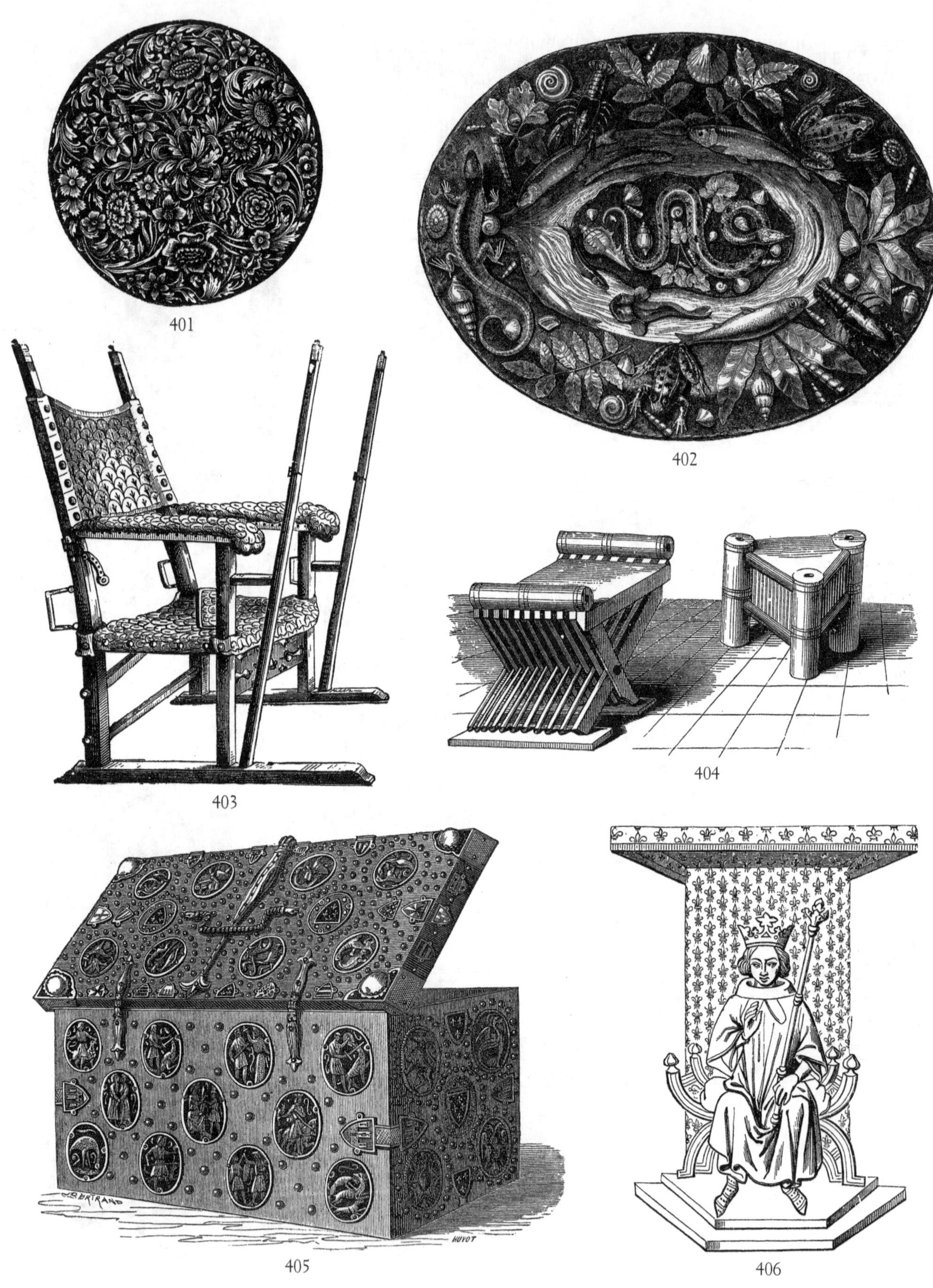

401. Scent-box, 15th century. **402.** Enameled dish. **403.** Sedan chair of Charles VI. **404.** Seats, 14th and 15th centuries. **405.** Coffer containing hair-cloths of St. Louis, 13th century. **406.** Louis IX in his regal chair, 14th century.

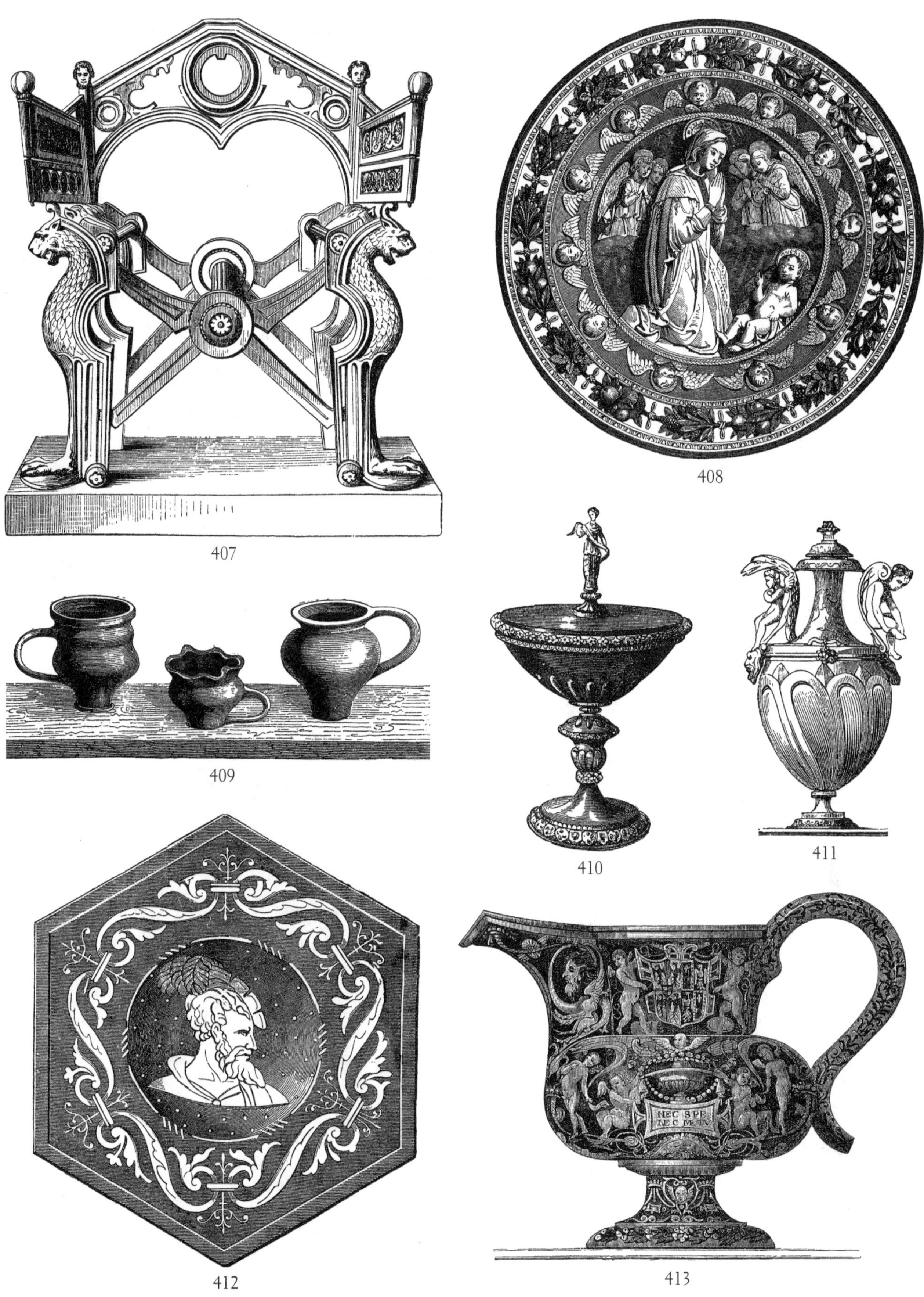

407. Curule chair called the Fauteuil de Dagobert. **408.** Enameled terra-cotta. **409.** Vases of ancient form, 12th century. **410.** Cup, lapis lazuli, 16th century. **411.** Vase, rock crystal, 16th century. **412.** Interior base of salt-cellar with portrait of Francis I. **413.** Italian ware cup.

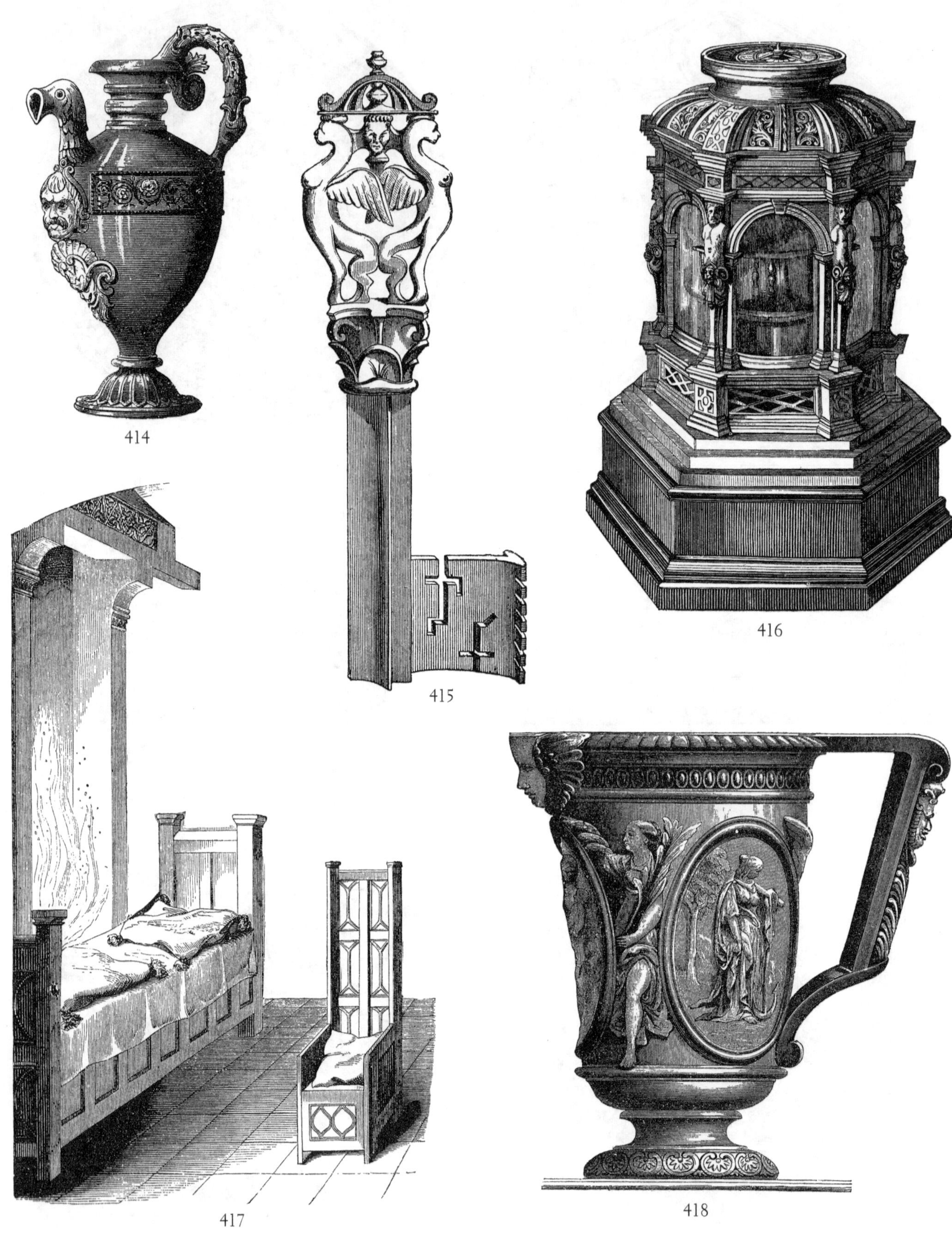

414. Egg-shaped coffeepot, 16th century. **415.** Key with back-to-back chimeras, 13th century. **416.** Portable clock of the Valois period. **417.** Chest shaped like a bed, in front of fireplace, and chair with cushions. **418.** Goblet.

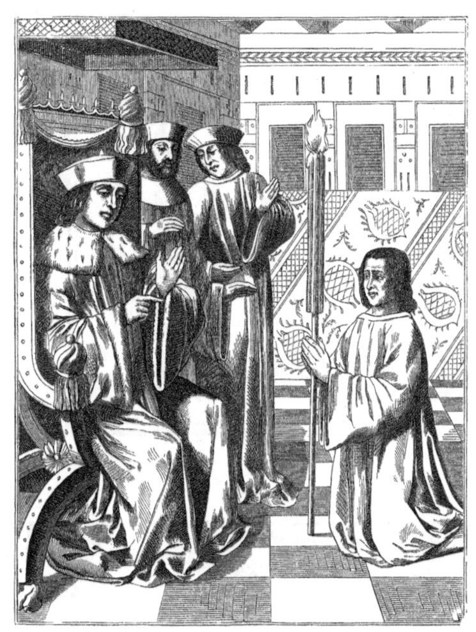

419

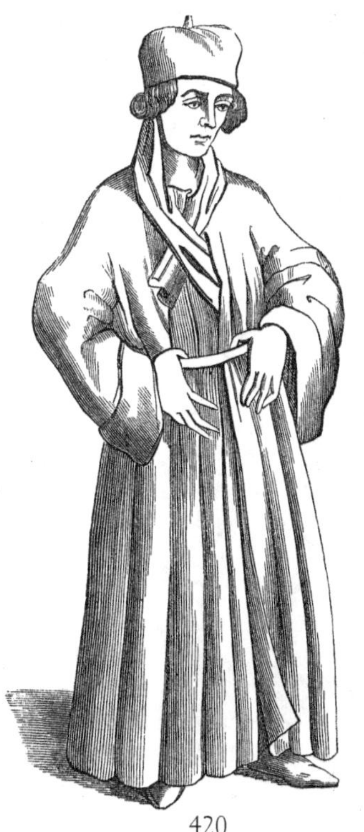

420

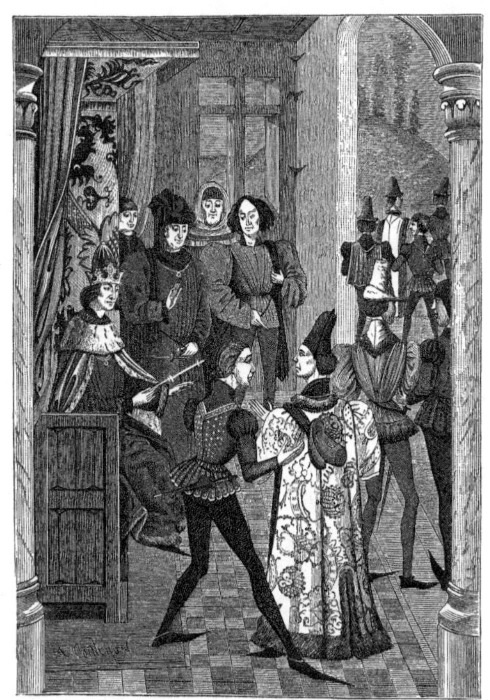

421

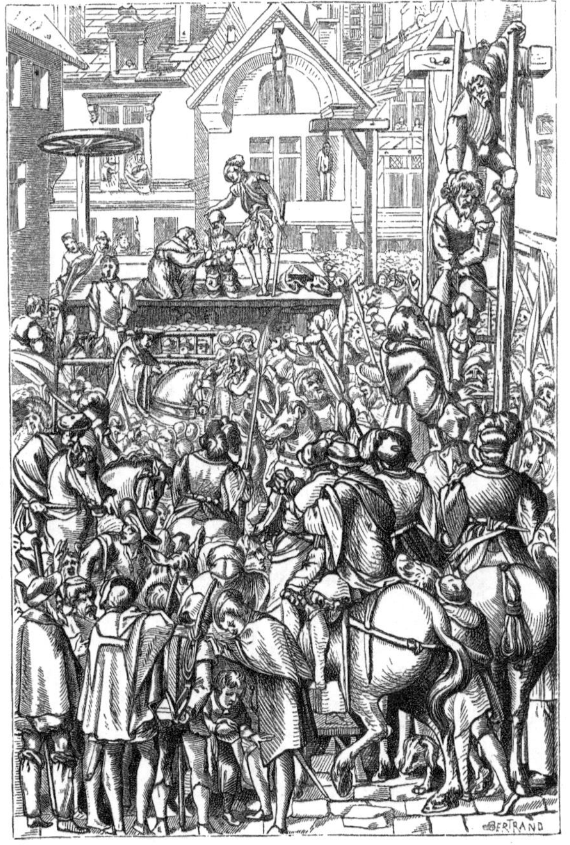

422

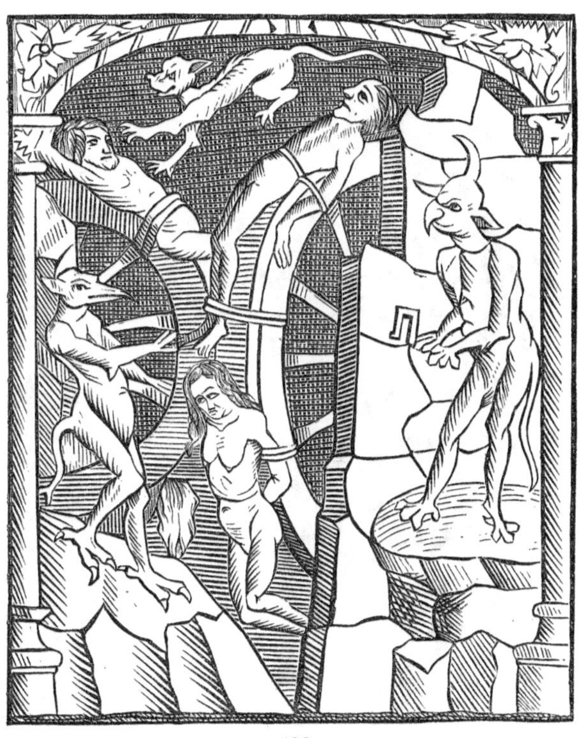

423

419. *Amende honorable* of Jacques Coeur before Charles VII, 15th century. **420.** Judge. **421.** The King's court, or grand council, 15th century. **422.** Public execution, 1541. **423.** Demons applying the torture of the wheel.

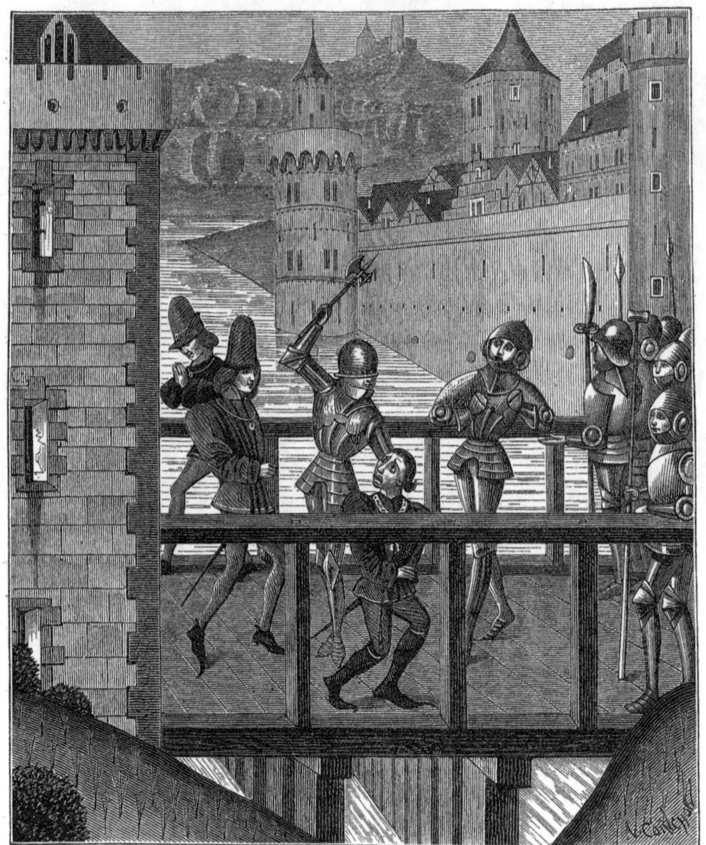

424

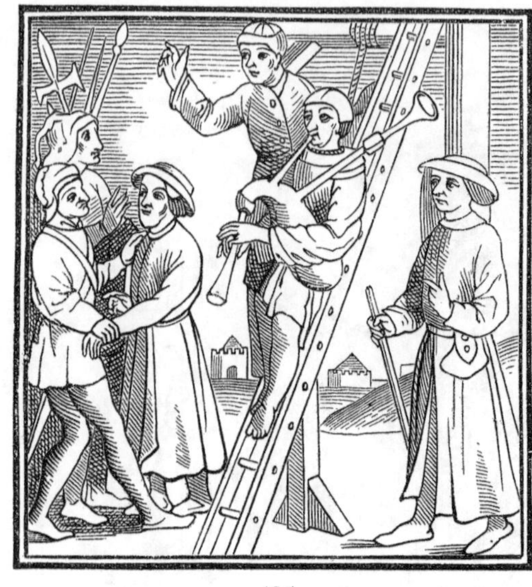

425

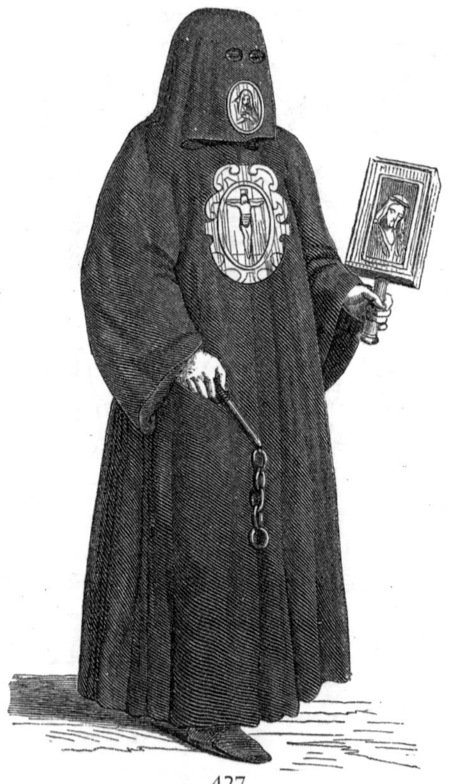

426

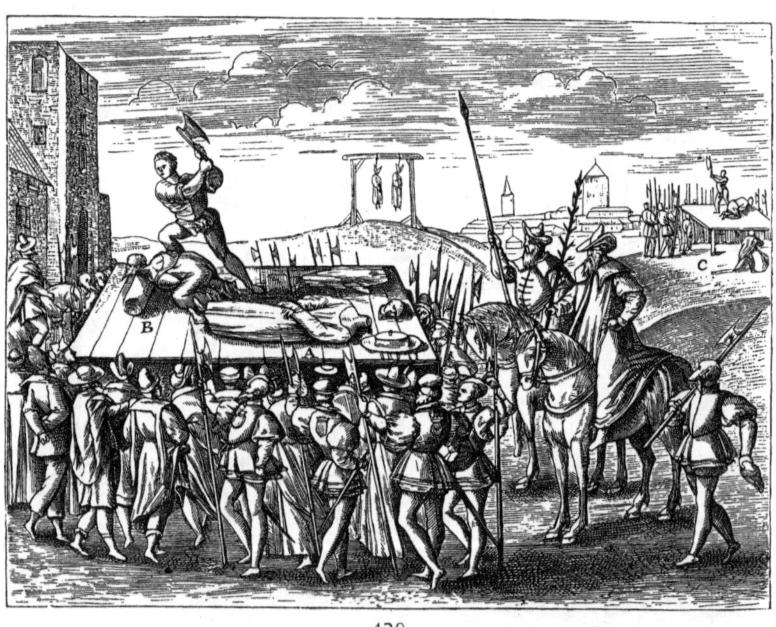

427

428

424. Assassination of the Duke of Burgundy, John the Fearless, on the bridge of Montereau. **425.** Hanging to music. **426.** Movable iron cage. **427.** Member of the Brotherhood of Death, whose duty it was to accompany those sentenced to death. **428.** Punishments decreed by Henry VIII against the Catholics, 1587.

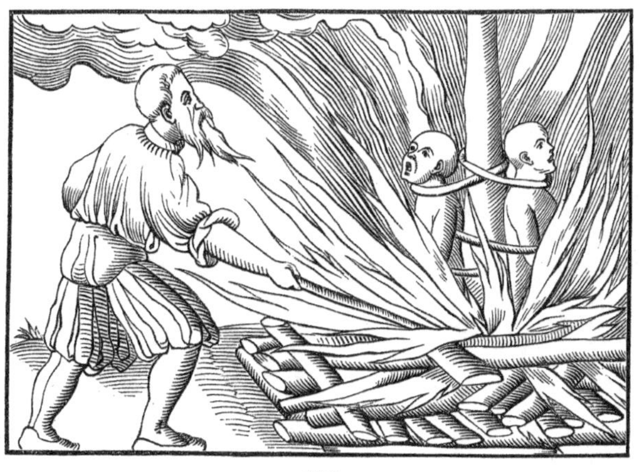

429

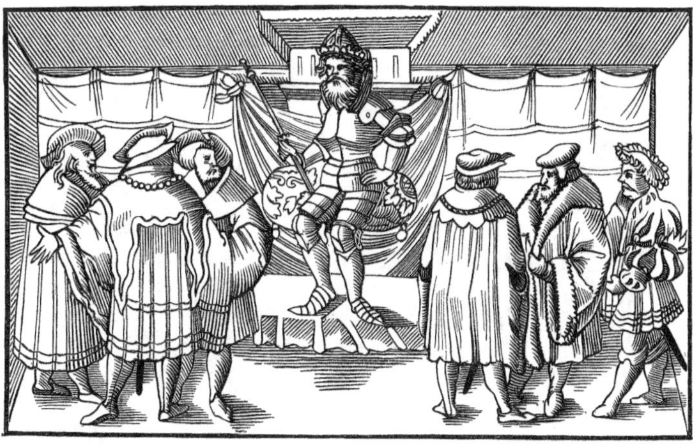

430

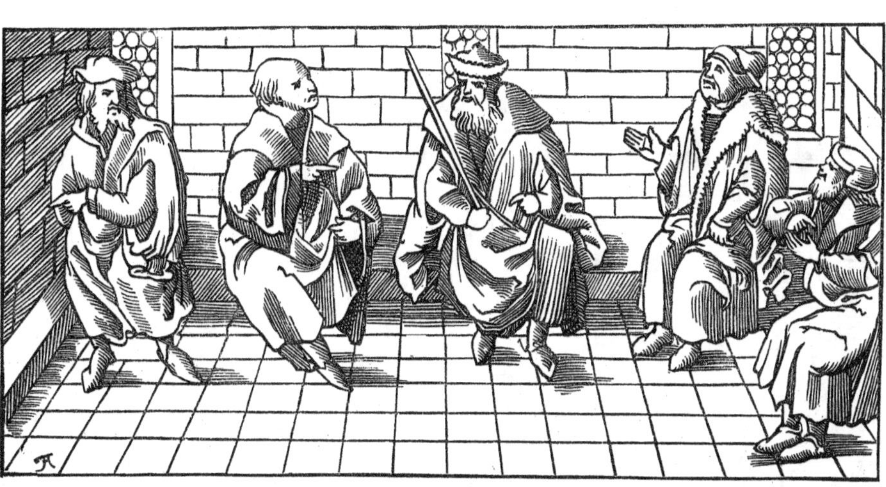

431

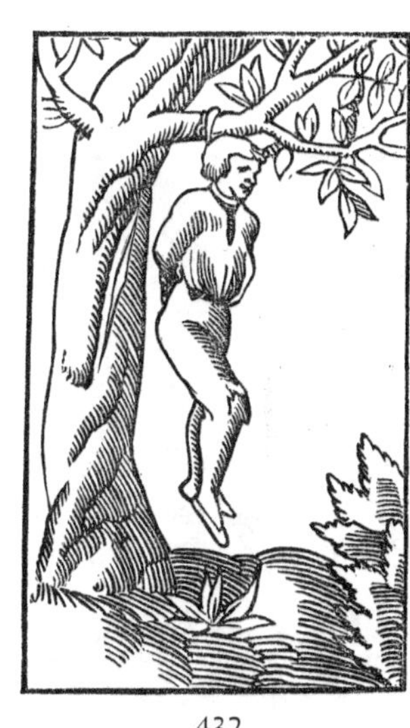

432

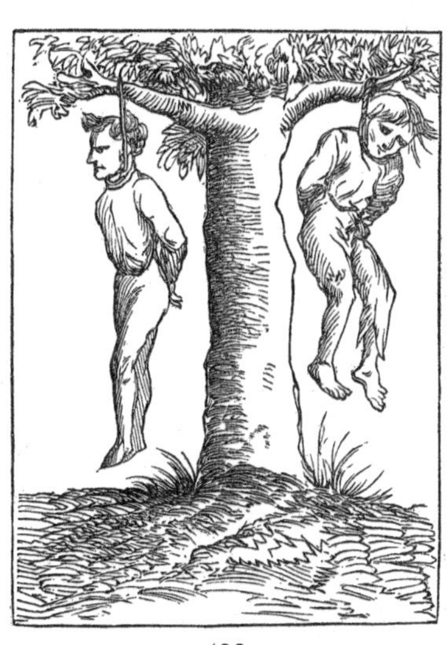

433

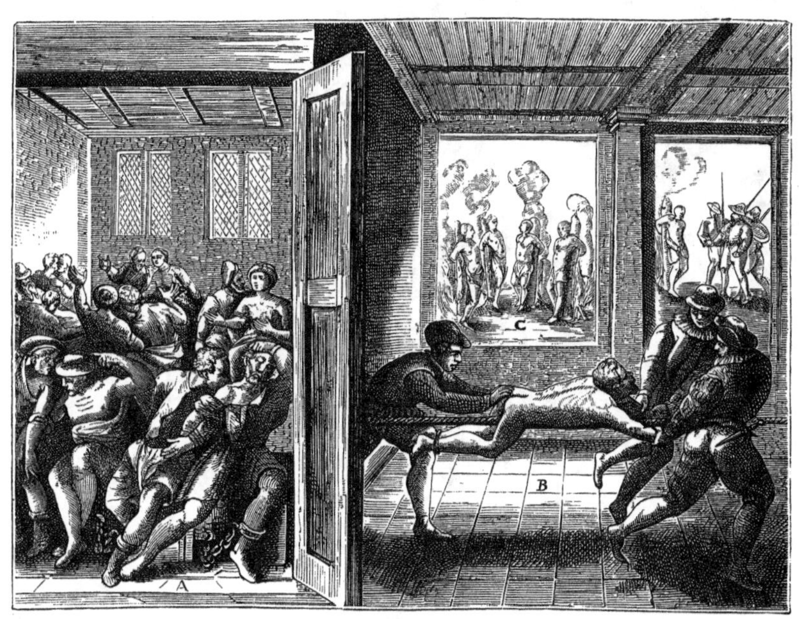

434

429. Punishment by fire. **430.** The court of a baron. **431.** Bailiwick, 1552. **432.** Execution of the sentence of the secret tribunal. **433.** Execution of the sentence of the secret tribunal. **434.** Tortures inflicted upon Catholics by the Huguenots in the south of France, 1587.

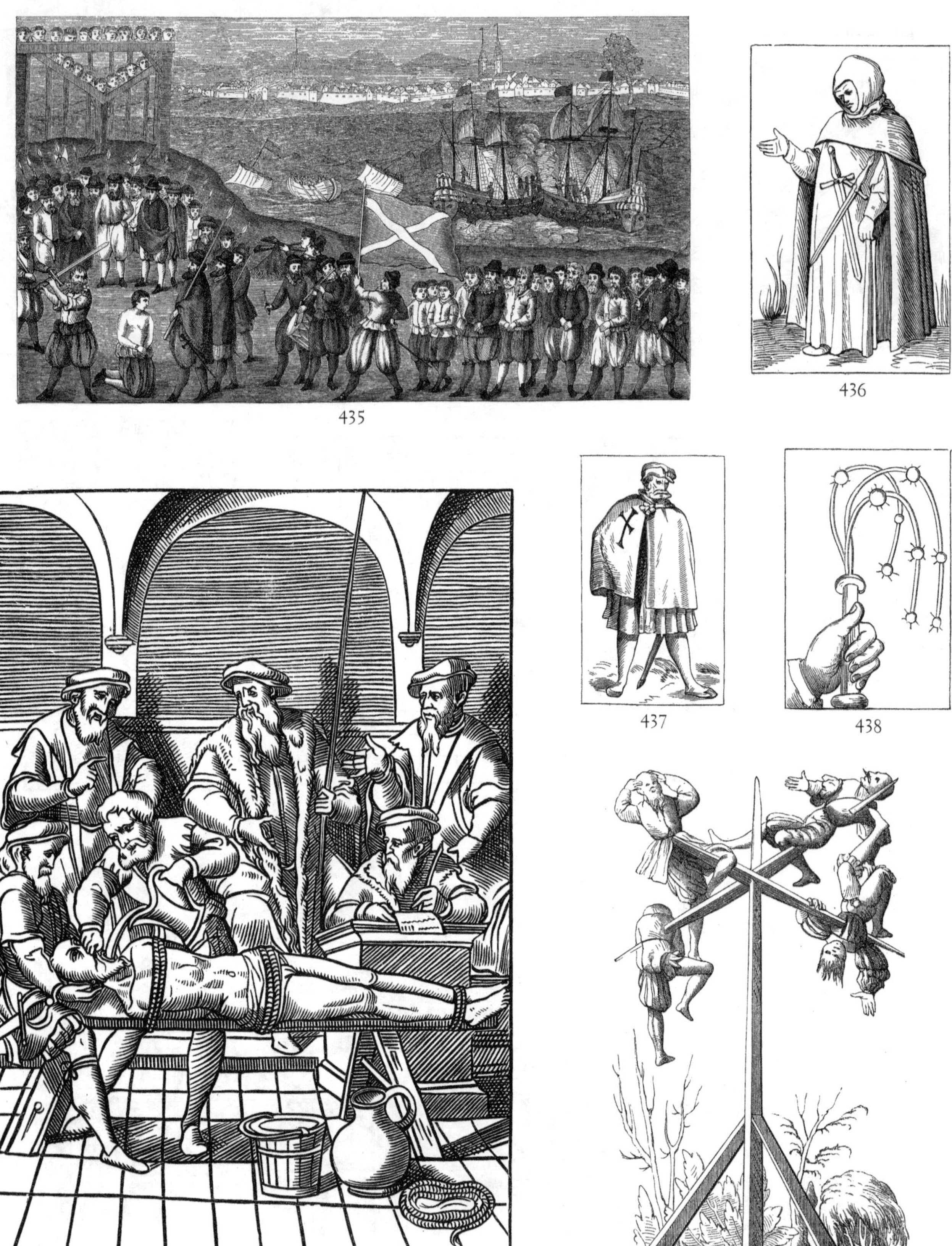

435. Execution of the celebrated pirate Stœrtebeck and his seventy accomplices in 1402 at Hamburg, 16th century. **436.** Free judge. **437.** Free judge. **438.** Cat-o'-nine-tails. **439.** The water torture. **440.** Impalement.

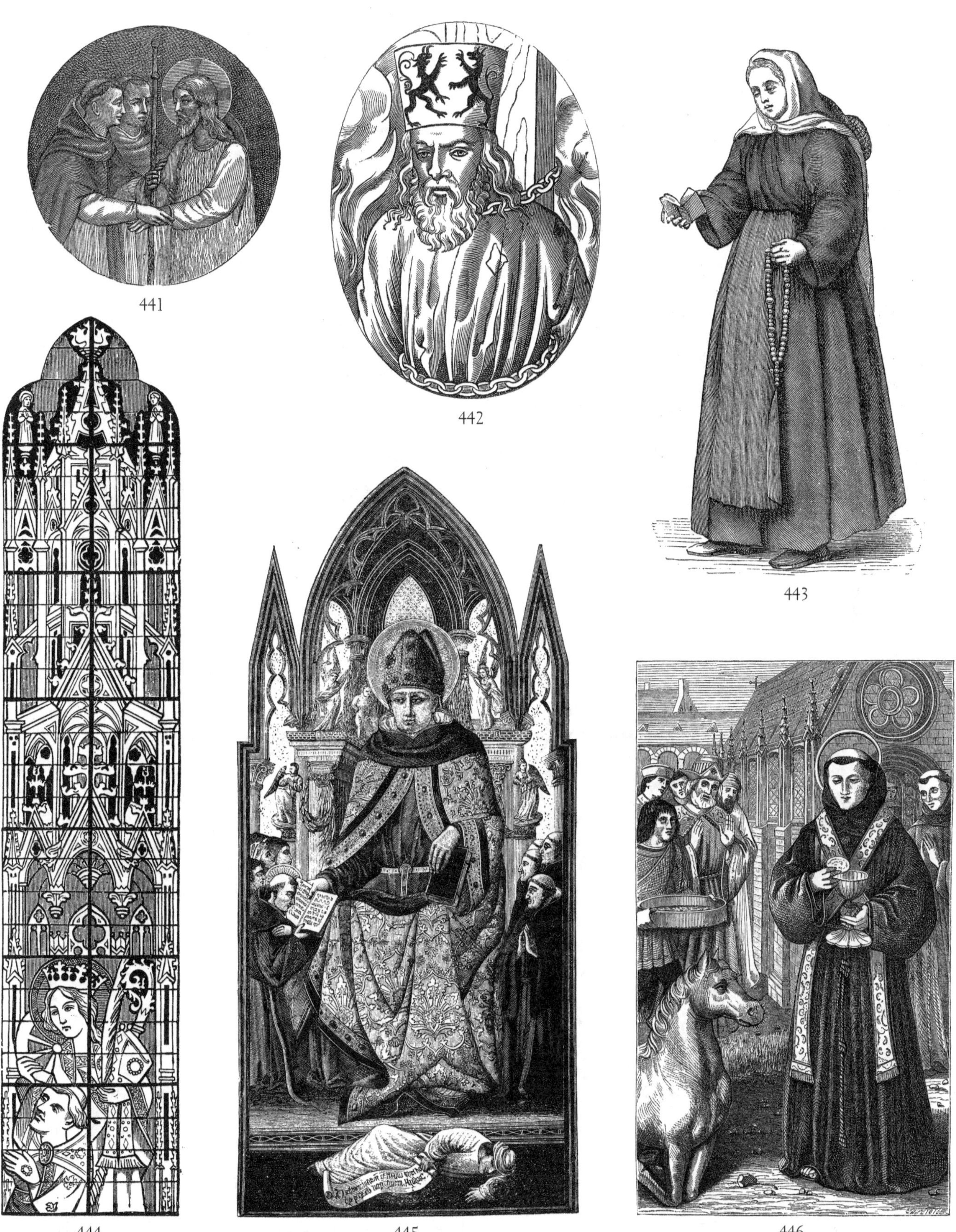

441. 442. 443. 444. 445. 446.

441. Hospitality: Jesus Christ being received as a pilgrim by Order of St. Dominic, 15th century. **442.** Jerome of Prague, a disciple of John Huss, burnt alive for heresy in 1416. **443.** Orphan of the Venice hospitals, 16th century. **444.** Fragment of a window, Cathedral of Evreux. **445.** St. Augustine, Bishop of Hippo, 15th century. **446.** St. Anthony of Padua, a Franciscan friar, 15th century.

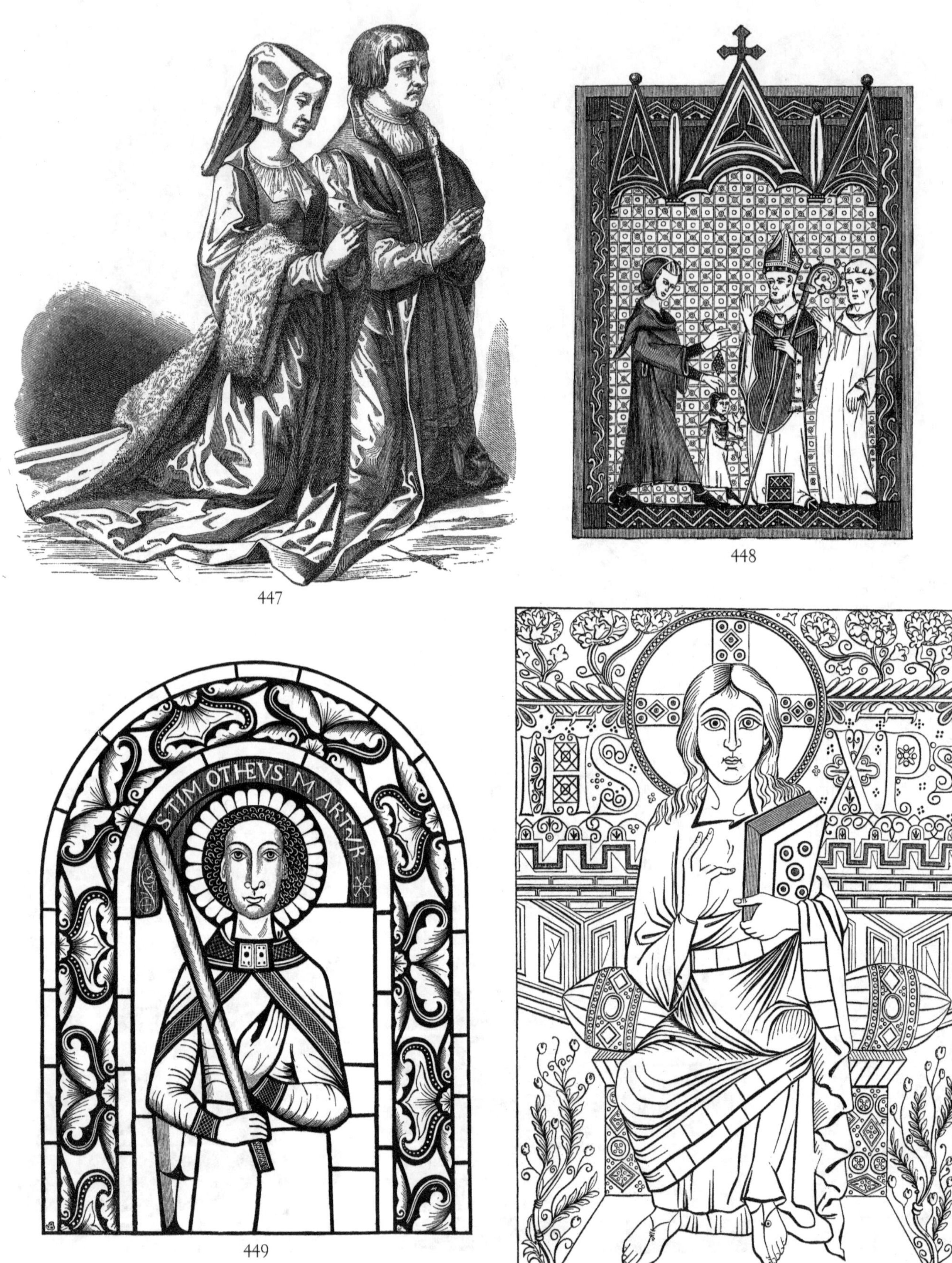

447. Burgess of Ghent and his wife, in ceremonial attire. **448.** The offering of a child to an abbot, 13th century, **449.** St. Timothy the Martyr, colored glass, 11th century. **450.** From Book of the Gospels.

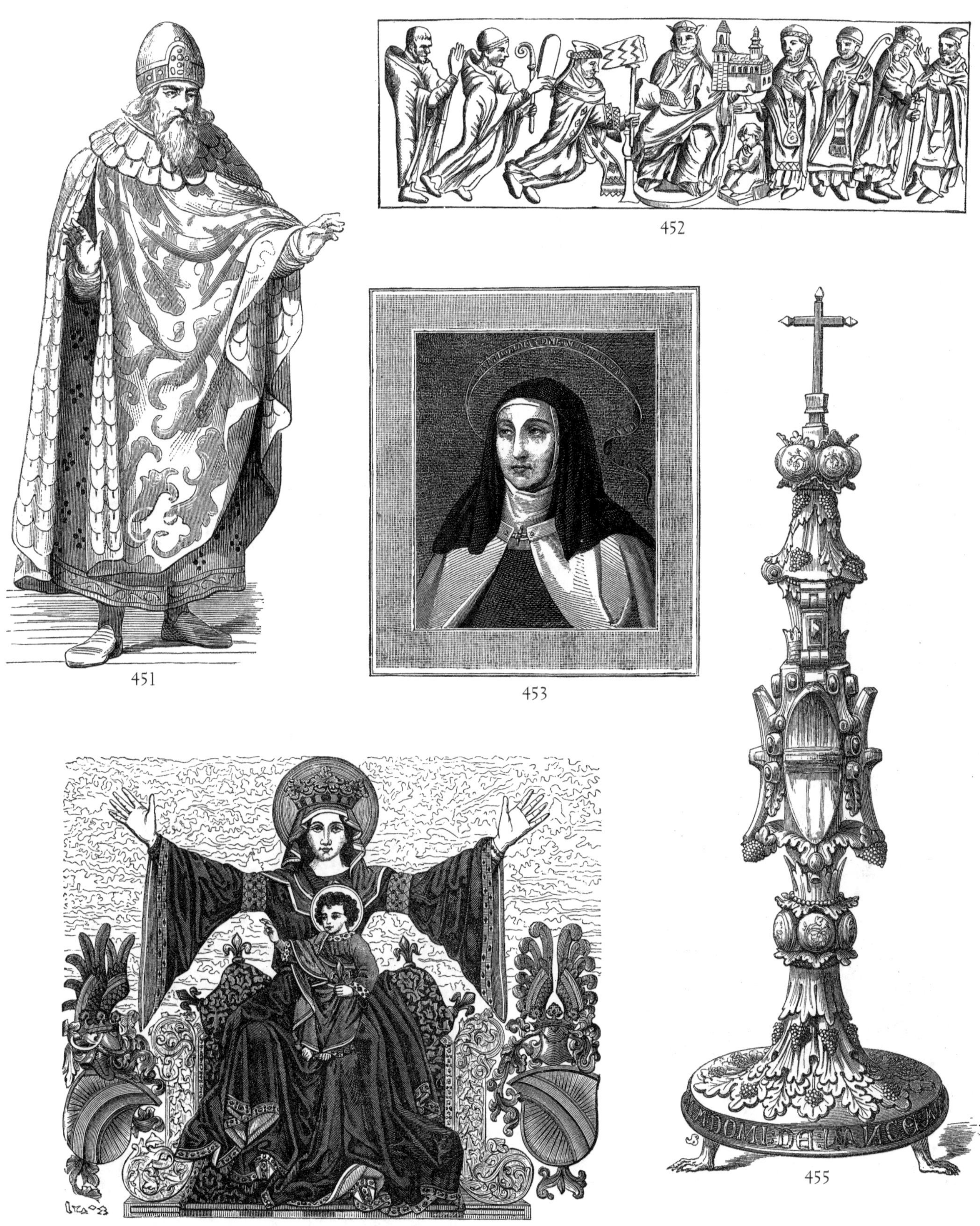

451 452 453 454 455

451. Doge of Venice, 16th century. **452.** Bas-relief on the tomb of Hincmar, Archbishop of Rheims, 10th or 11th century. **453.** St. Theresa, reformer of the Carmelites, 16th century. **454.** Ancient banner of the city of Strasburg with image of Our Lady, the Virgin, 13th century. **455.** Reliquary of the Holy Thorn, 13th century.

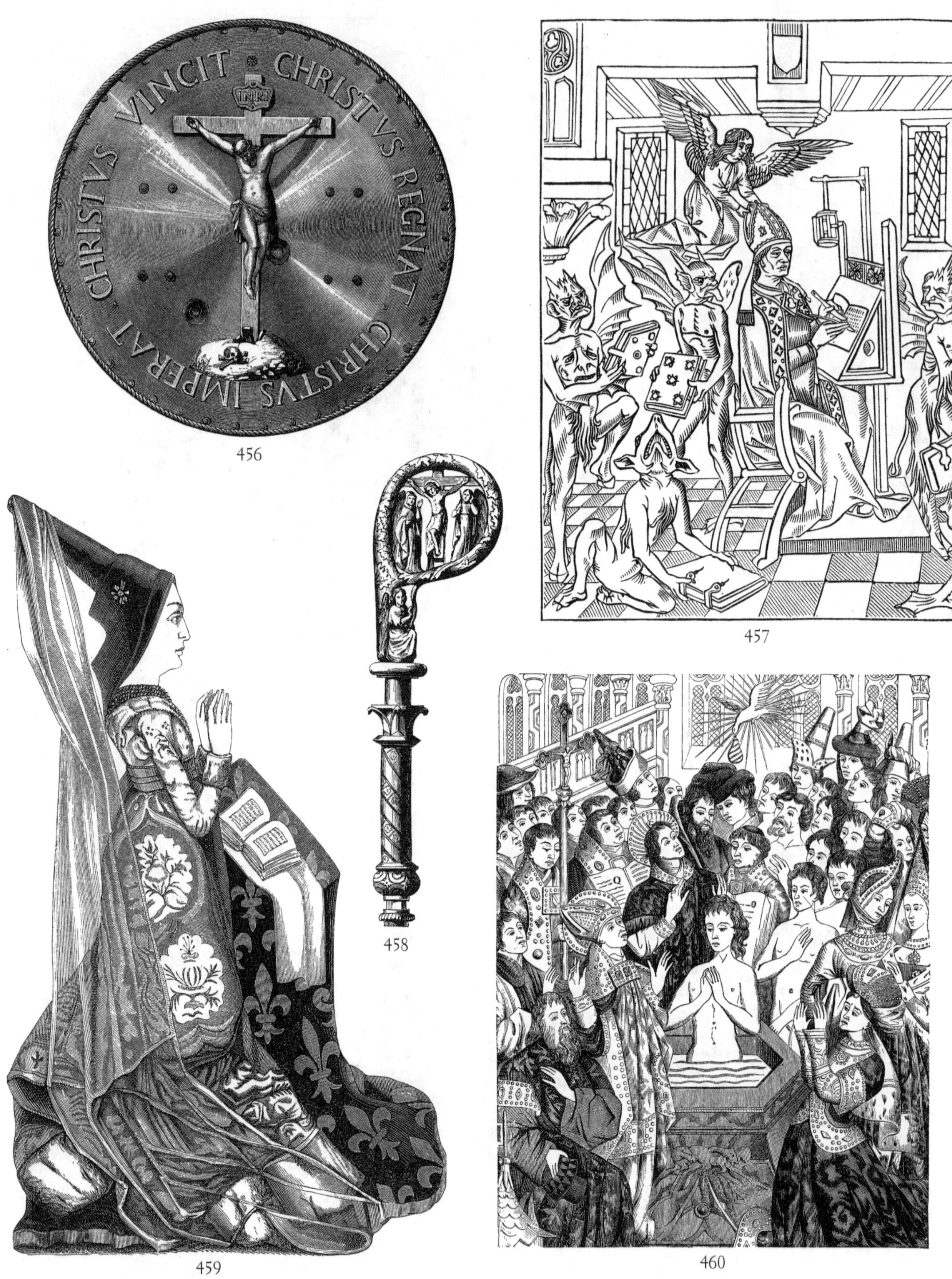

456. Iron shield presented to Don John of Austria by Pius V. **457.** Orthodoxy surrounded by the Snares of Heresy. **458.** Bishop's crozier. **459.** Costume of Charlotte of Savoy, second wife of Louis XI. **460.** Baptism of King Clovis, 15th century.

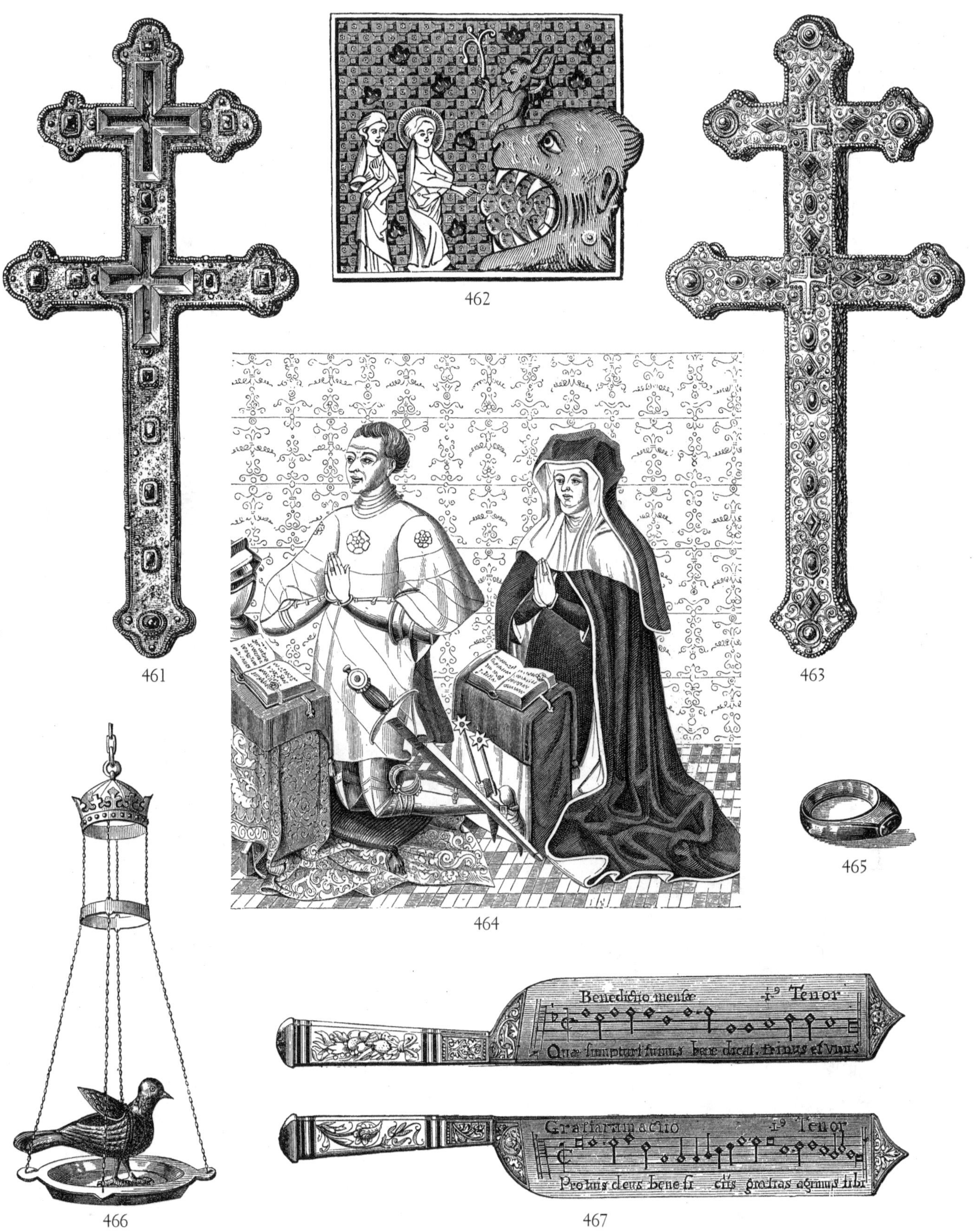

461. Abbatial cross of St. Waudru (front). **462.** The Purgatory of Monsignor St. Patrick, 14th century. **463.** Abbatial cross of St. Waudru (back). **464.** Jean Jouvenal des Ursins, provost of the merchants of Paris, and Michelle de Vitry, his wife. **465.** Abbatial ring of St. Waudru. **466.** Dove suspended above the altar, containing the Eucharistic box, 13th century. **467.** Knife for cutting consecrated bread, music on blade, 16th century.

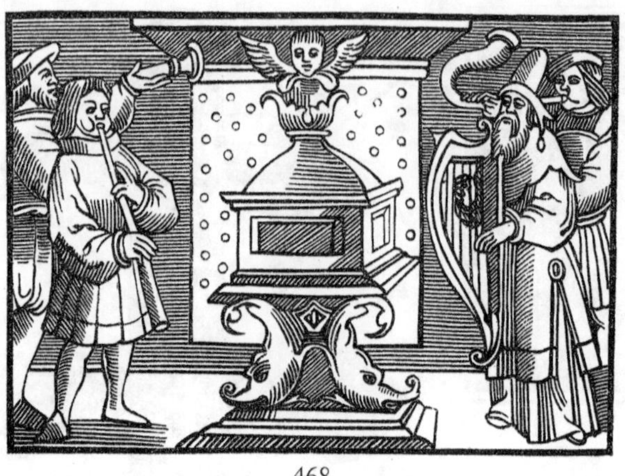

468

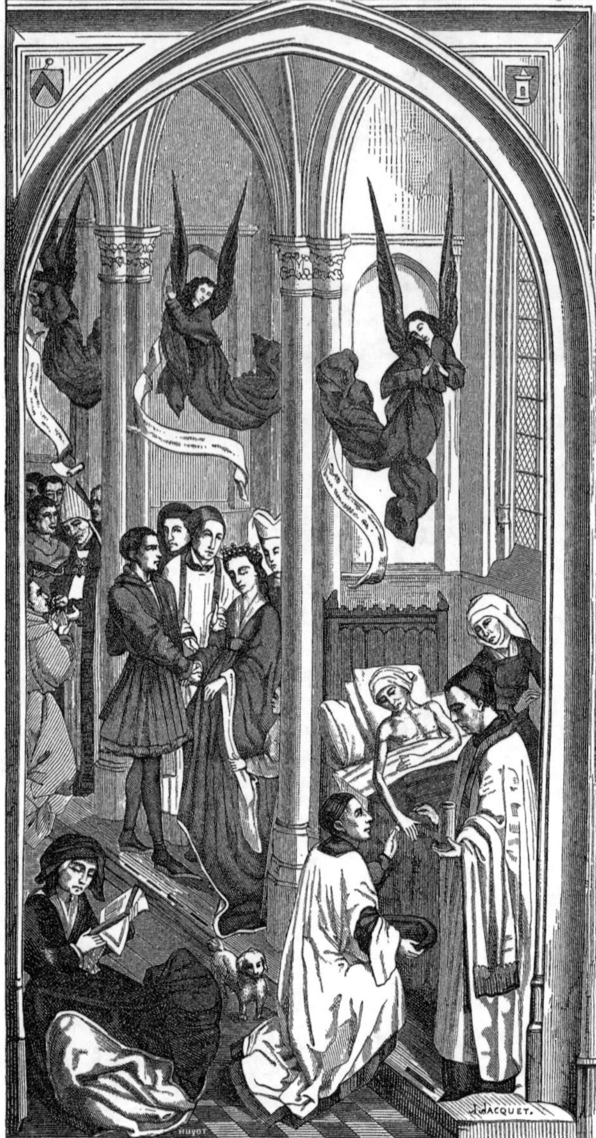

469

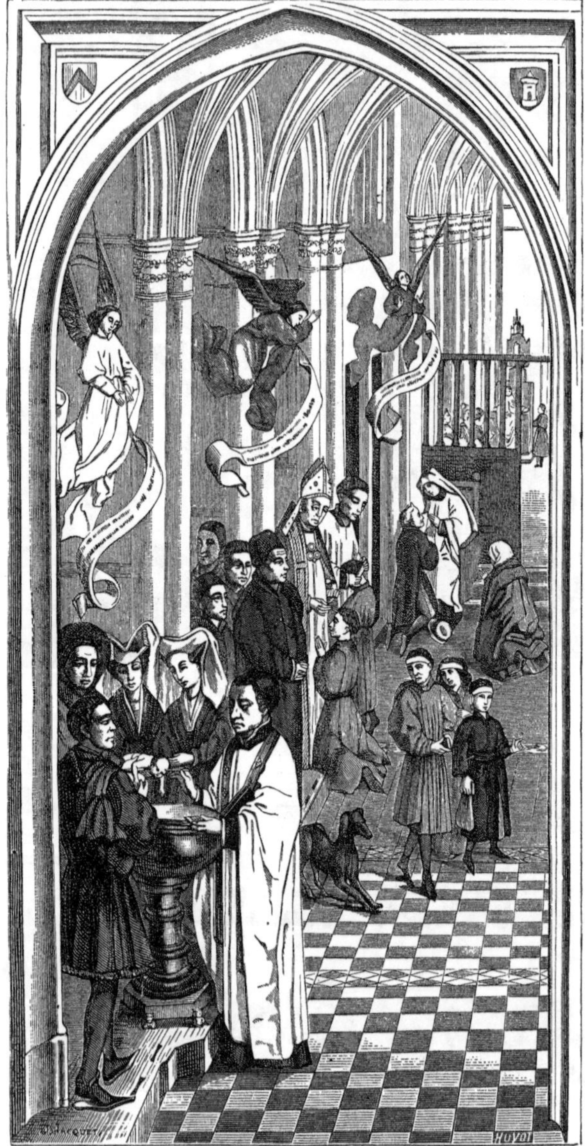

470

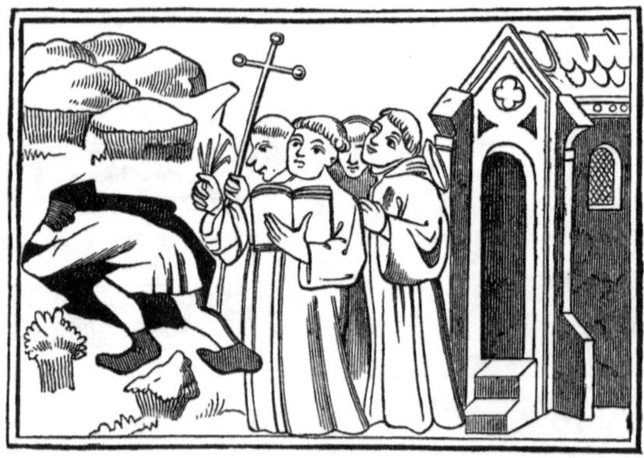

471

468. Jewish ceremony before the ark. **469.** Three Sacraments: *Marriage, Orders,* and *Extreme Unction,* 15th century. **470.** Three Sacraments: *Baptism, Confirmation,* and *Penance,* 15th century. **471.** Owen, accompanied by monks, creeps into the Aperture of the Gap, 15th century.

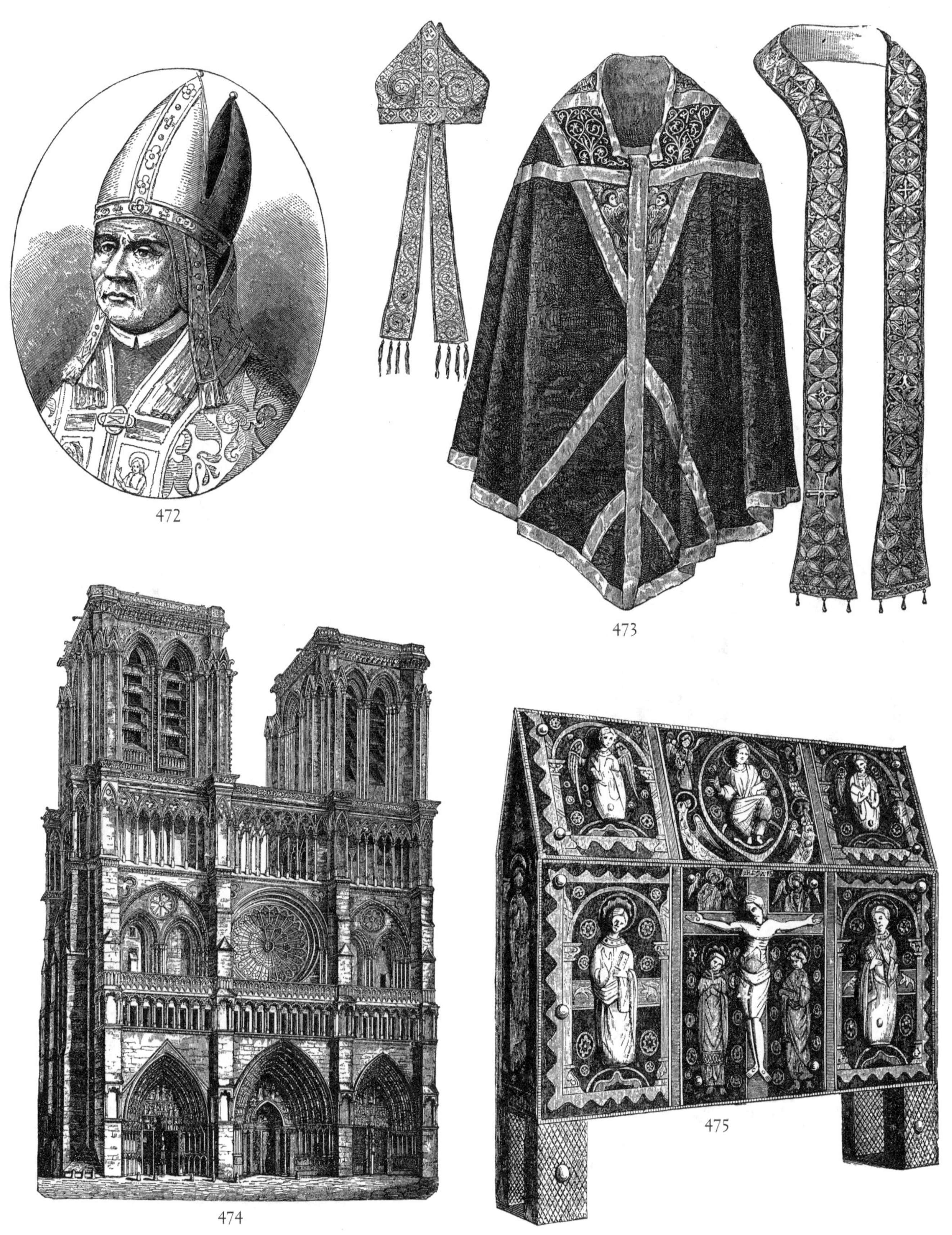

472. Portrait of Pope Sylvester I. **473.** Chasuble, mitre, and stole of St. Thomas à Becket, Archbishop of Canterbury, 12th century. **474.** Notre-Dame, Paris, 12th and 13th centuries. **475.** Enameled shrine, 12th century.

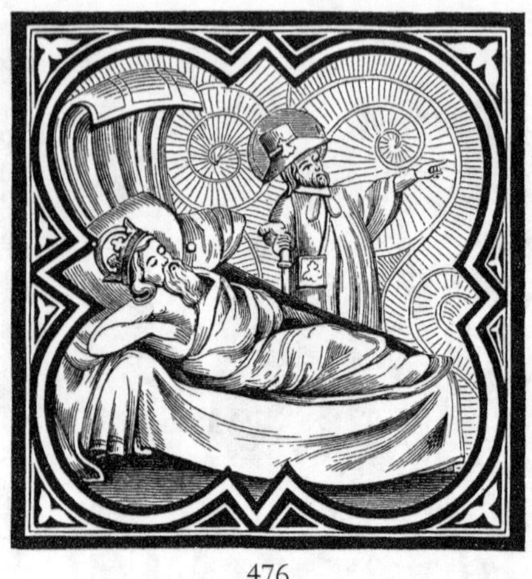

476

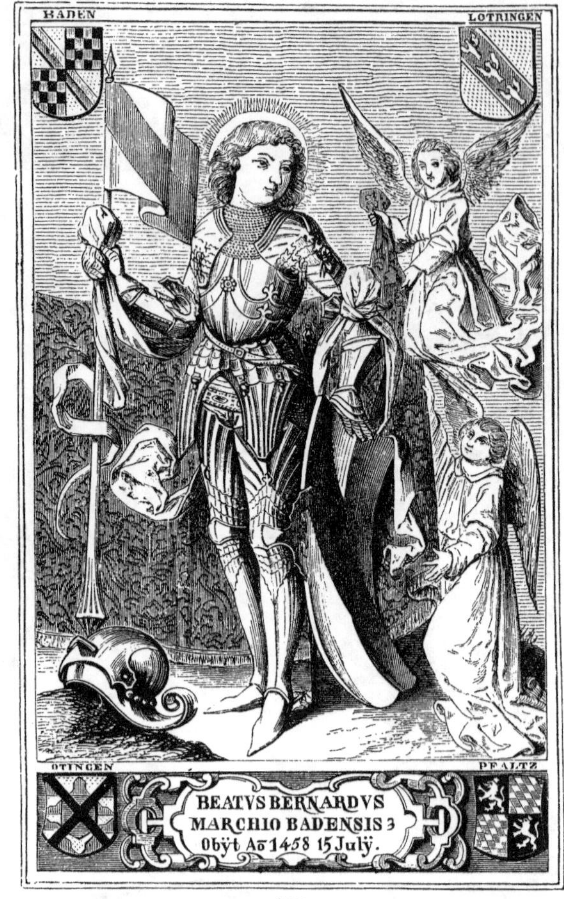

477

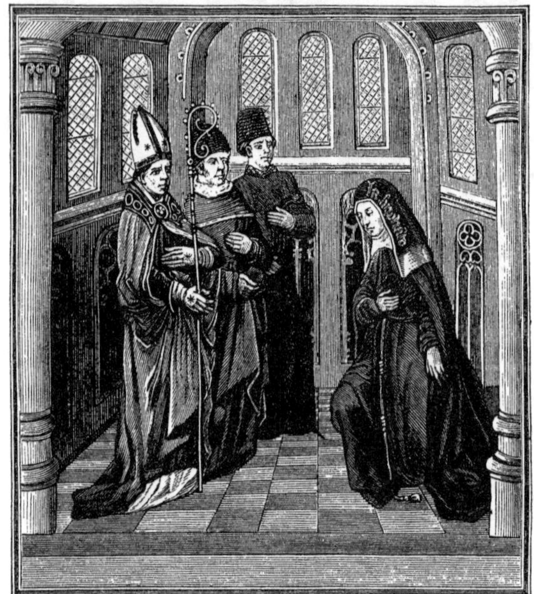

478

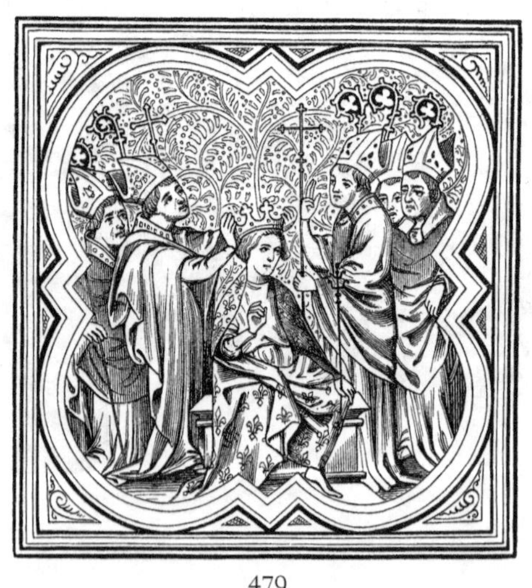

479

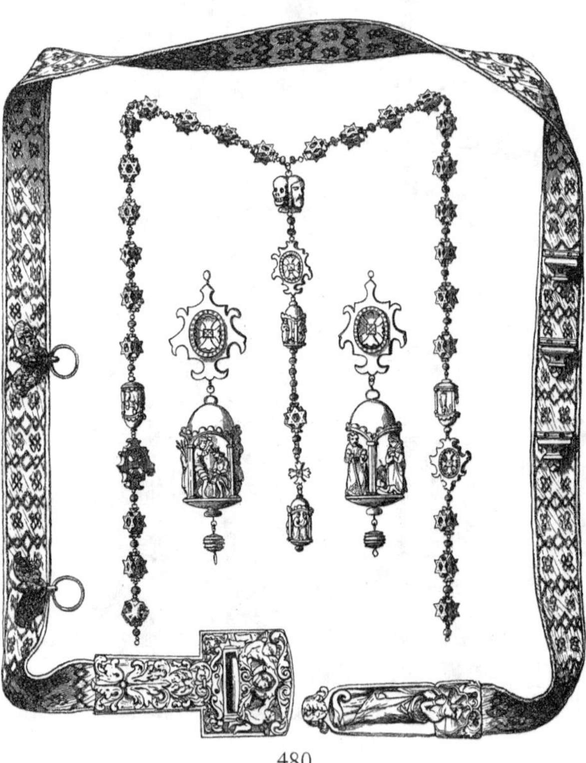

480

476. The Vision of Charlemagne, 14th century. **477.** Miniature, the *Livre d'Heures*. **478.** Sacred oratory, with Bishop, doctor of theology, clerk, and supplicant, 1466. **479.** Coronation of Charlemagne. **480.** Carved ivory chaplet of beads; girdle of an abbess, 16th century.

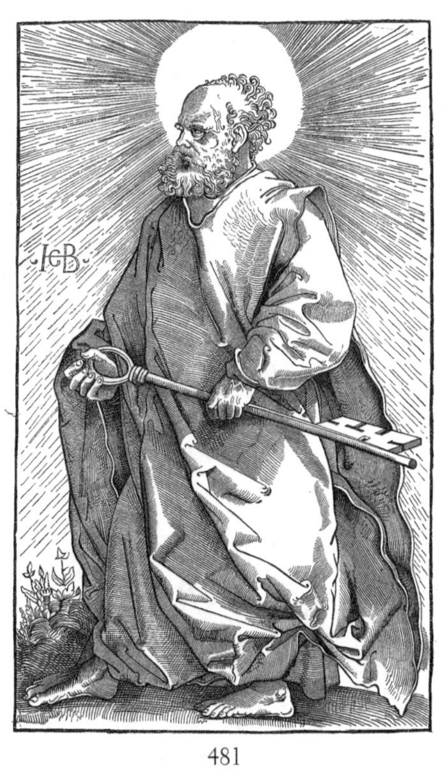

481

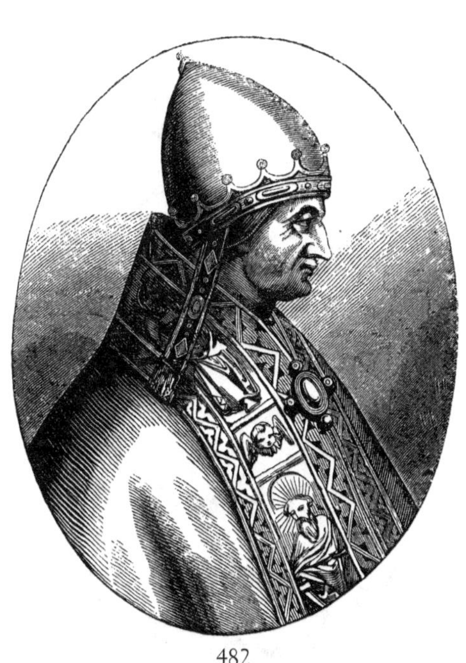

482

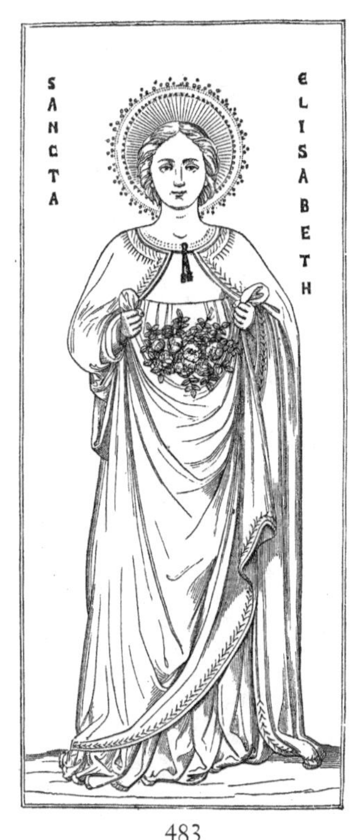

483

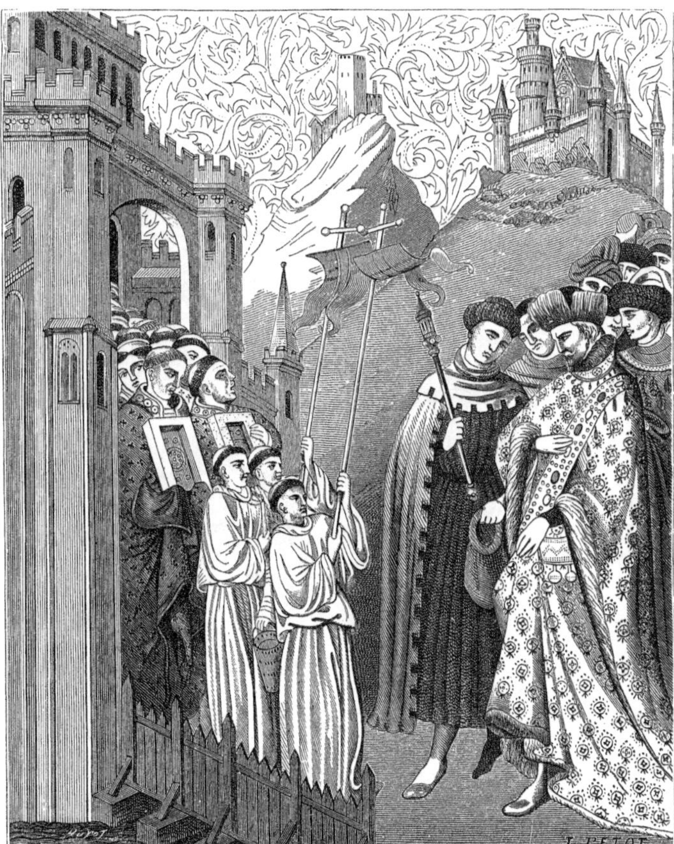

484

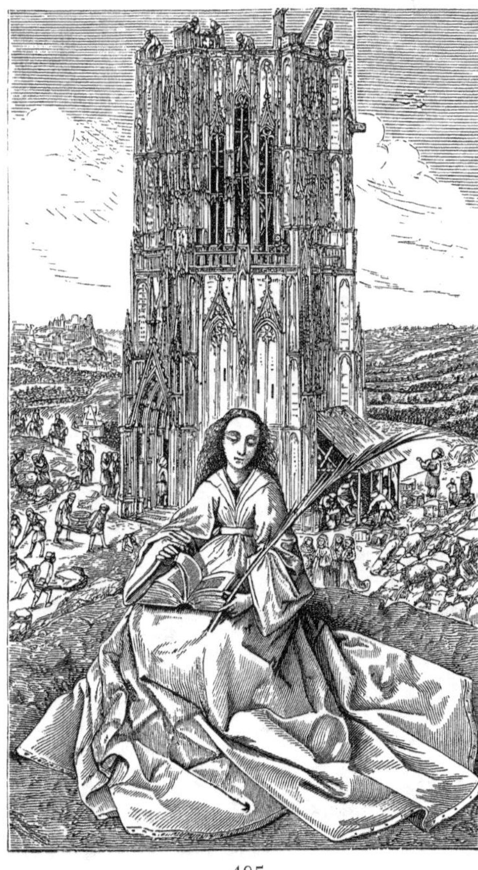

485

481. St. Peter, 15th or 16th century. **482.** Portrait of Innocent IV, elected Pope in 1243. **483.** St. Elizabeth of Hungary, with roses, 15th century. **484.** Clergy, with cross and holy images, 14th century. **485.** St. Barbara, who suffered martyrdom in the third century; 15th century.

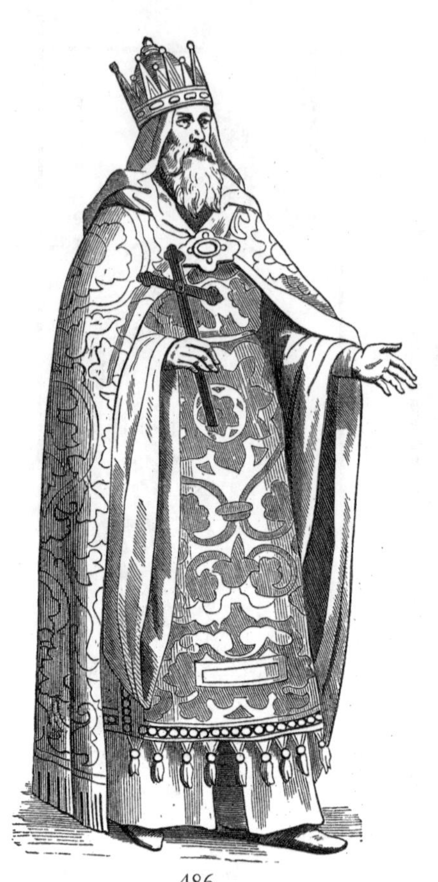

486

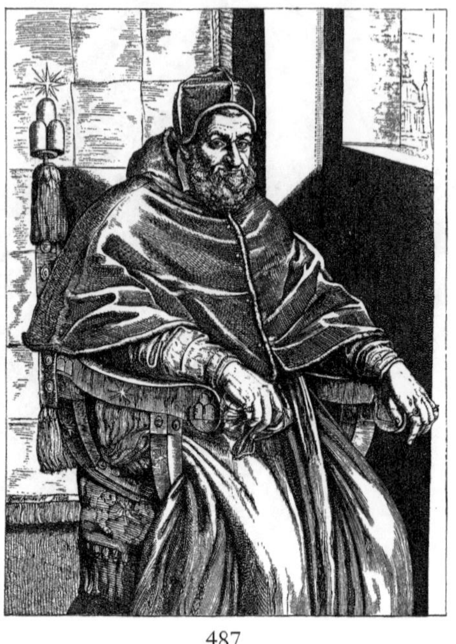

487

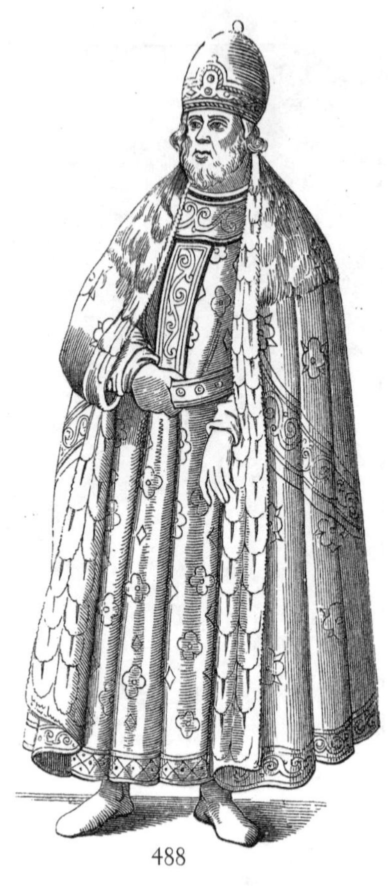

488

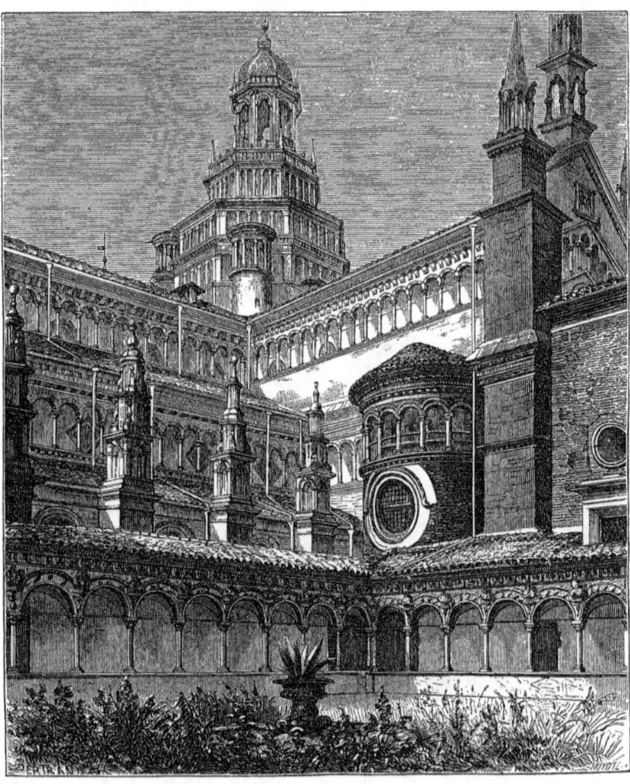

489

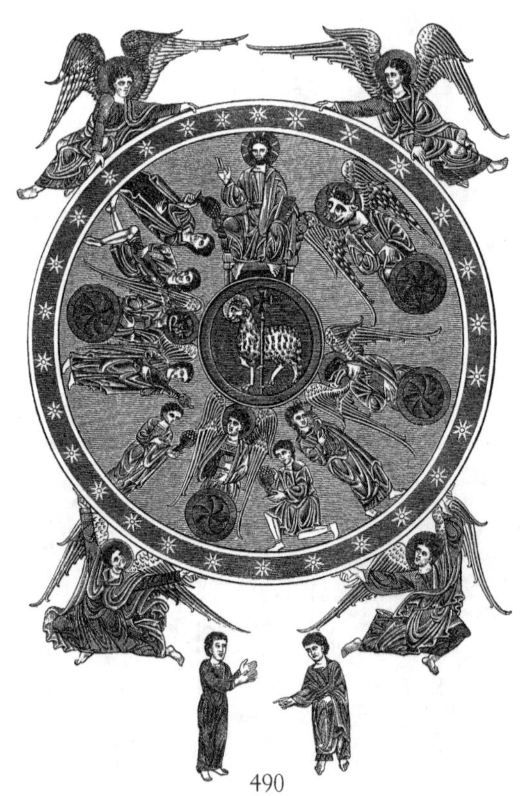

490

486. Prester-John, Chief of a Christian tribe in Tartary. **487.** Portrait of Sixtus Quintus (1521–1590). **488.** Doge of Venice, ceremonial costume, 16th century. **489.** Small Cloister of the Chartreuse at Pavia, 14th century. **490.** The Triumph of the Lamb, Christ, 12th century.

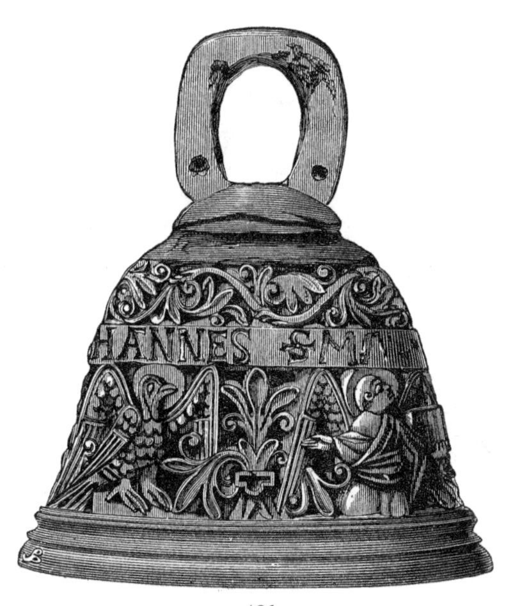

491

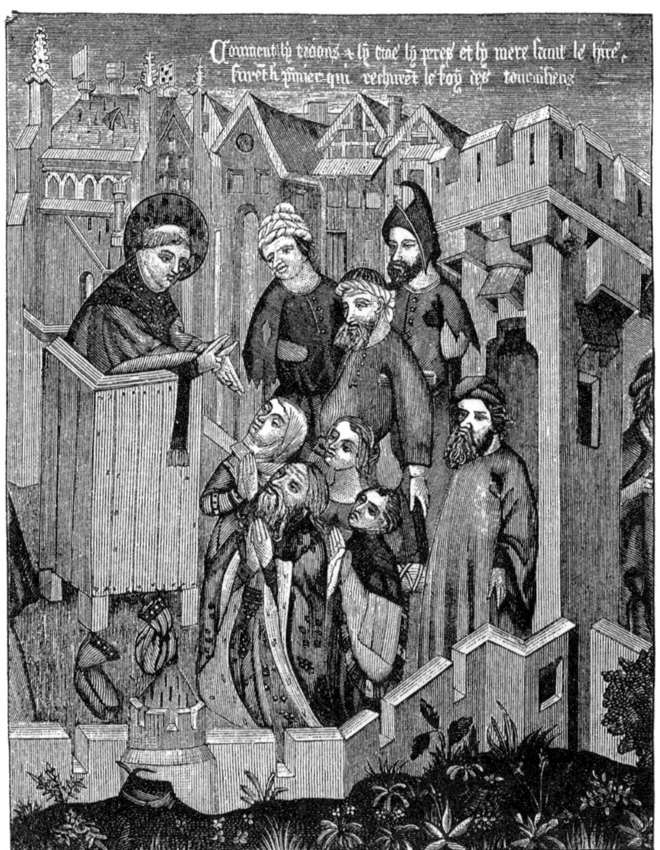

492

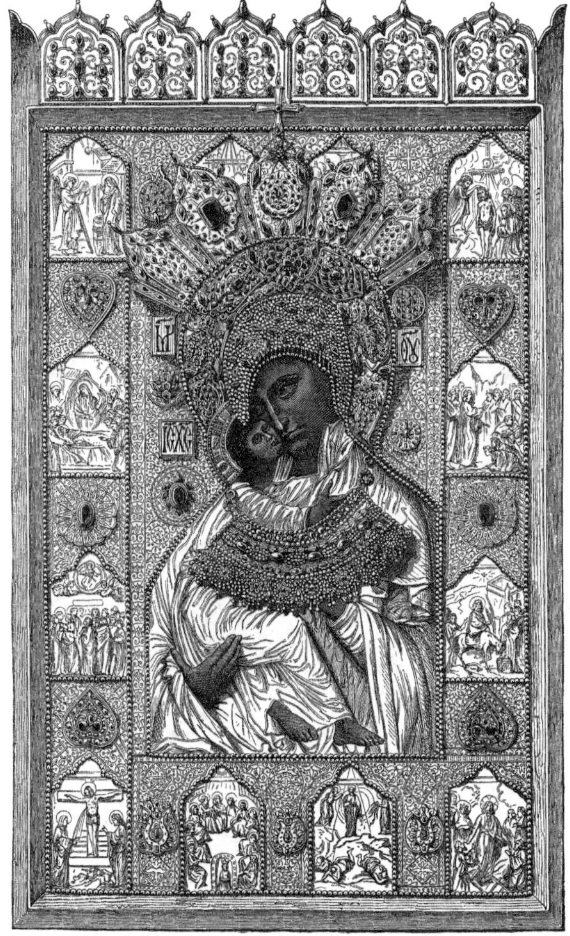

493

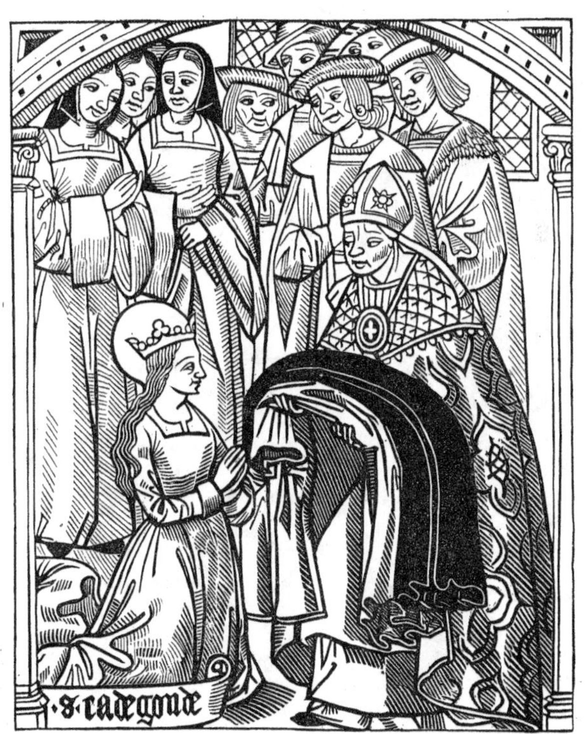

494

491. Romanesque perforated handbell, 12th century. **492.** Preaching of the first missionary apostles, 1402. **493.** Miraculous image of Our Lady of Vladimir, 12th century. **494.** St. Radegonde, Wife of King Clotaire, 1513.

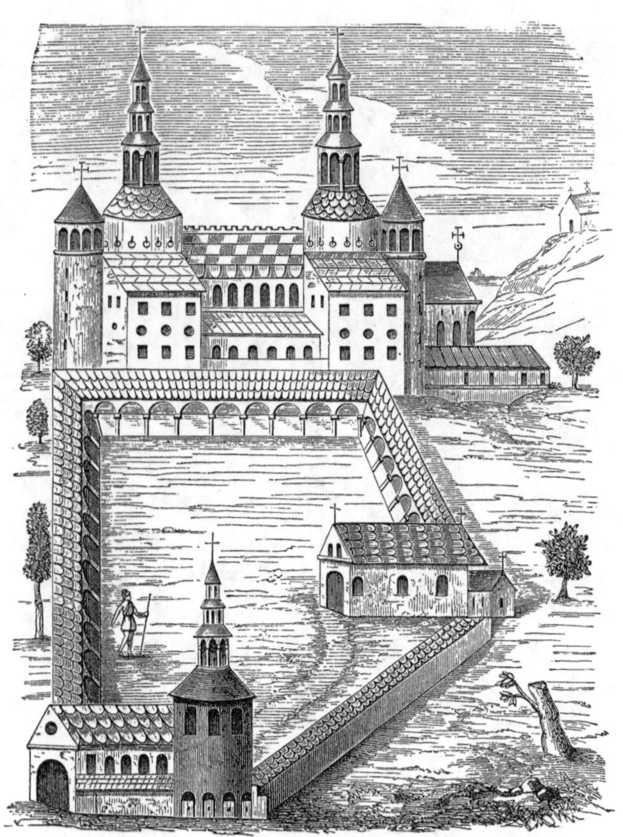

495

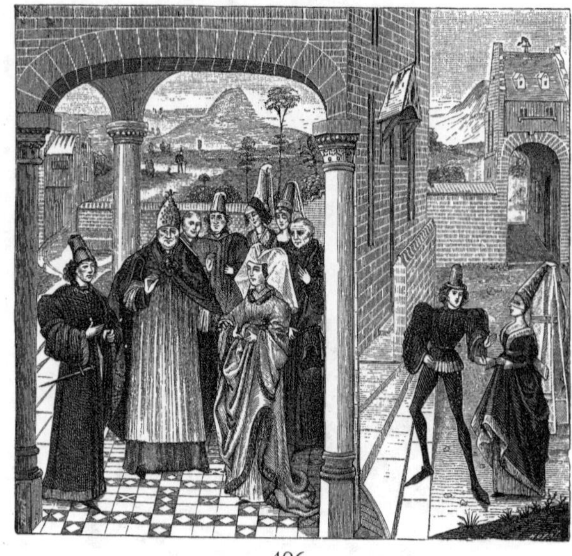

496

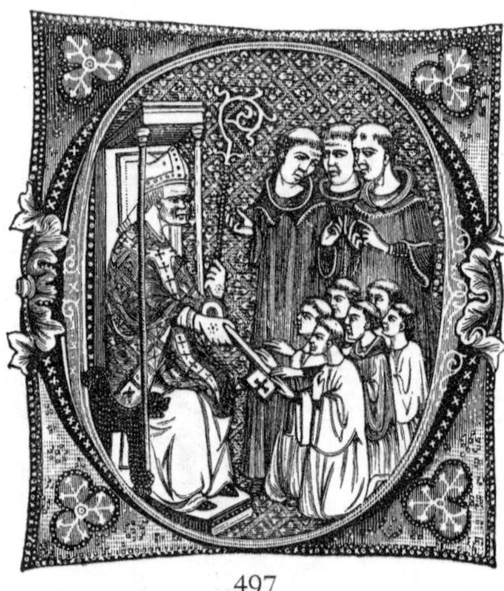

497

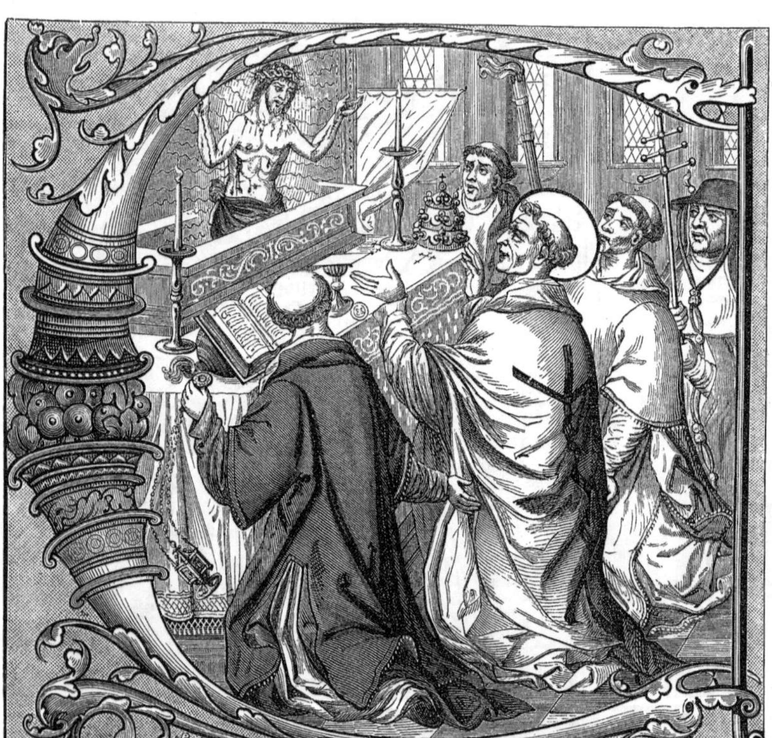

498

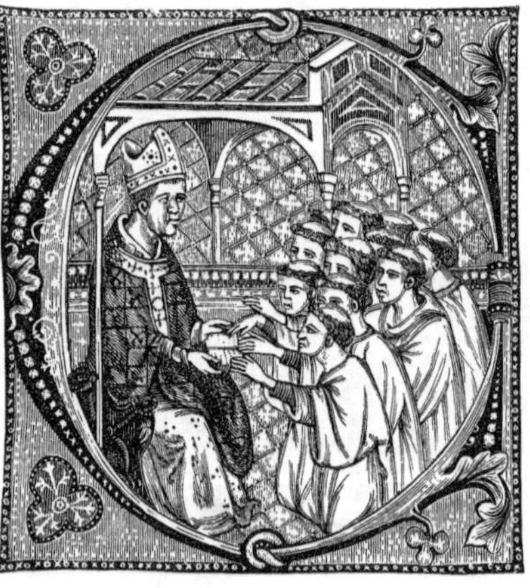

499

495. Abbey of St. Riquier, founded in 799; 1612. **496.** Treaty of Arras, concluded in 1191; 15th century. **497.** The exorcist, minor order, 14th century. **498.** Miraculous Mass of St. Gregory the Great, 15th century. **499.** The doorkeeper, minor order, 14th century.

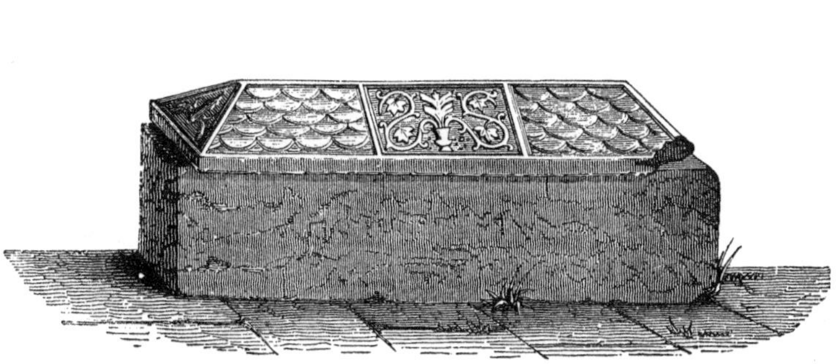

500

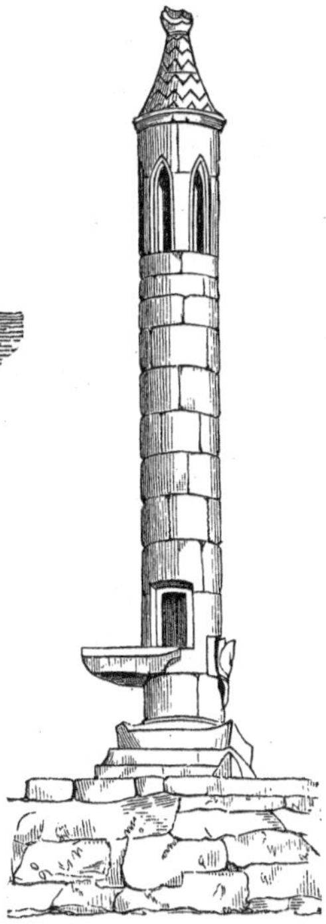

501

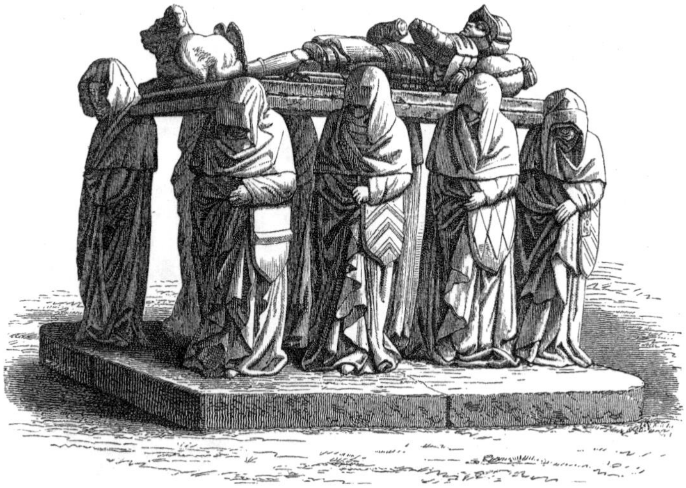

503

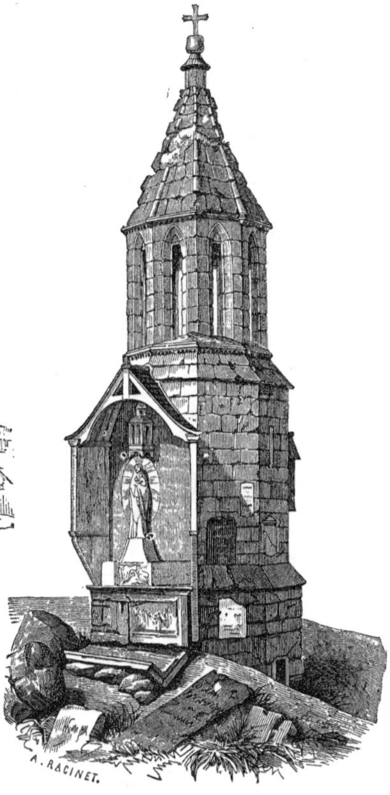

502

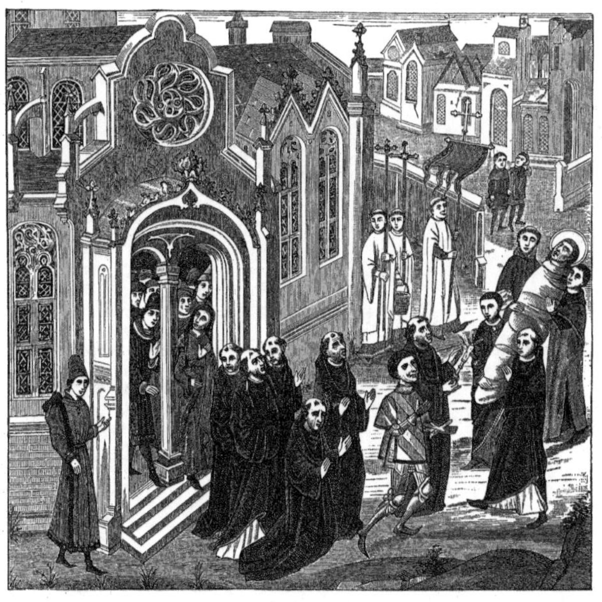

504

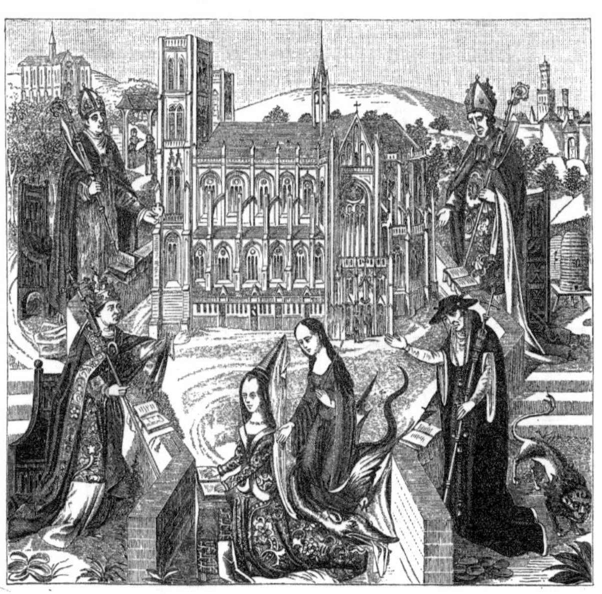

505

500. Stone tomb for one of the first abbots of St. Germain-des-Près, Paris. **501.** Beacon in the cemetery of Ciron, 12th century. **502.** Tower of Notre-Dame-du-Bois, demolished in 1786. **503.** Tomb of Philip Pot, Grand Seneschal of Burgundy. **504.** Removal of the body of Mary Magdalene to the church of Vézelay (Yonne), 15th century. **505.** Margaret of York, one of the most charitable princesses of her time, 15th century.

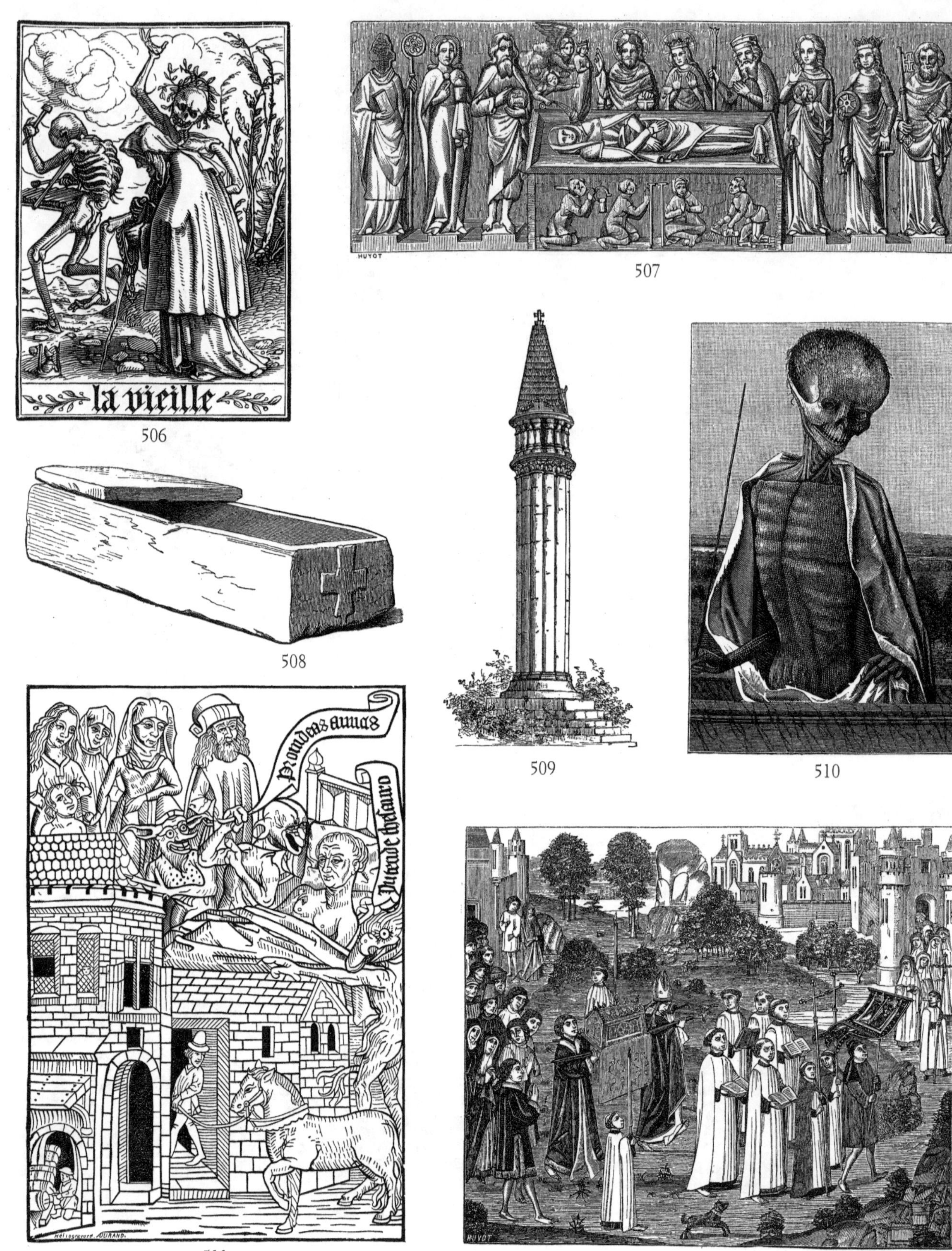

506. The Dance of Death, after Holbein's drawings. **507.** Tomb of St. Elizabeth of Hungary, 13th century. **508.** Stone coffin of Gallo-Roman origin. **509.** Beacon in the cemetery of Feniou, 11th century. **510.** Doctor Death, from a *Book of Hours,* 16th century. **511.** Facsimile of the fifth page of the first xylographic edition of the *Ars Moriendi,* representing the sinner on his deathbed. **512.** Count Renier bearing the body of St. Veronica to the church of St. Waudru, 15th century.

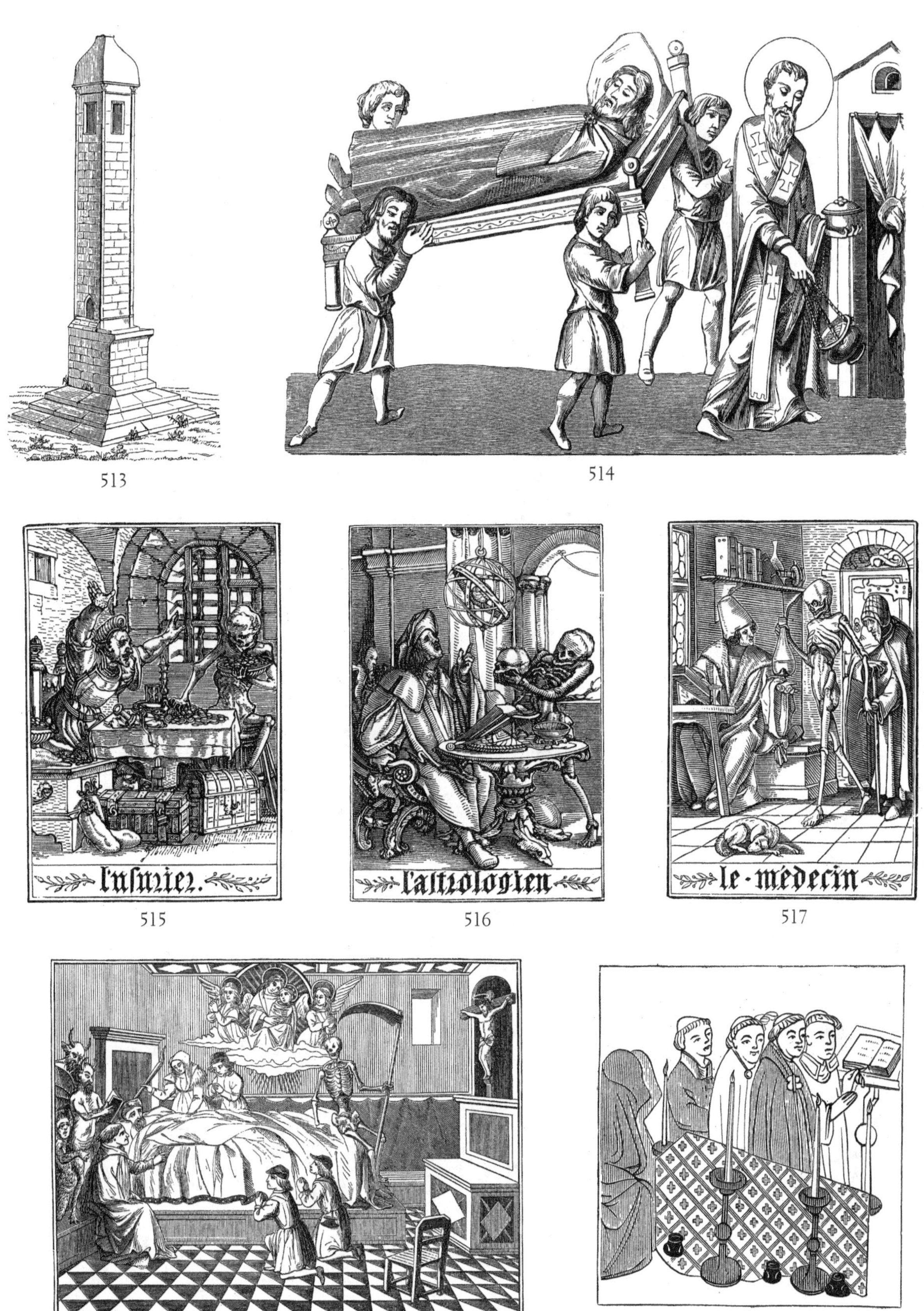

513. Beacon in the cemetery of Antigny, Vienne, 15th century. **514.** Obsequies of St. Cesarius, physician to the emperors Constantius and Julian, 9th century. **515, 516, 517.** The Dance of Death, after Holbein's drawings. **518.** The Christian professor on his death-bed. **519.** Funeral service, 14th century.

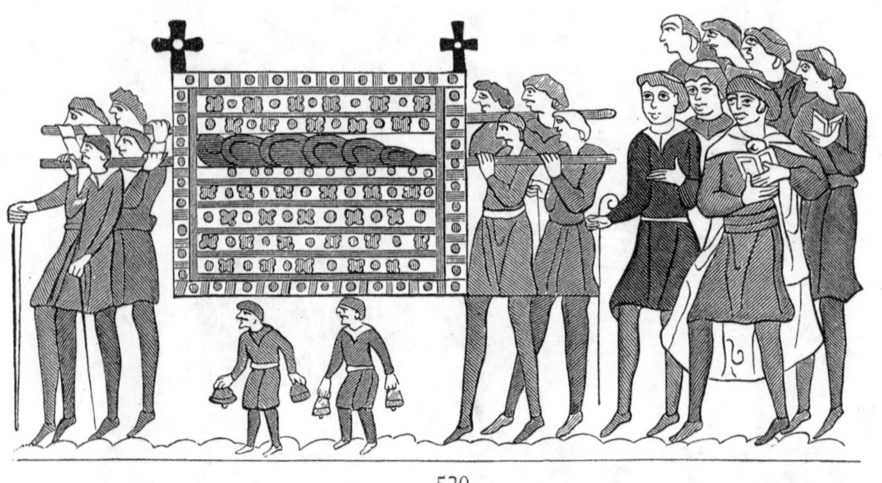

520

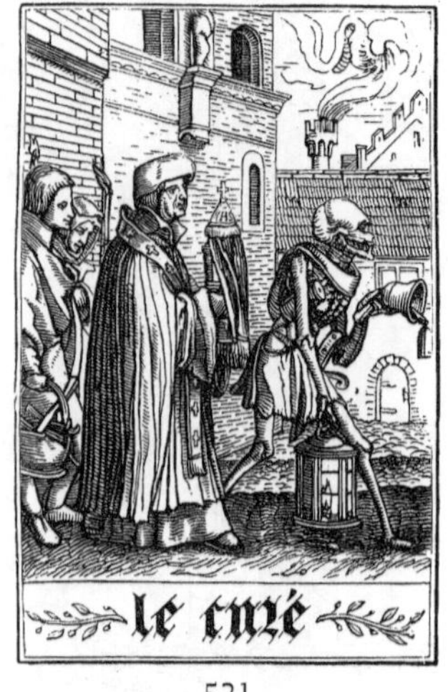

521

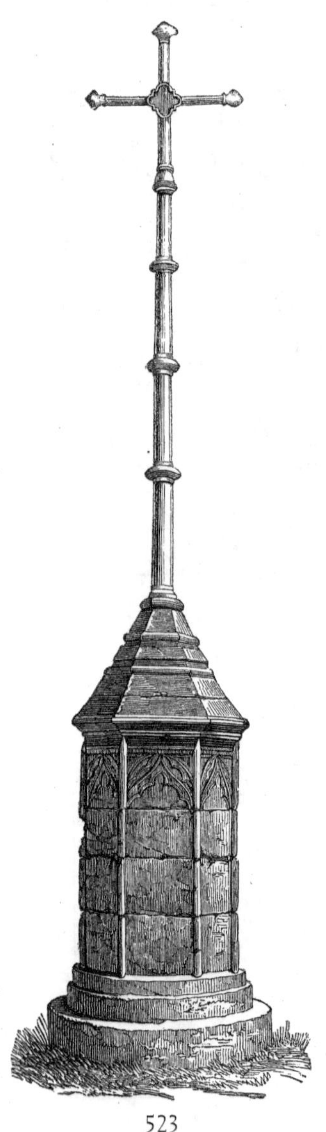

523

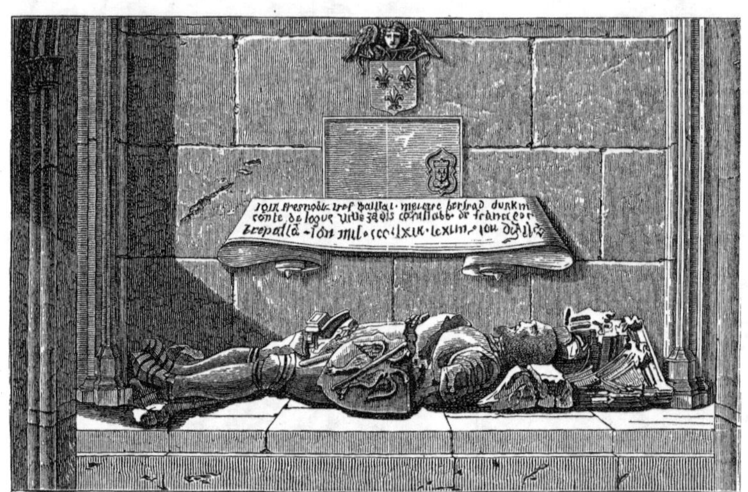

522

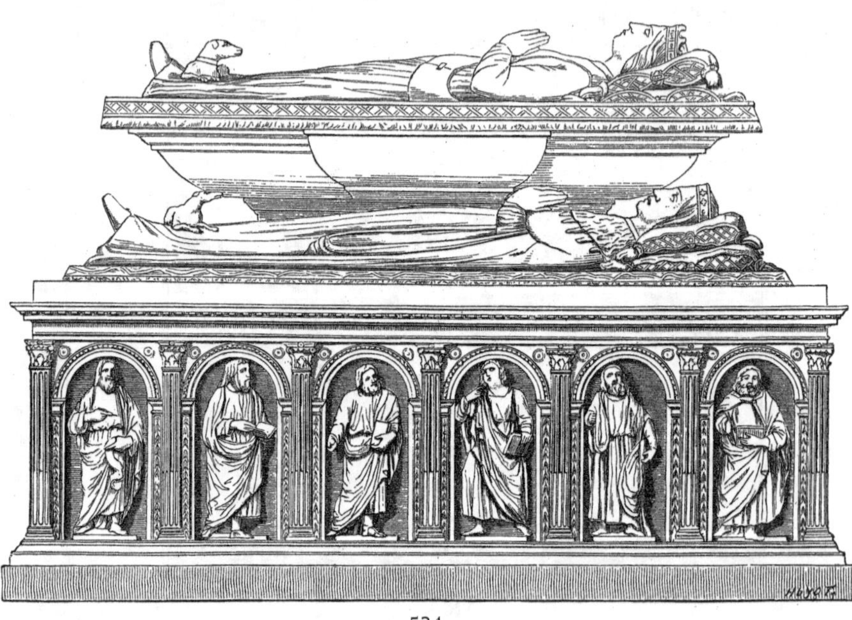

524

520. Funeral of St. Edward the Confessor, from the Bayeux tapestry, 12th century. **521.** The Dance of Death, after Holbein's drawings. **522.** Tomb erected in the Church of the Dominicans, 14th century. **523.** Cross of the Bureau family, Paris. **524.** Tomb of Louis, Duke of Orleans, and Valentine, his spouse, 16th century.

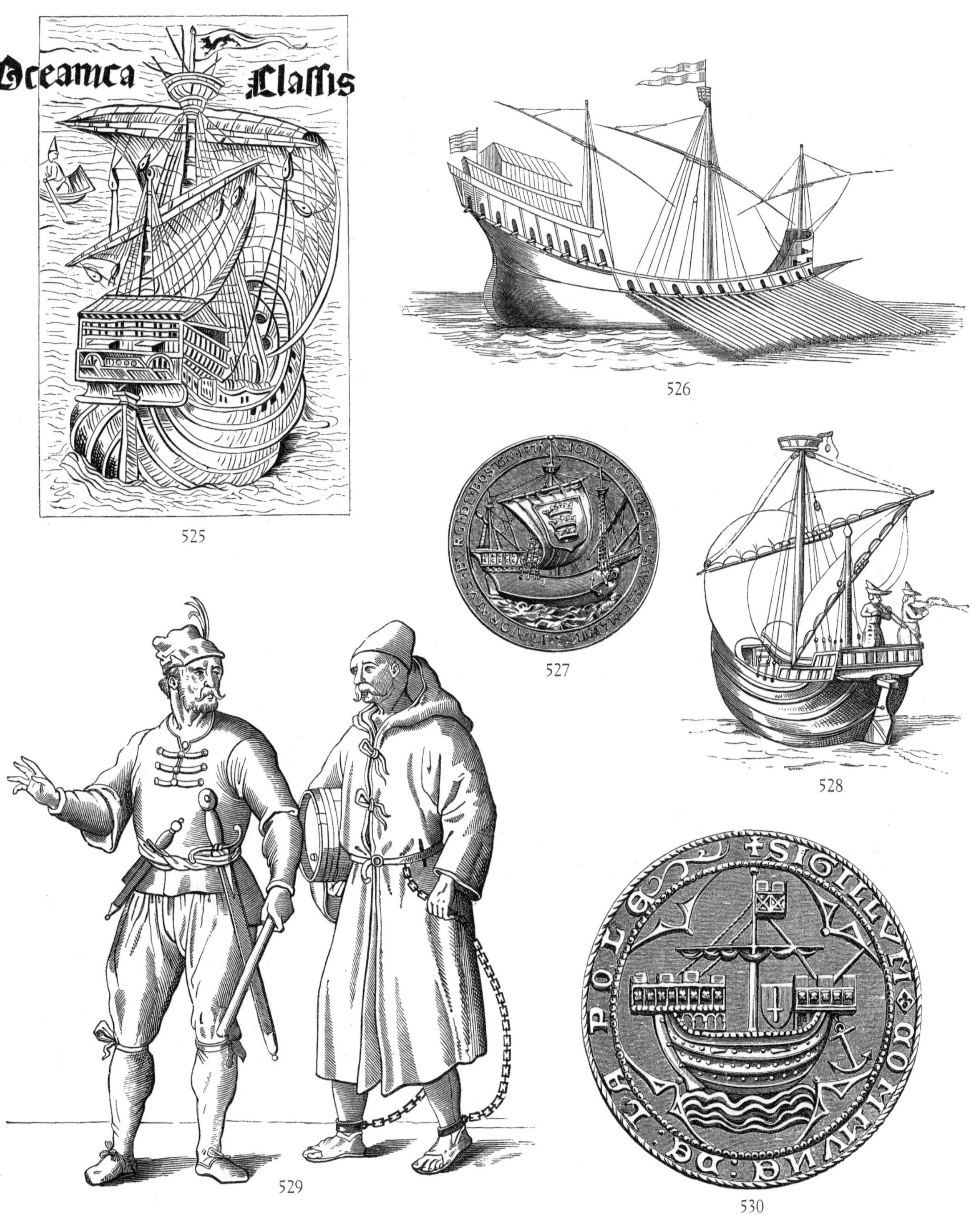

525. Spanish caravel in which Columbus discovered America, from a drawing attributed to Columbus, 1494(?). **526.** Sketch of a galley, 16th century. **527.** Seal of the town of Boston, 1575. **528.** Coque, 15th century. **529.** Galley soldier and galley slave, 16th century. **530.** Seal of the town of Poole, 13th century.

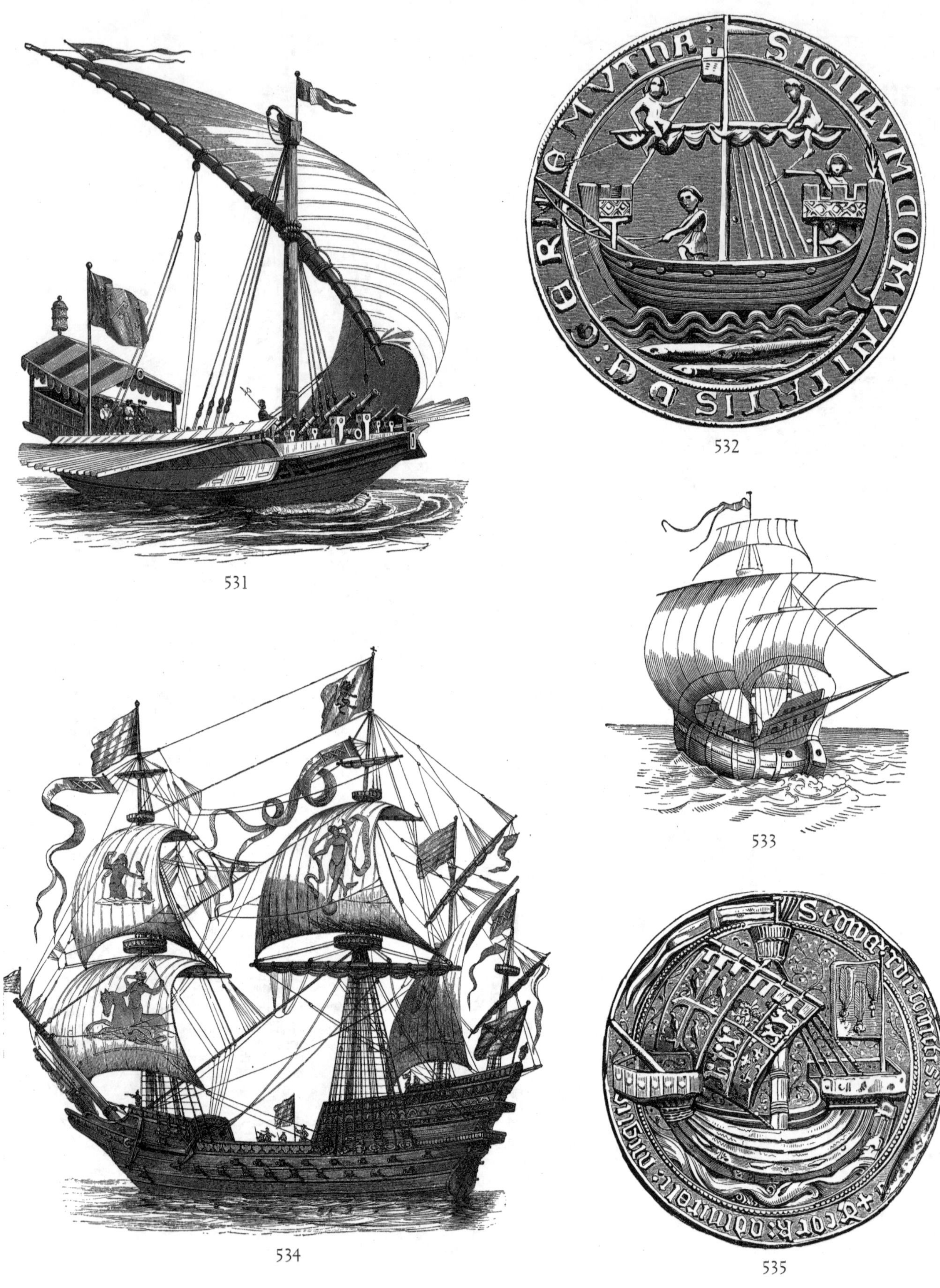

531. Pontifical galley with sails, oars, and heavy artillery, Brueghel the Elder, 1550. **532.** Seal of the town of Yarmouth, 13th century. **533.** Spanish ship, 15th century. **534.** Man-of-War, 16th century. **535.** Seal of Edward, Count of Rutland, 1395.

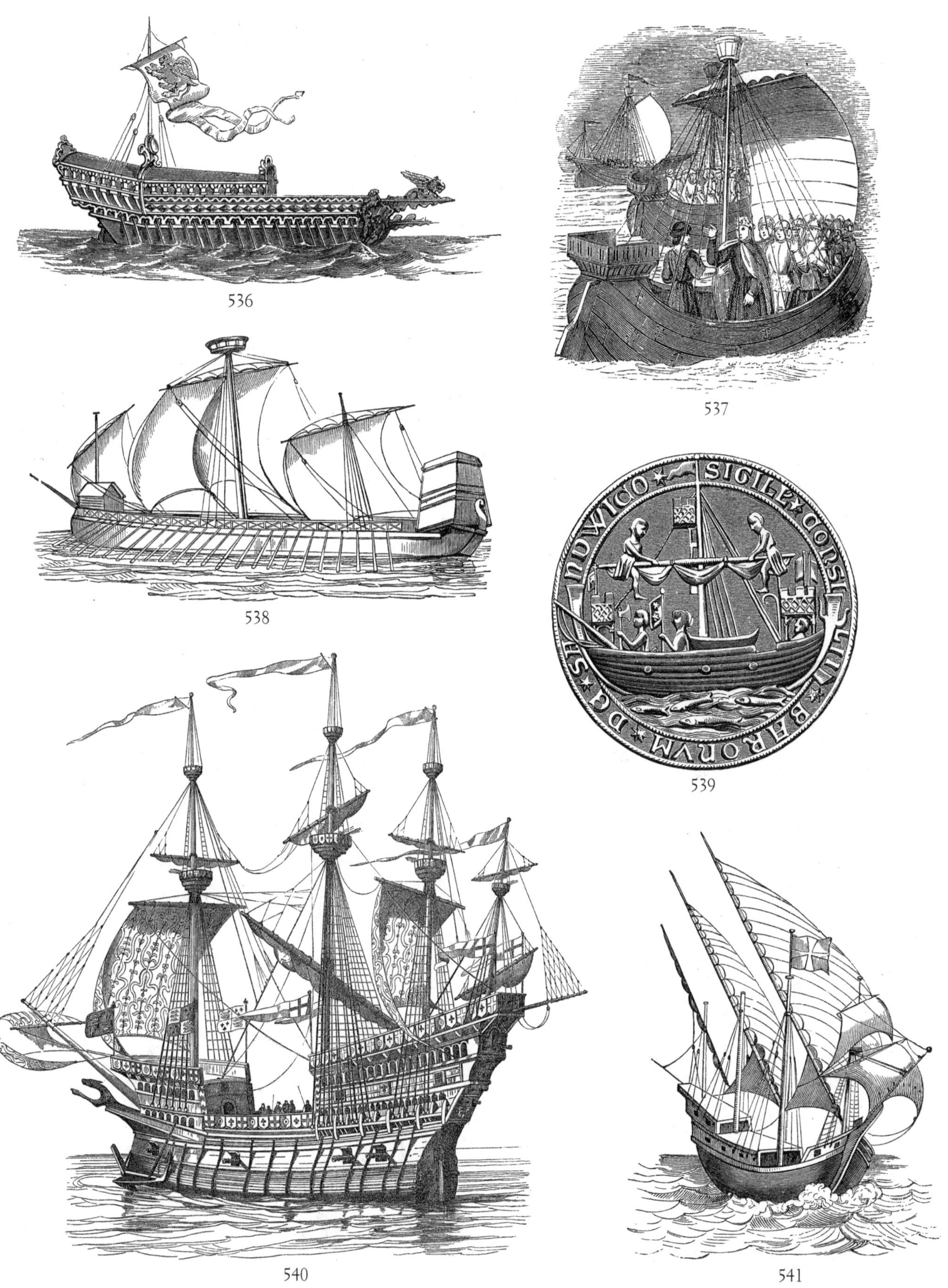

536. The *Bucentaur*, state barge used for the symbolic marriage of Venice with the sea. **537.** English ships of war, 15th century. **538.** Three-masted galley with square sails, 16th century. **539.** Seal of the town of Sandwich, 13th century. **540.** Man-of-war, 1520. **541.** French caravel, 16th century.

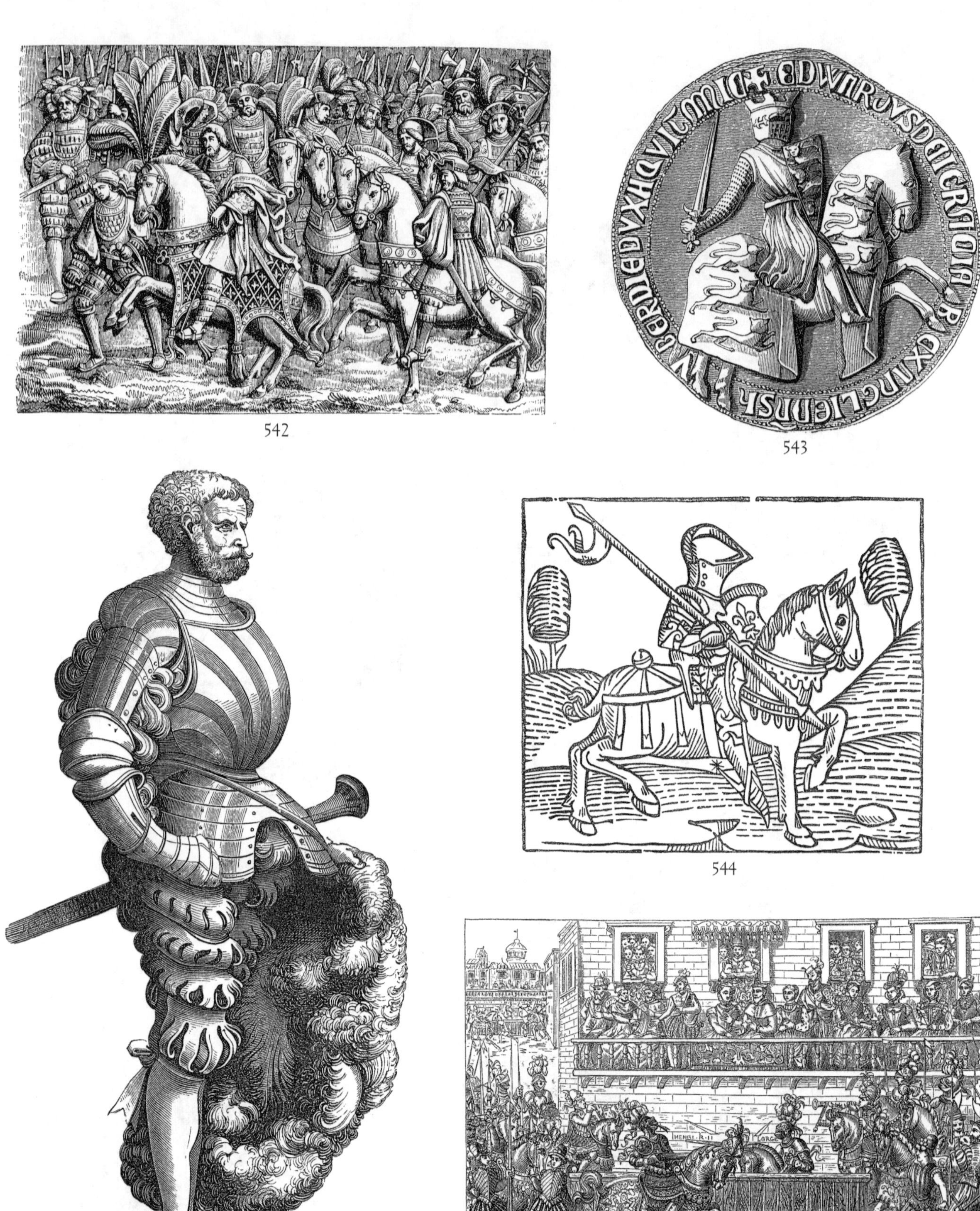

545

546

542. Interview between Francis I and Henry VIII on the Field of the Cloth of Gold. **543.** Great seal of Edward I. **544.** Knight. **545.** German knight, 15th century. **546.** King Henry II wounded by Montgomery in a tournament, 1559.

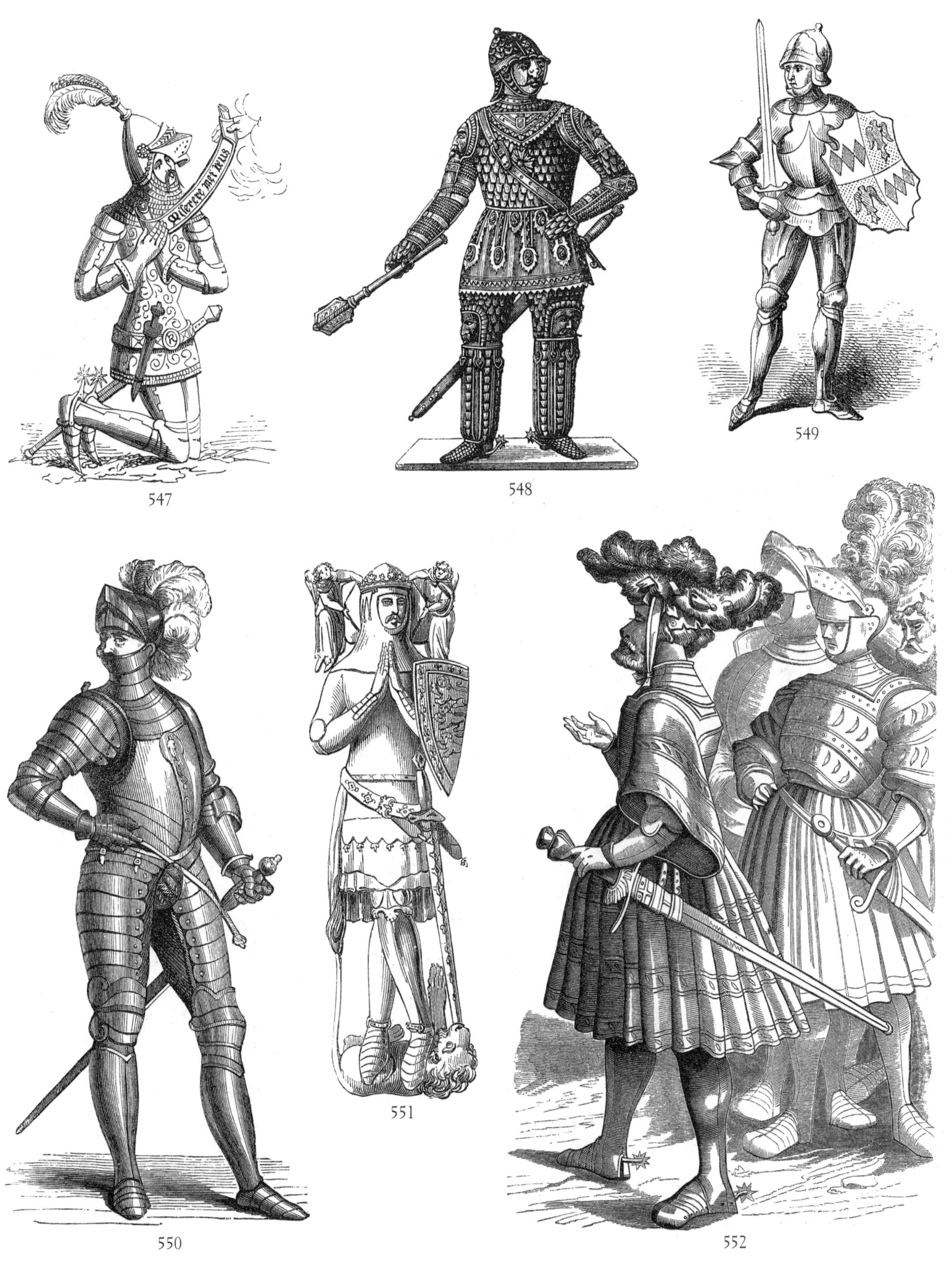

547. Robert Chamberlain, esquire to Henry V. **548.** Polish knight, 15th century. **549.** Richard Nevil, Earl of Warwick. **550.** Knight in complete armor. **551.** John of Eltham. **552.** German knights.

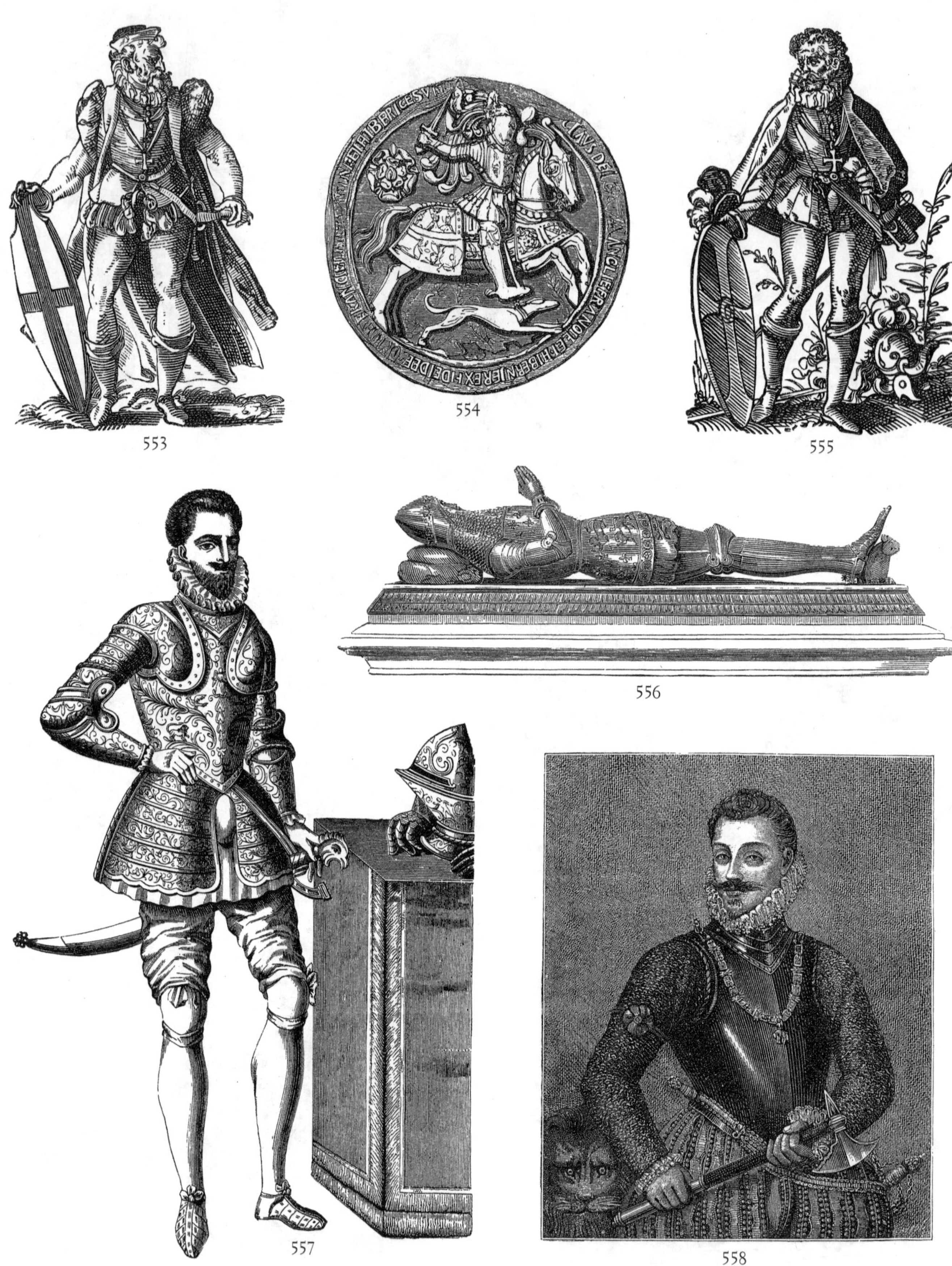

553. Teutonic knight, 1585. **554.** Great seal of Henry VIII. **555.** Knight of the Order of Rhodes. **556.** Monument of Edward the Black Prince in Canterbury Cathedral. **557.** Damascened armor. **558.** Don Juan of Austria, 16th century.

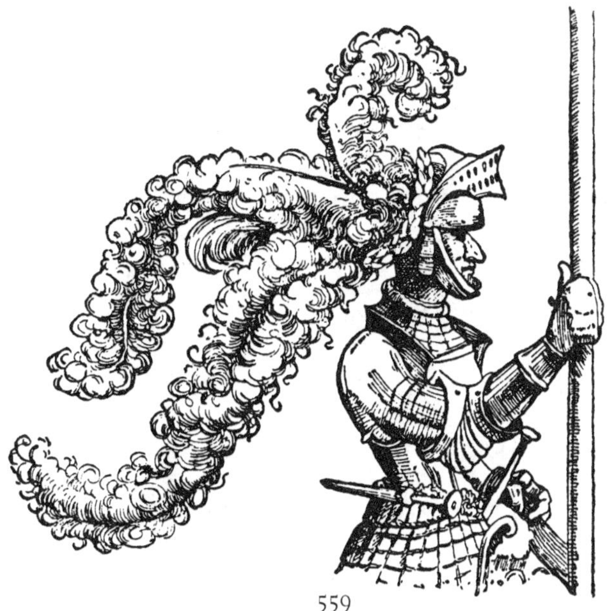
559

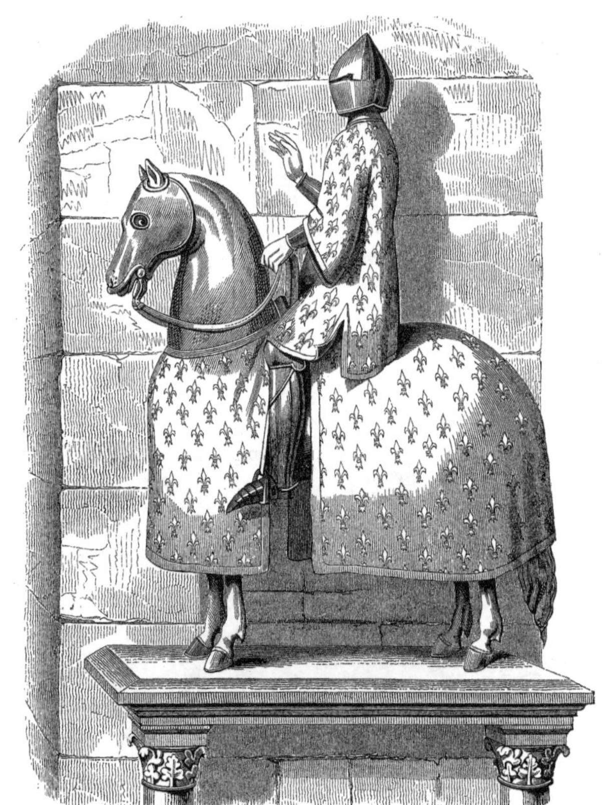
560

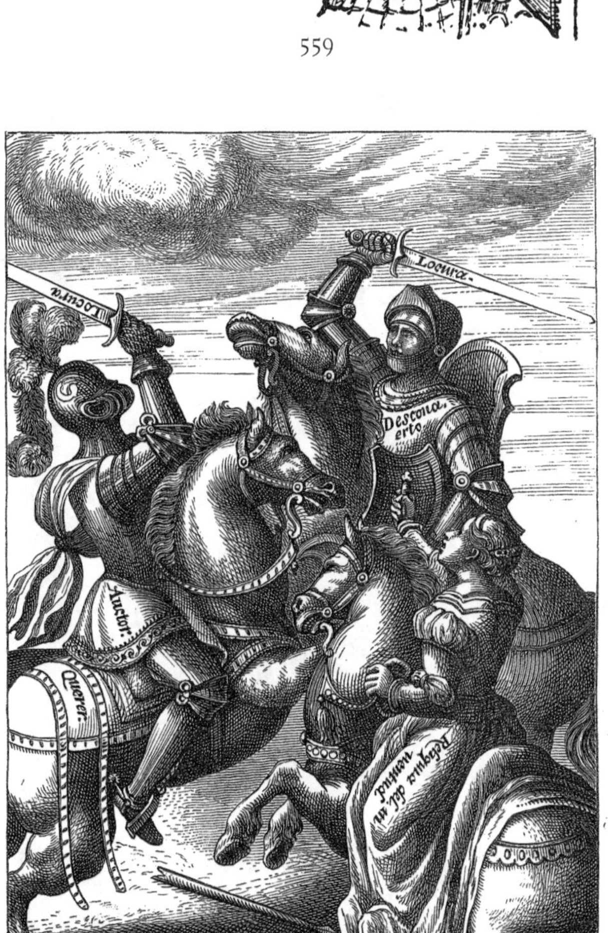

561

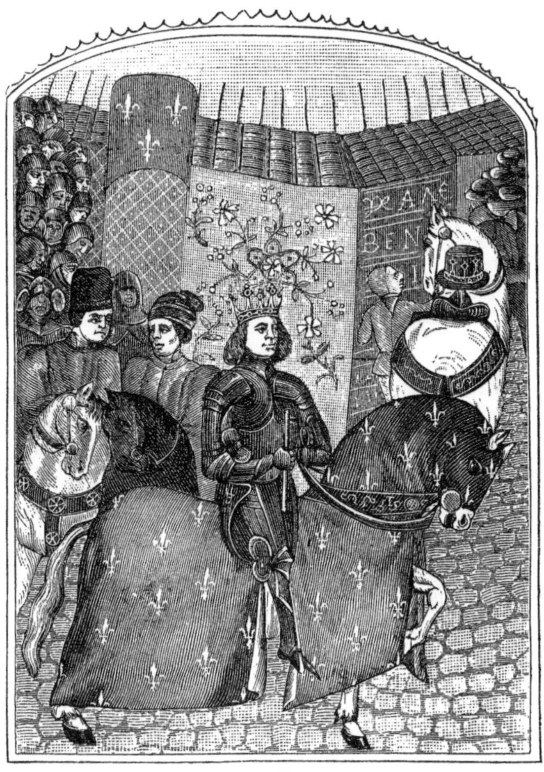
562

559. Plumed helmet. **560.** King Philip le Bel in war dress, on the occasion of his entering Paris in 1304. **561.** Chivalry represented by allegorical figures, 1573. **562.** Entry of Charles VII into Rouen in 1450.

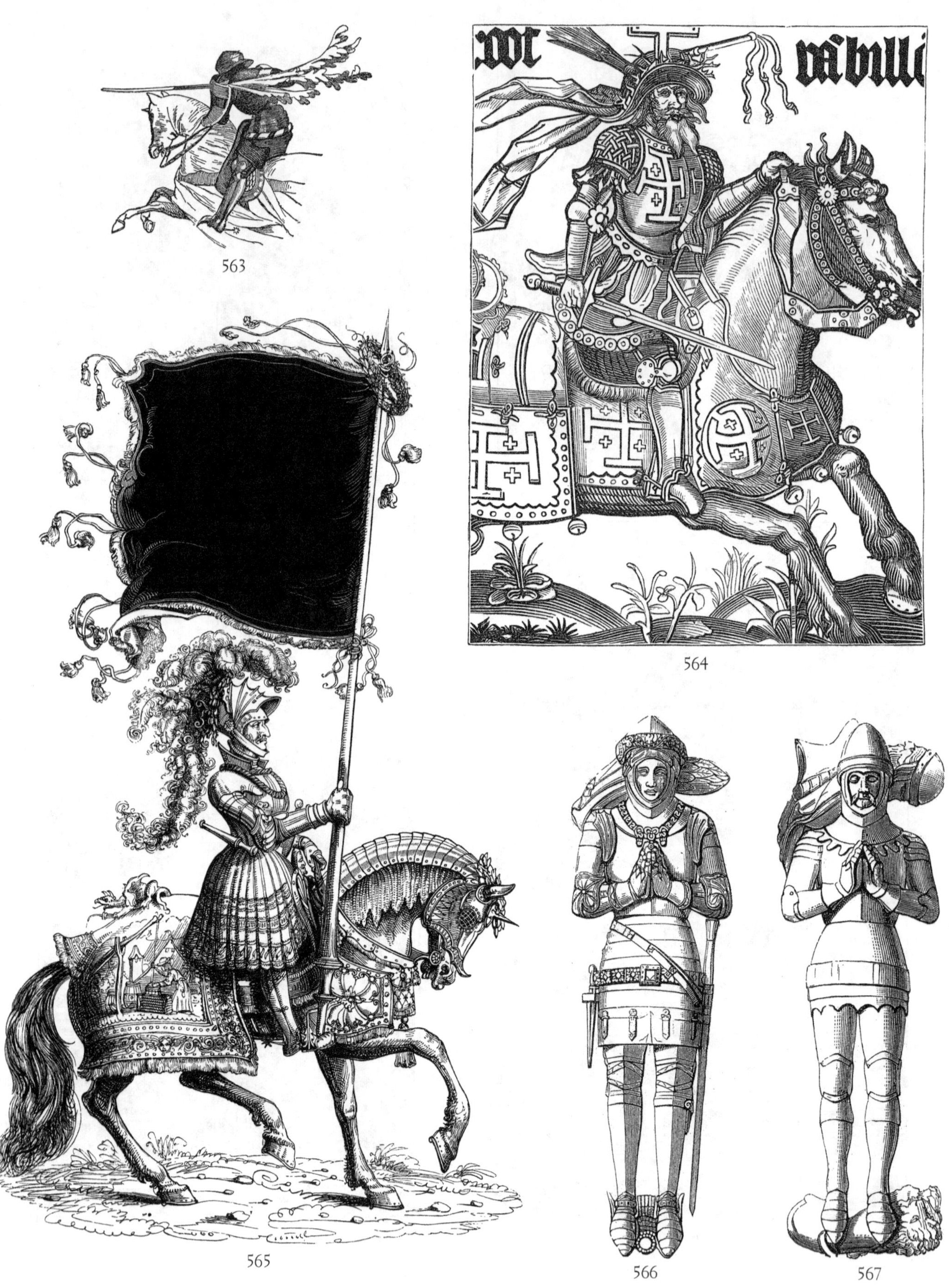

563 564 565 566 567

563. Knight in battle. **564.** Godefroy de Bouillon, 15th century. **565.** Knight. **566.** Effigy of Sir Robert Grushill. **567.** Effigy of Michael de la Pole, Earl of Suffolk.

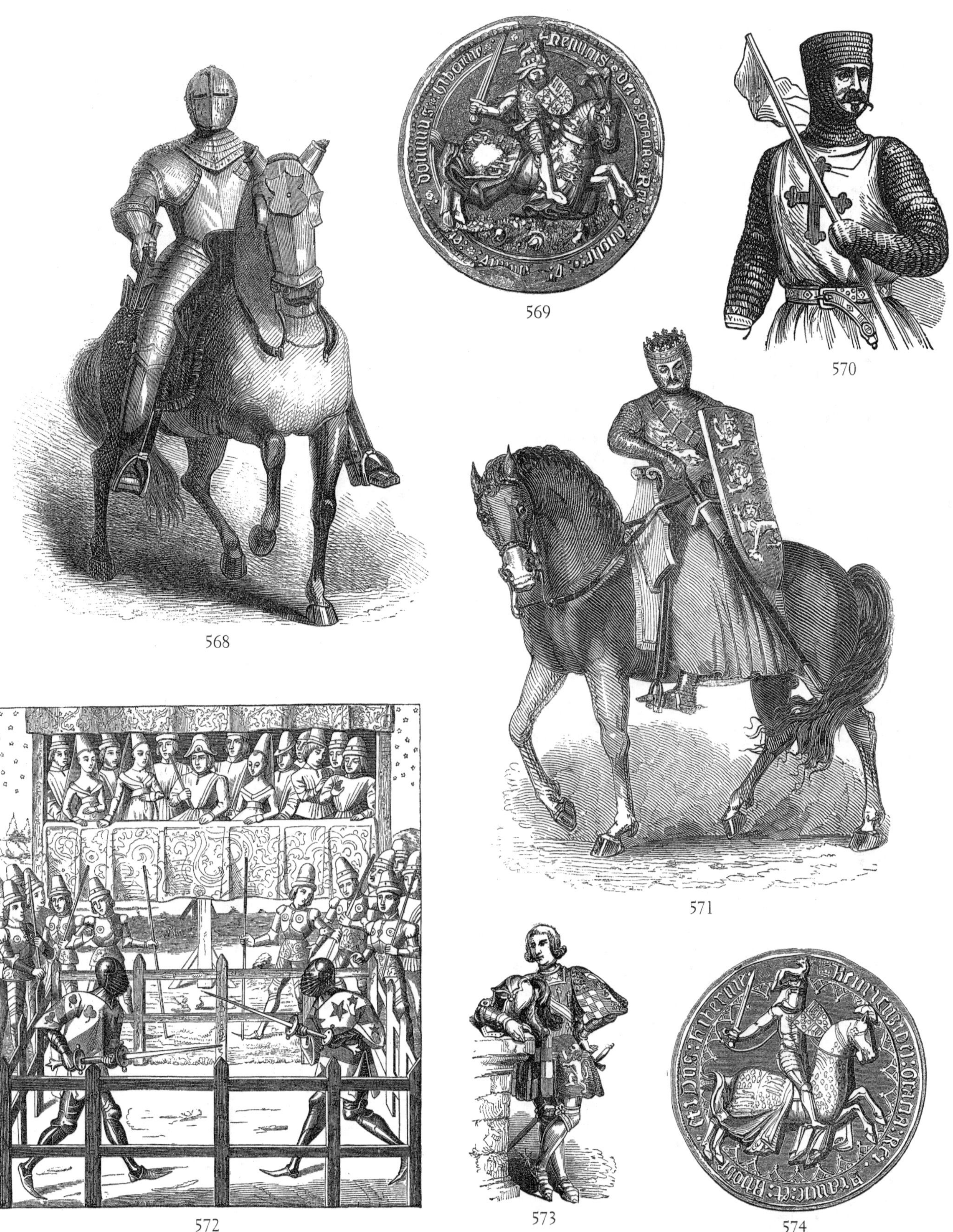

568. Sir Horace Vere. **569.** Great seal of Henry VII. **570.** Knight Templar, 13th century. **571.** Edward I. **572.** "How both parties are out of their tents, armed and ready to do their duty at the signal from the marshal, who has thrown the glove," 15th century. **573.** John Howard, first duke of Norfolk. **574.** Great seal of Henry IV.

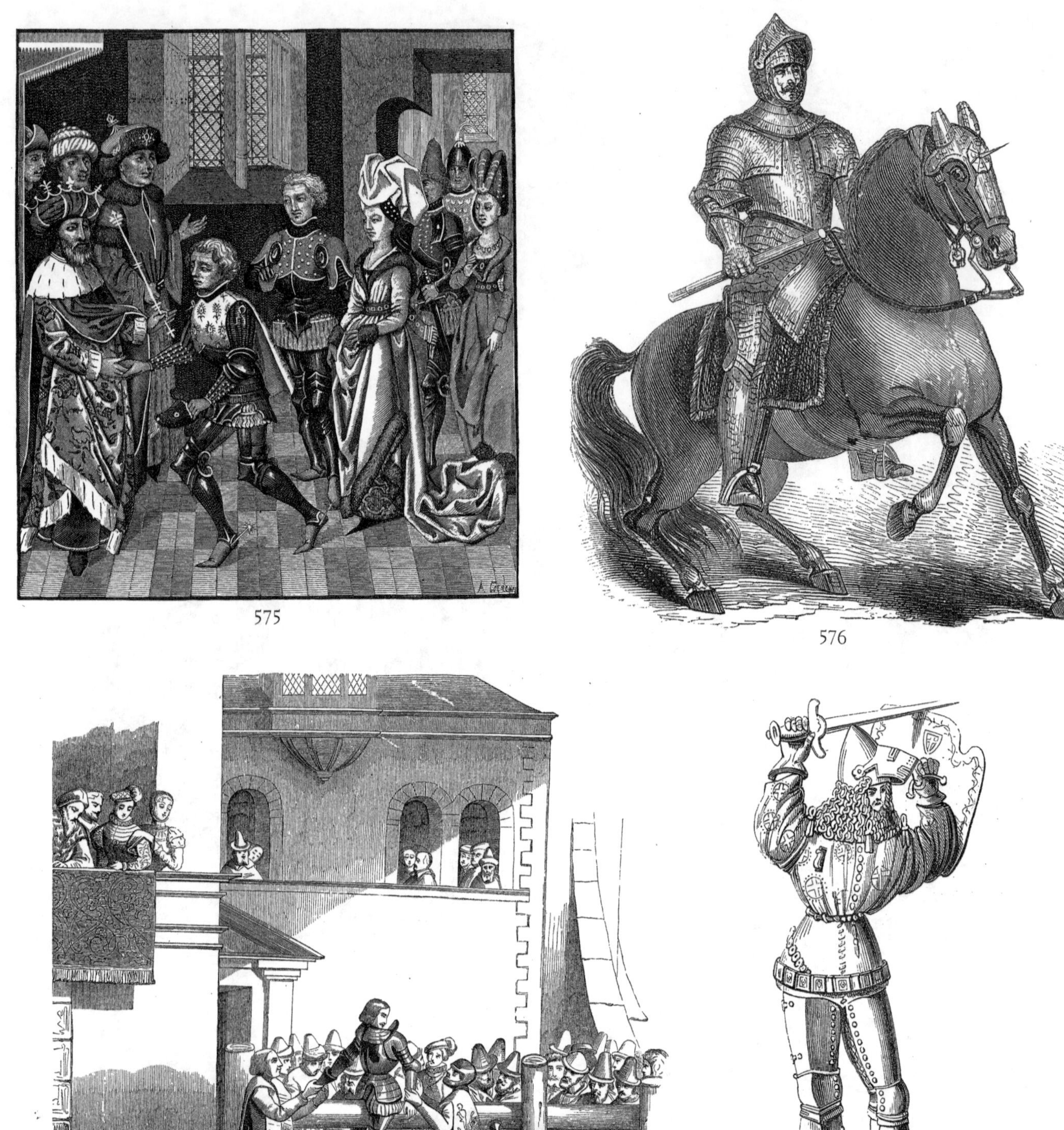
575 576 577 578

575. Reception of Gautier-sans-Avoir by the King of Hungary, 15th century manuscript. **576.** Charles I. **577.** Degradation of a knight, 1565. **578.** St. George at Dijon.

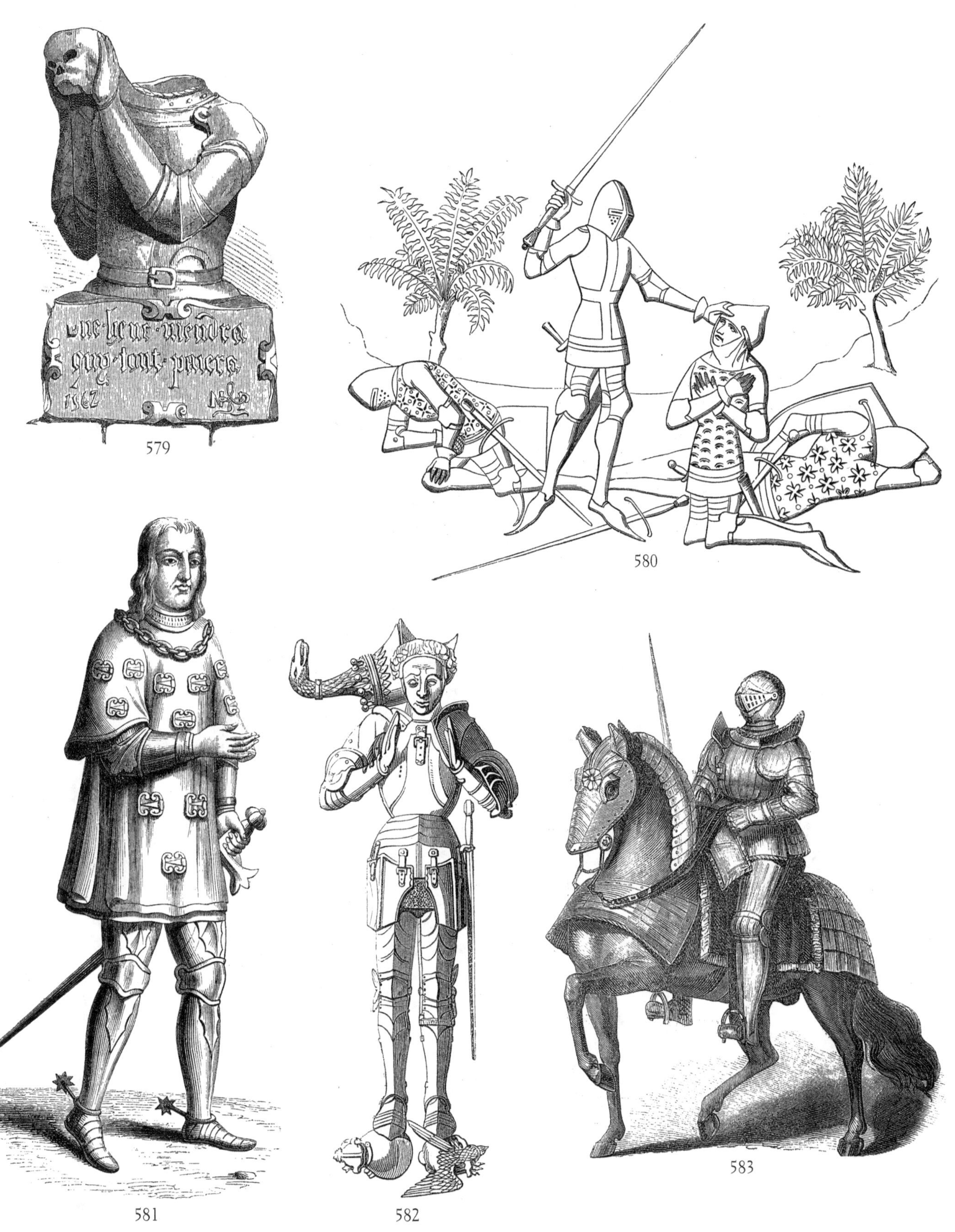

579. Beheaded knight holding his fleshless head in his hands, 1562. **580.** Conferring knighthood on the field of battle, 13th century. **581.** Louis de Mallet, Lord of Granville, Admiral of France, in costume of war and tournament. **582.** Effigy of Richard Beauchamp, Earl of Warwick. **583.** Henry VII.

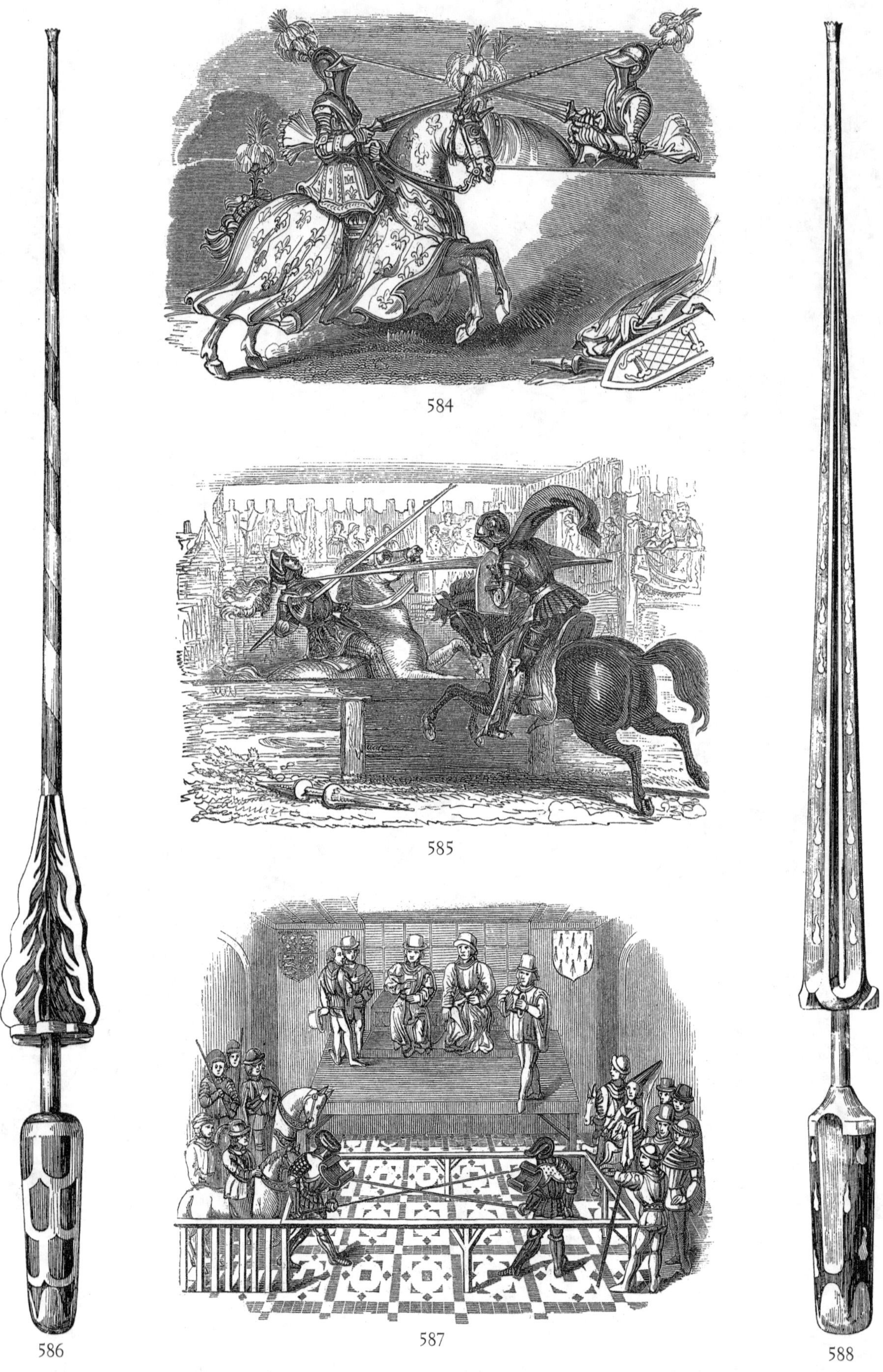

584

585

586

587

588

584. Tournament. **585.** Bertrand du Guesclin at the tournament. **586, 588.** Tilting lances, 16th century. **587.** Tilting match between Nich. Clifford and J. Boucmell.

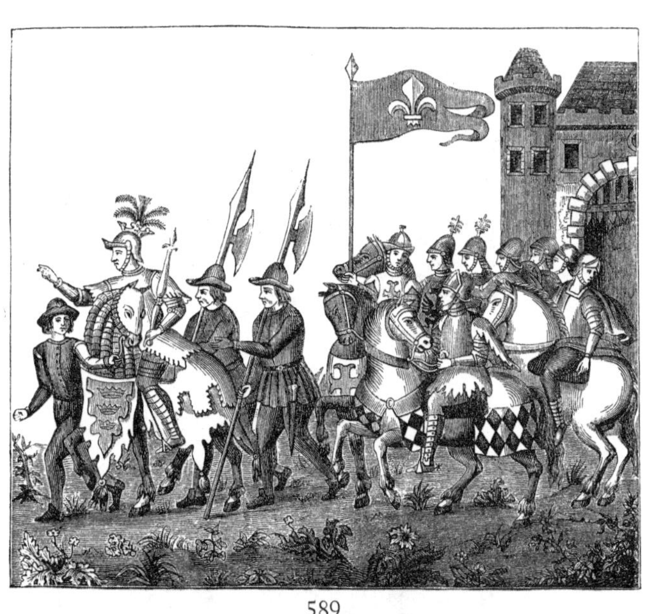

589

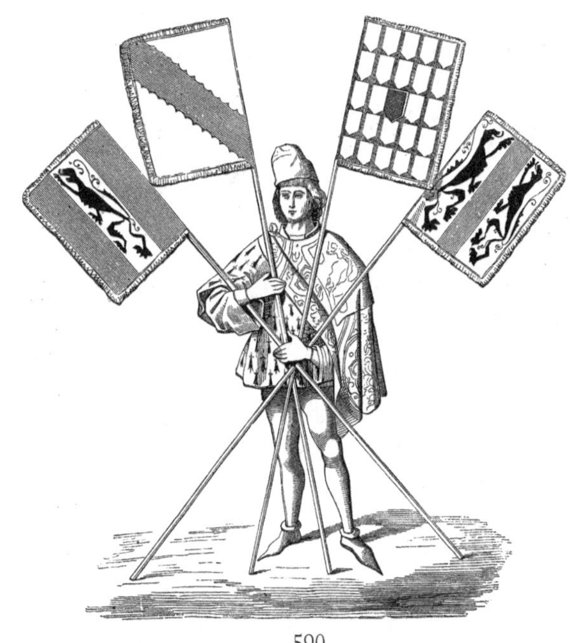

590

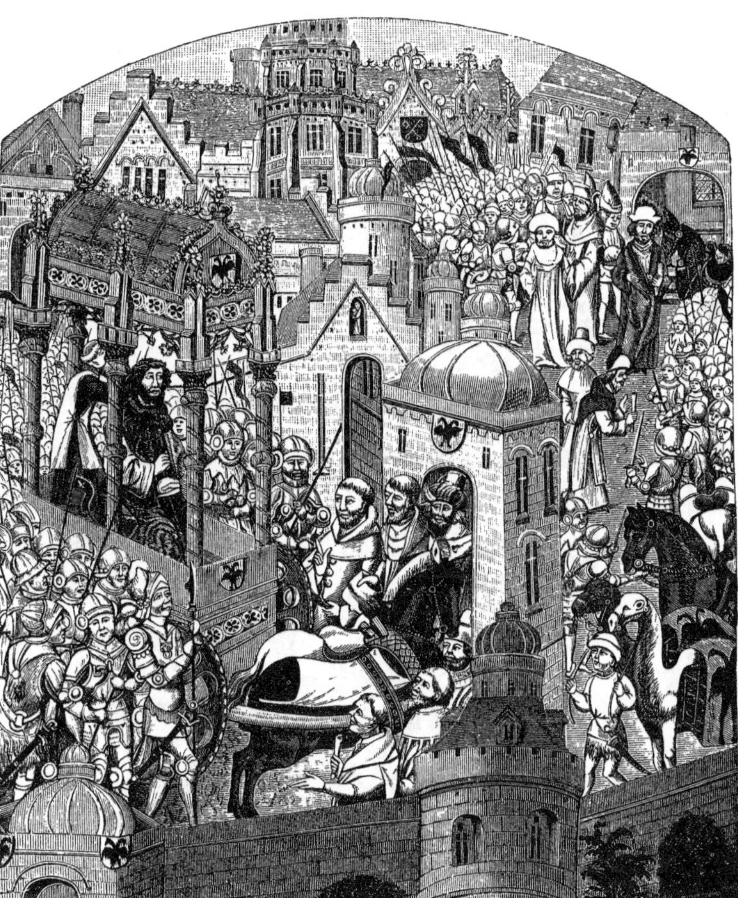

592

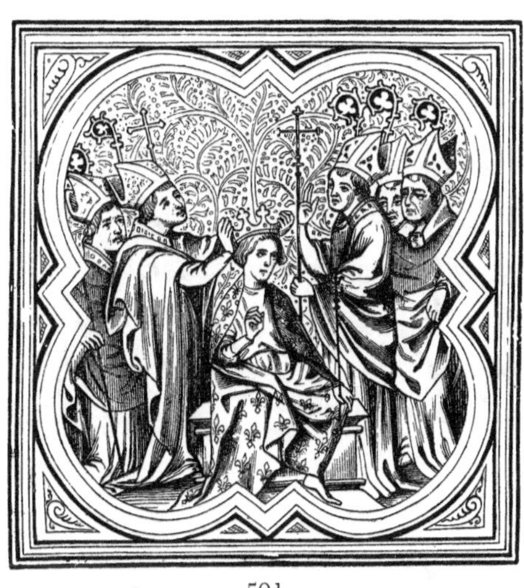

591

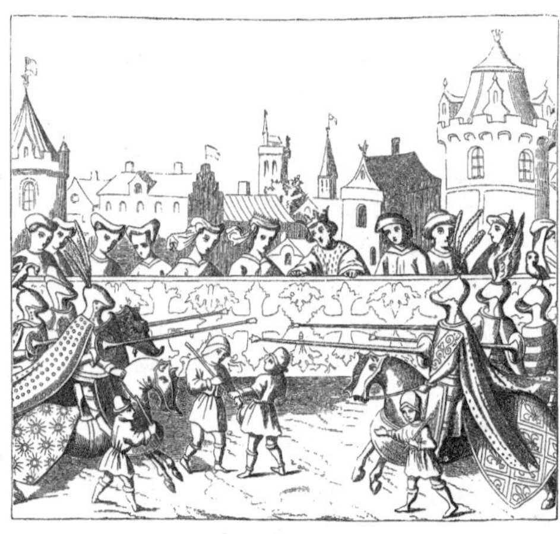

593

589. Entry of the Roi de l'Epinette at Lille. **590.** Herald holding banners of the four tournament referees, 15th century. **591.** Coronation of Charlemagne, 14th century manuscript. **592.** Coronation of Charlemagne in the city of Jerusalem, 15th century manuscript. **593.** Tournaments in honor of the entry of Queen Isabel into Paris.

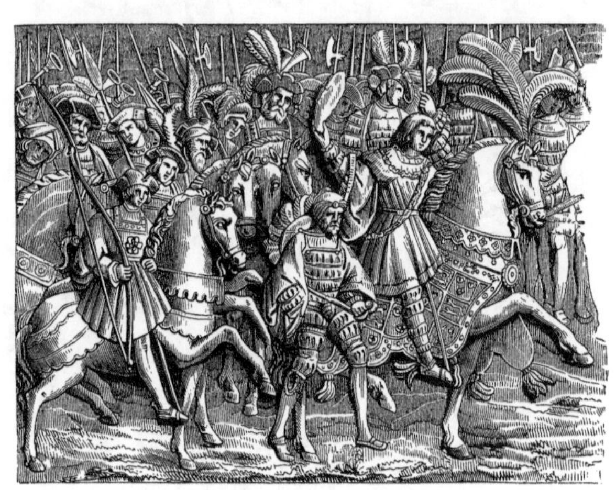

594

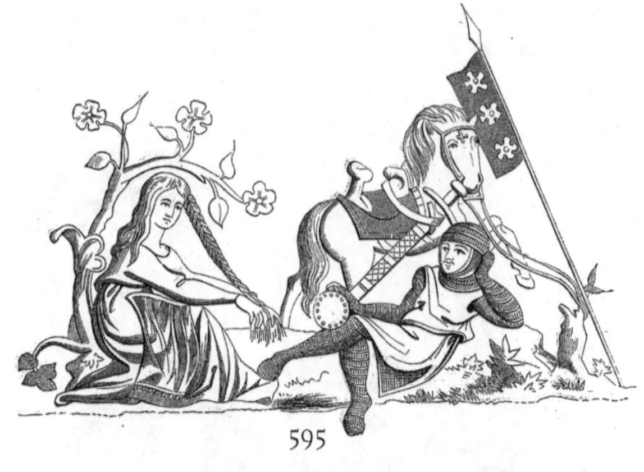

595

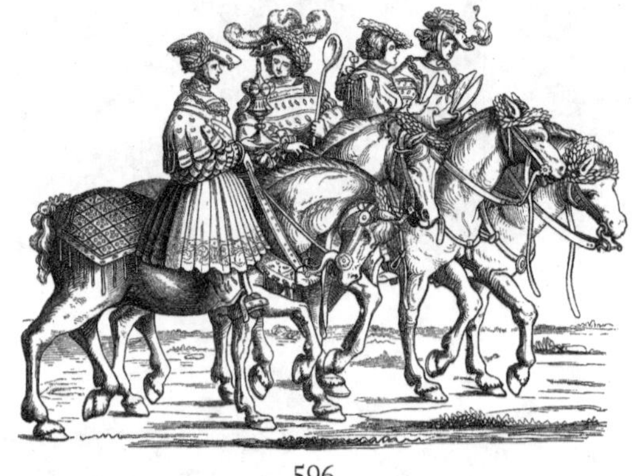

596

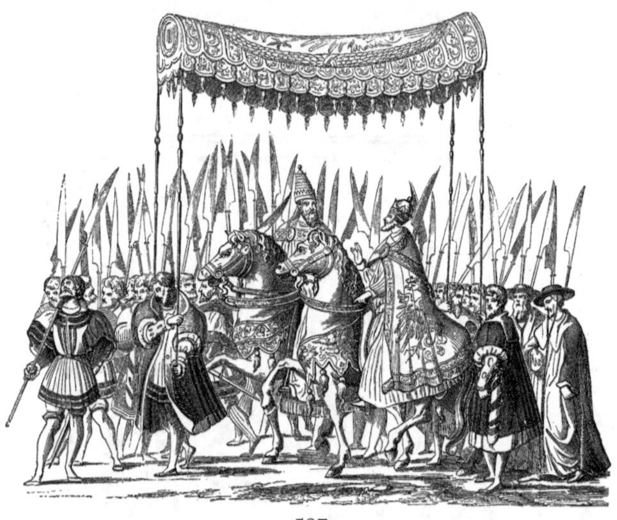

597

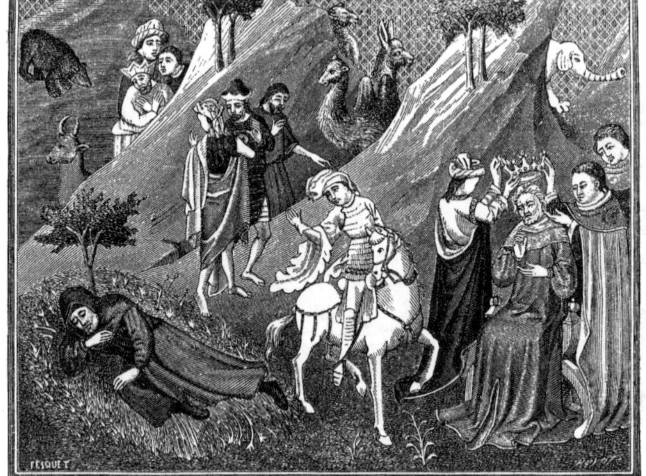

598

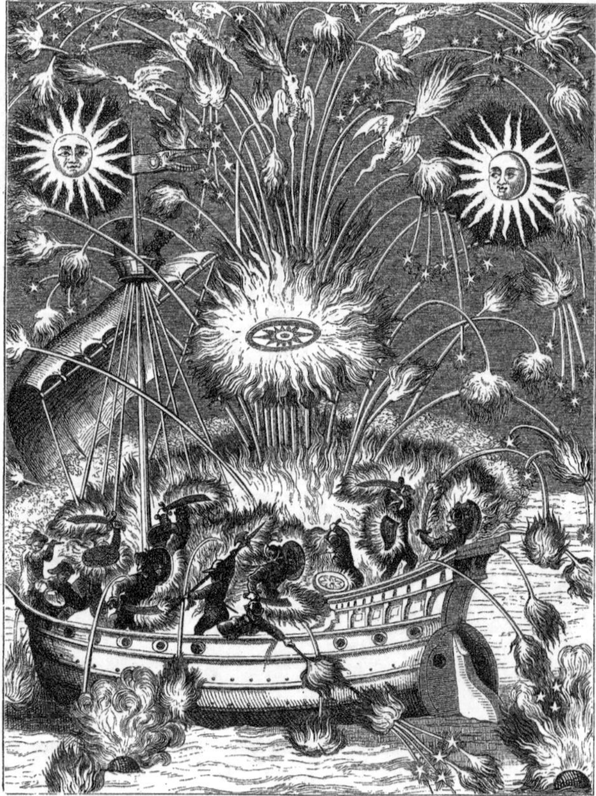

599

594. Henry VIII in the camp of the Field of the Cloth of Gold. **595.** Woman under the safeguard of knighthood. **596.** Officers of the table and of the chamber of the Imperial Court. **597.** Imperial procession. **598.** Coronation of the Great Khan, first king of Tartary, 15th century manuscript. **599.** Fireworks on the water, with an imitation of a naval combat.

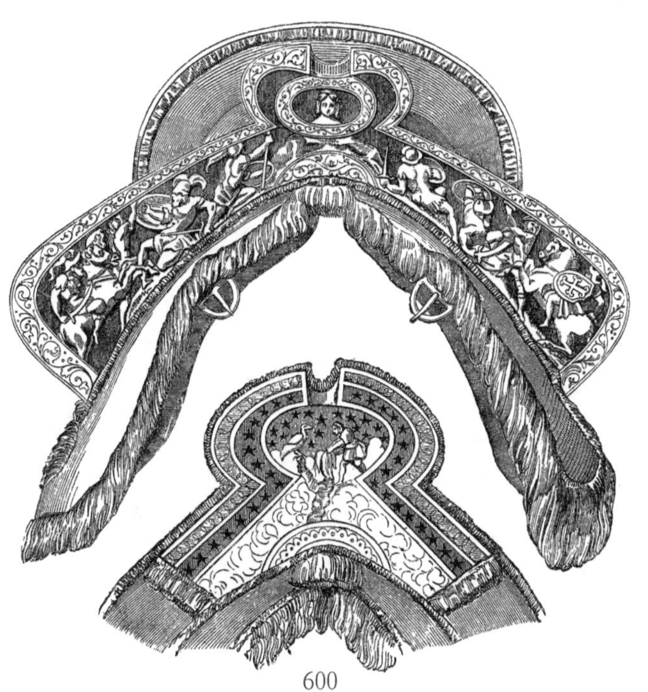

600

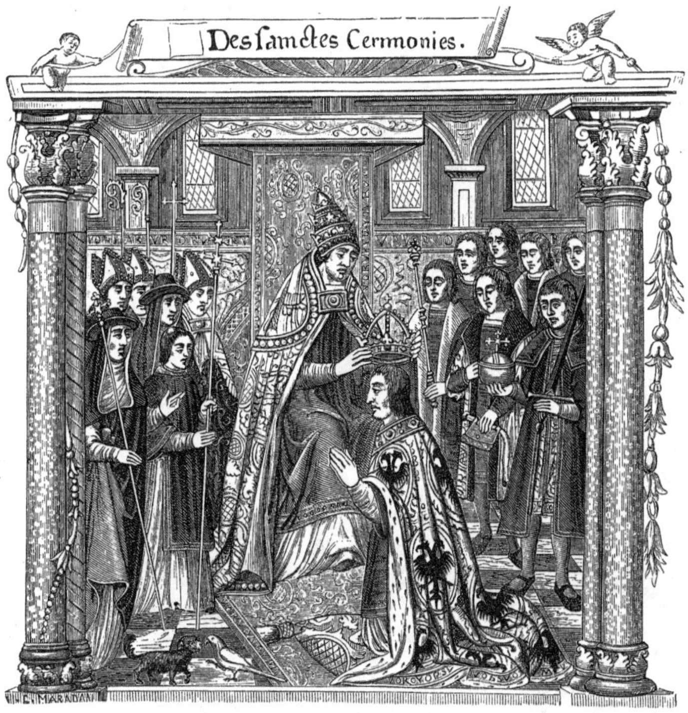

601

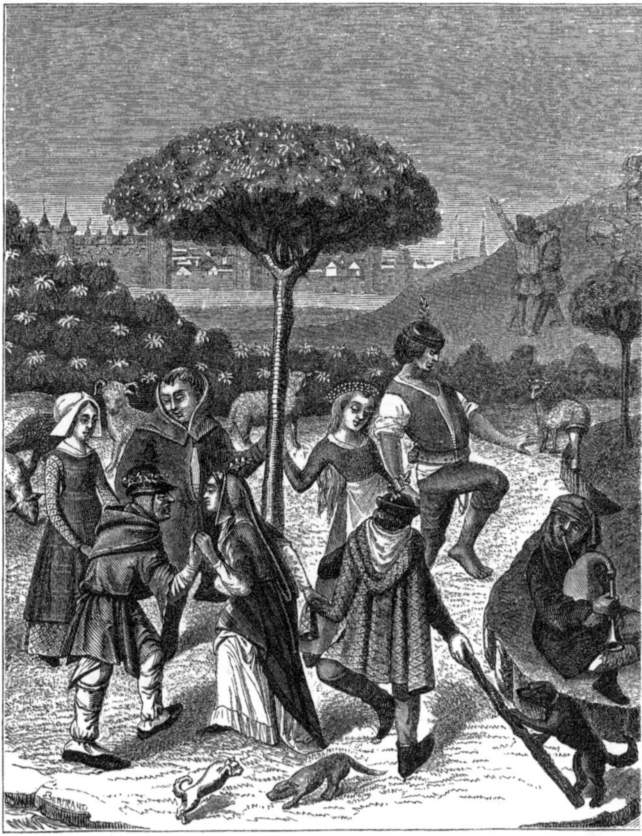

602

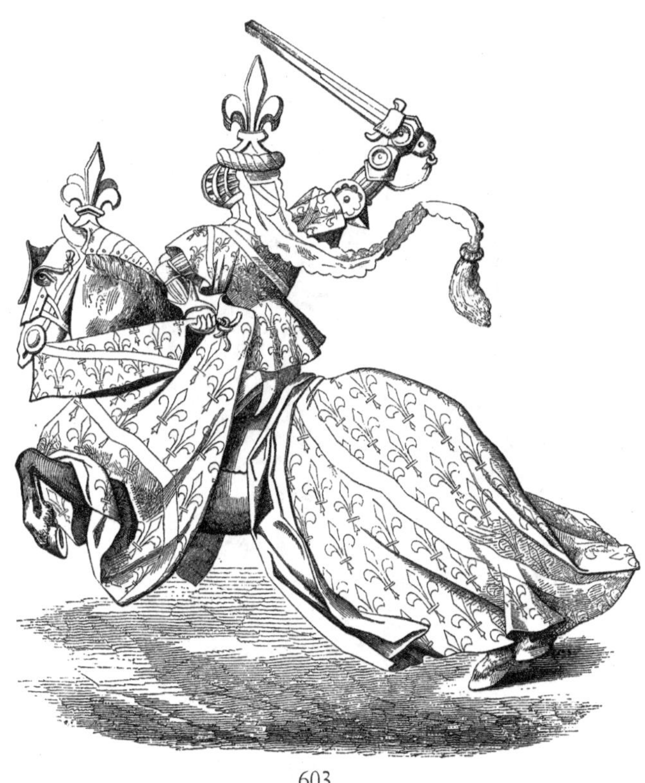

603

600. (top and bottom) Tournament saddles. **601.** Coronation ceremony. **602.** Peasant dances at the May fields. **603.** The Duc de Bourbon, armed cap-à-pie for the tournament.

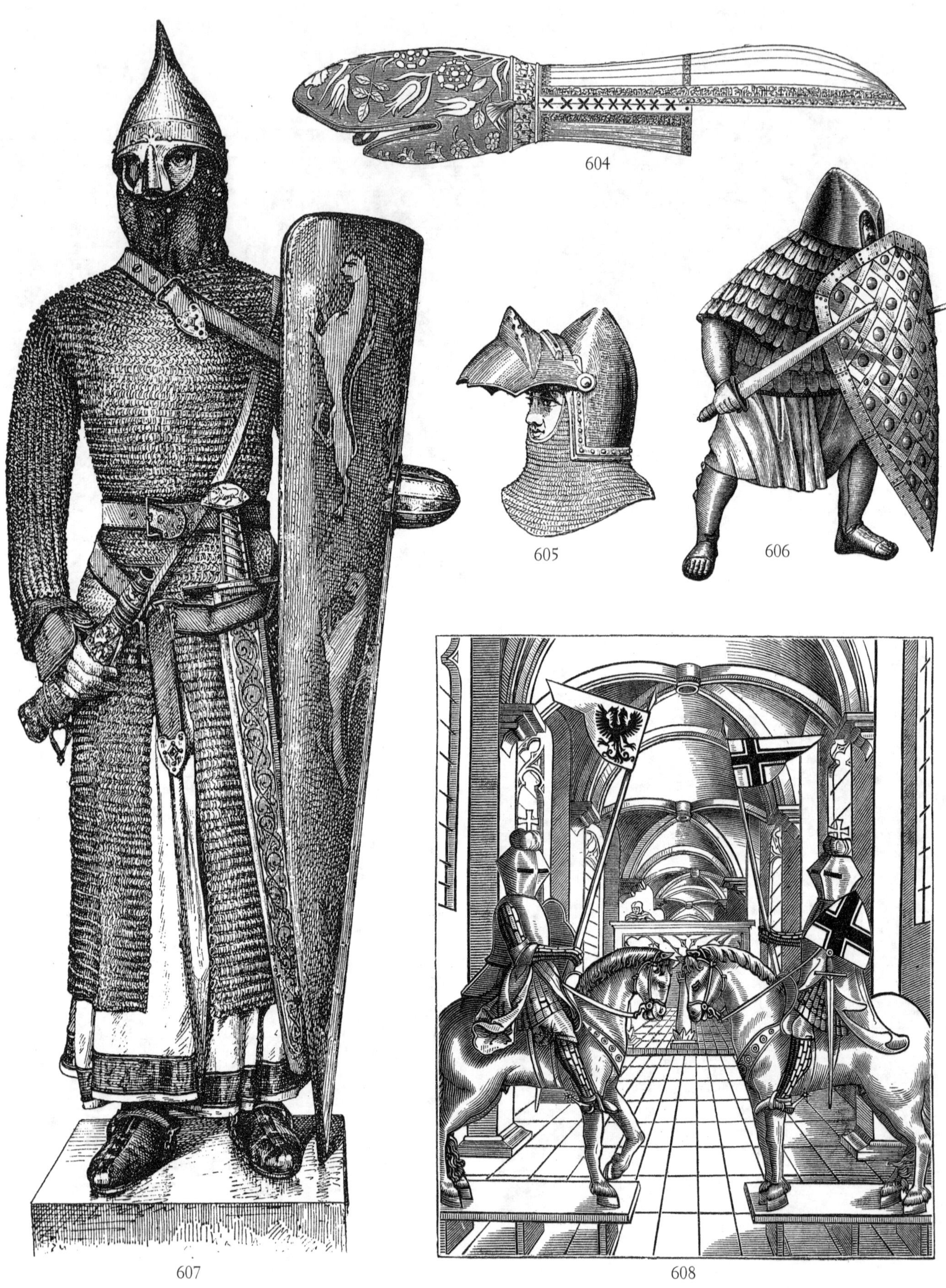

604. Moorish arm, 11th–14th centuries. **605.** French basinet, 14th century. **606.** Frankish warrior, 9th century. **607.** Armor, 12th century. **608.** Henry I and General Gautier Von der Hoye, 1530.

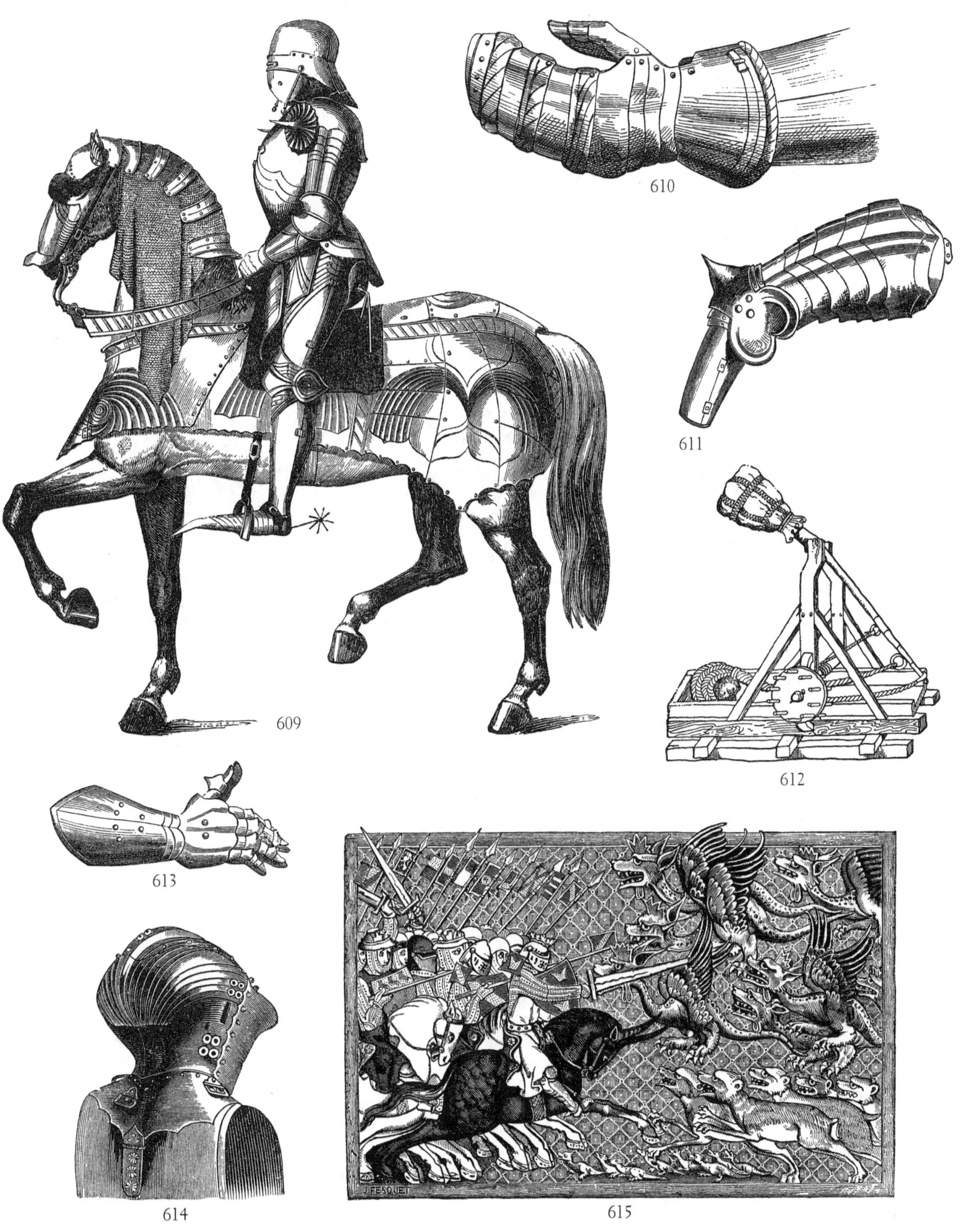

609. Knight armed and mounted for war. **610.** French gauntlet, 15th century. **611.** Armor, 15th century. **612.** Ballista, 14th century. **613.** Armor, 15th century. **614.** Tournament helmet screwed on the breastplate, 15th century. **615.** How Alexander fought the dragons and a species of beast called Scorpion, 13th century.

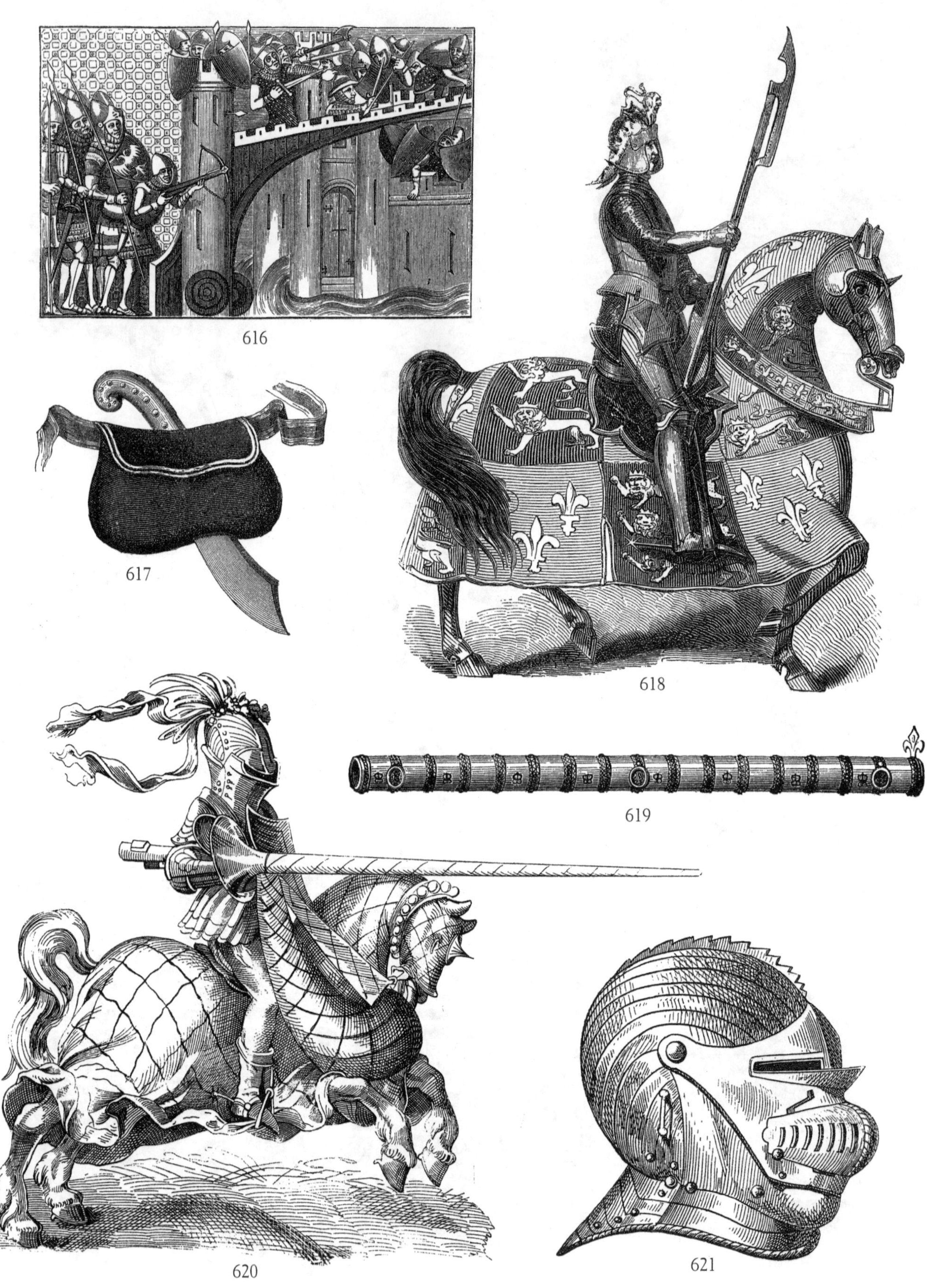

616. Rolling tower for scaling the walls of towns, 14th century. 617. Purse or leather bag, with knife or dagger, 15th century. 618. Henry VI, 1450. 619. Earliest models of cannon, Tower of London. 620. Knight. 621. French helmet, 15th century.

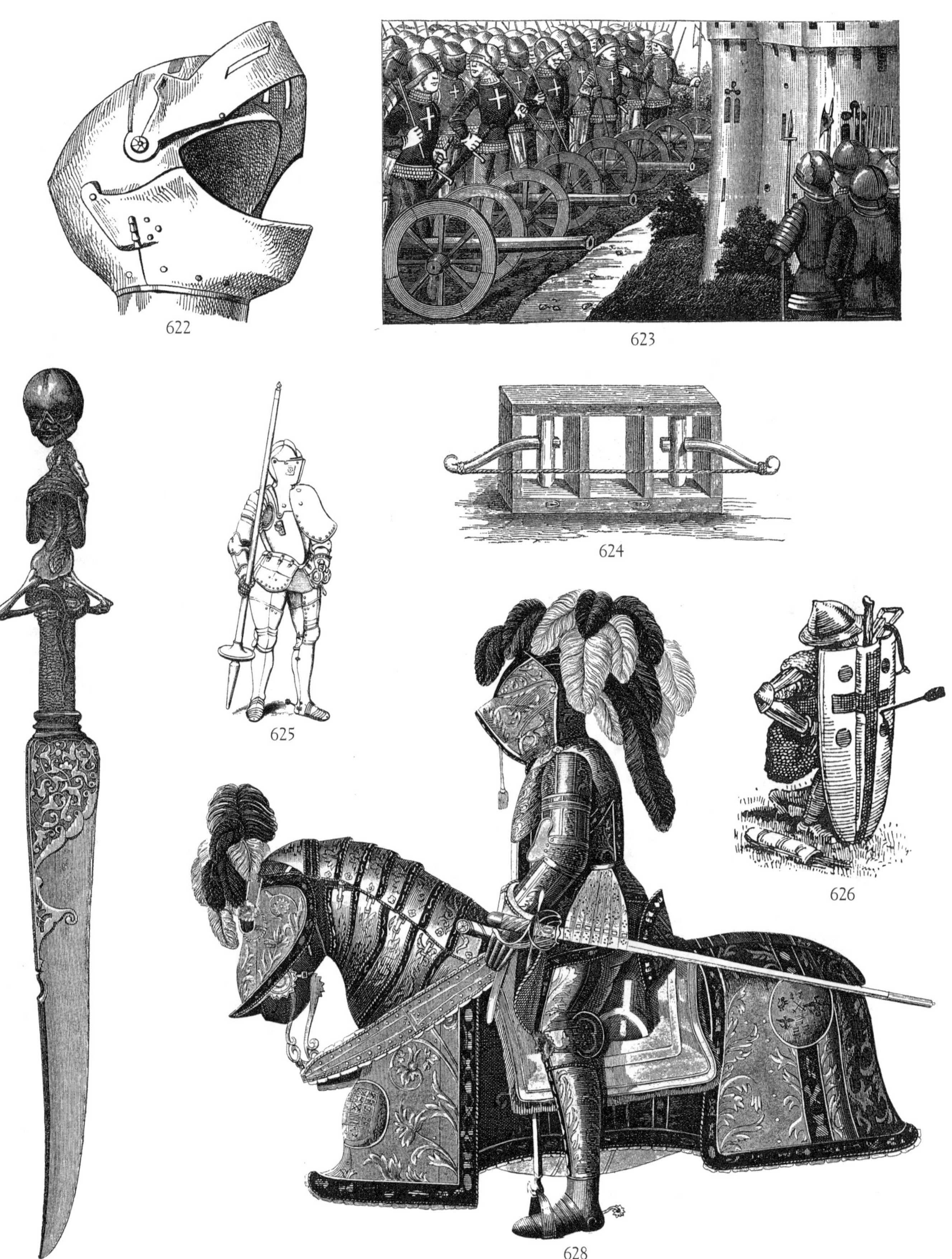

622. French helmet, 15th century. **623.** "How the Comte de Foix took strong places on Guienne," 1484. **624.** Ballista. **625.** Tournament armor, 1586. **626.** Pavise, 14th century. **627.** Dagger with Moorish blade and Flemish handle, 14th century. **628.** Tournament armor.

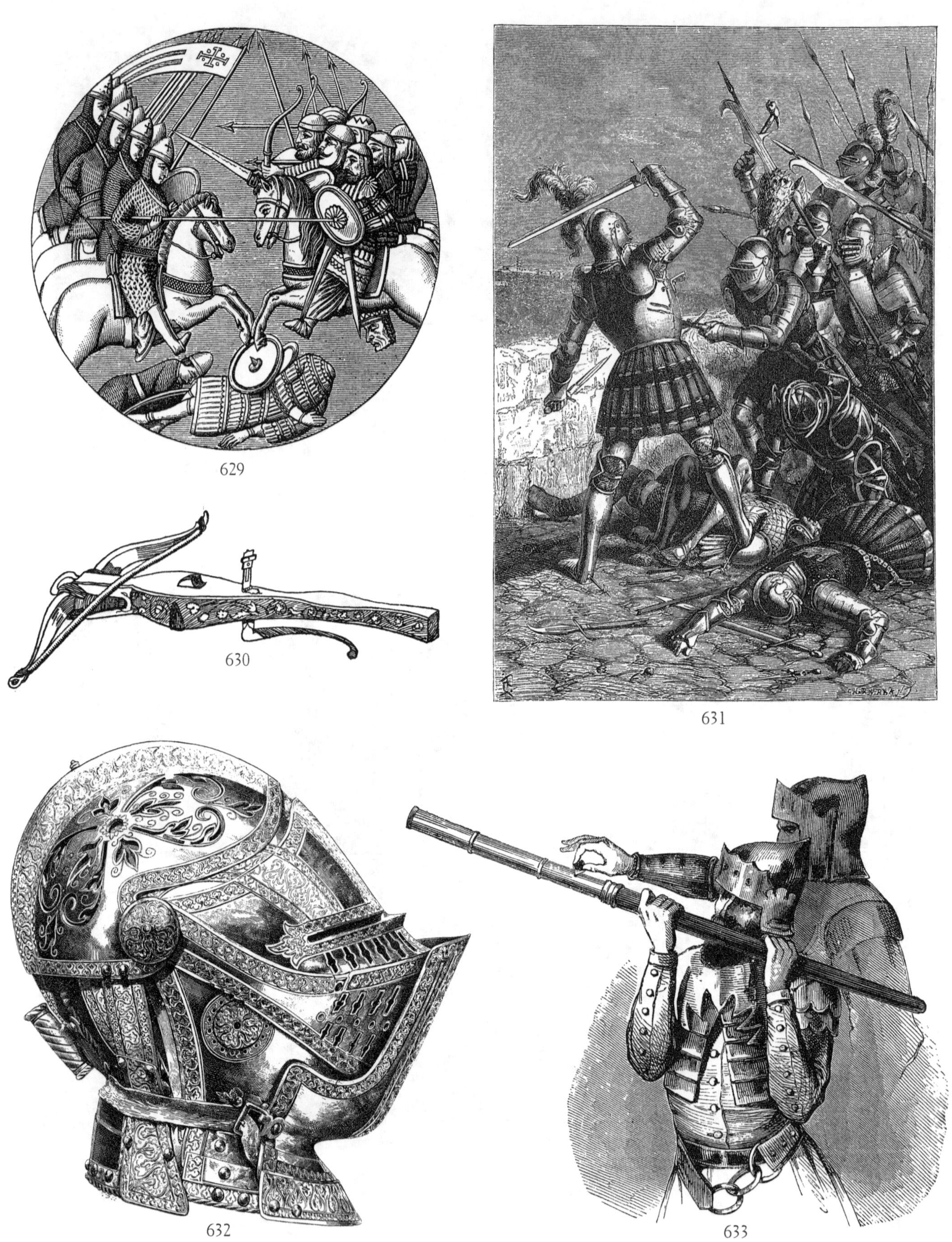

629. Holy Roman Empire battle scene. **630.** Crossbow, 13th century. **631.** Knight fending off an attack, 15th century. **632.** Spanish helmet, 16th century. **633.** Hand cannon.

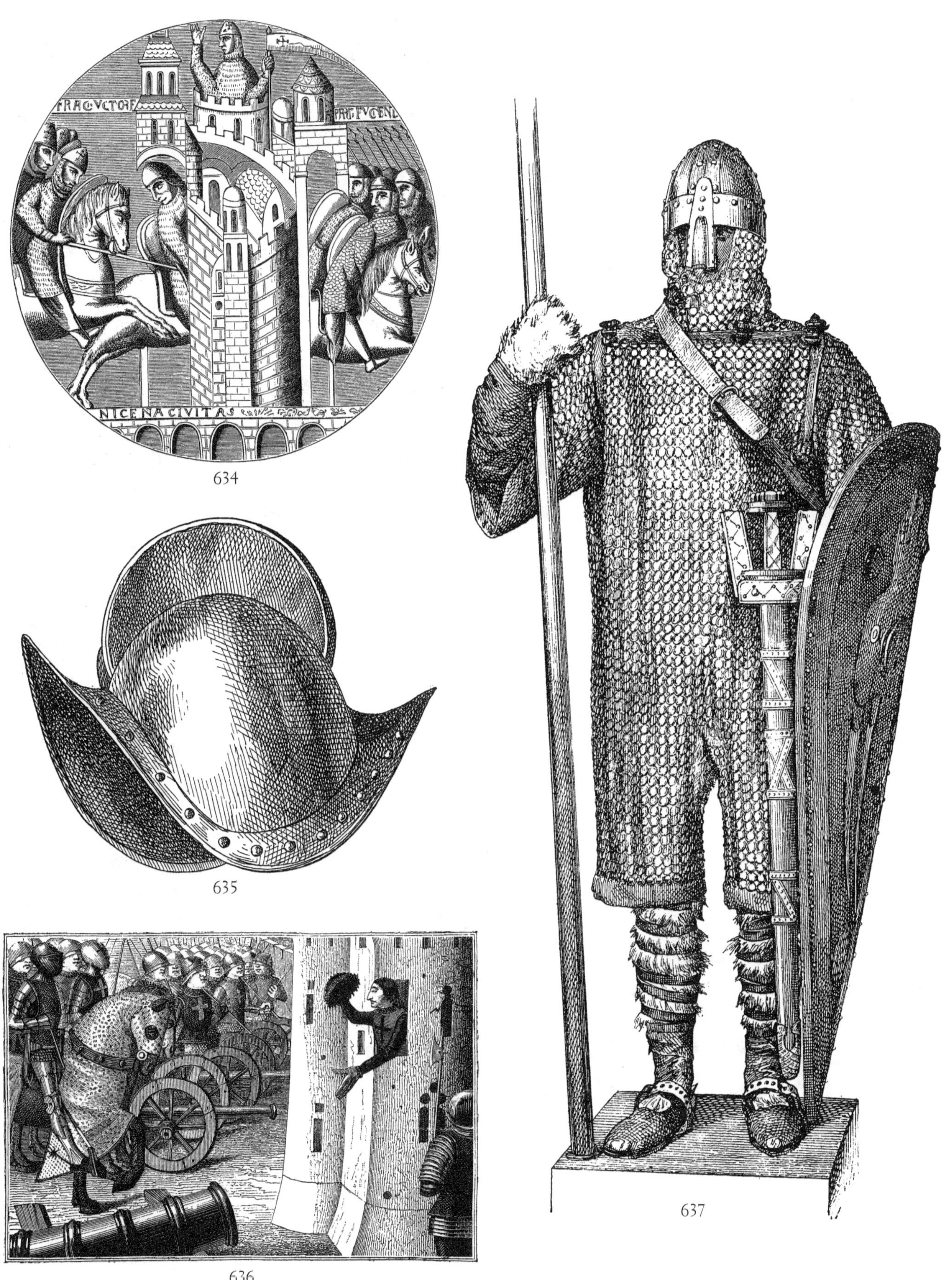

634. Taking of Nicaea by the Crusaders, 12th century. **635.** French casque, 15th century. **636.** How the Duc d'Alançon took the town of Alançon. **637.** Armor, 11th century.

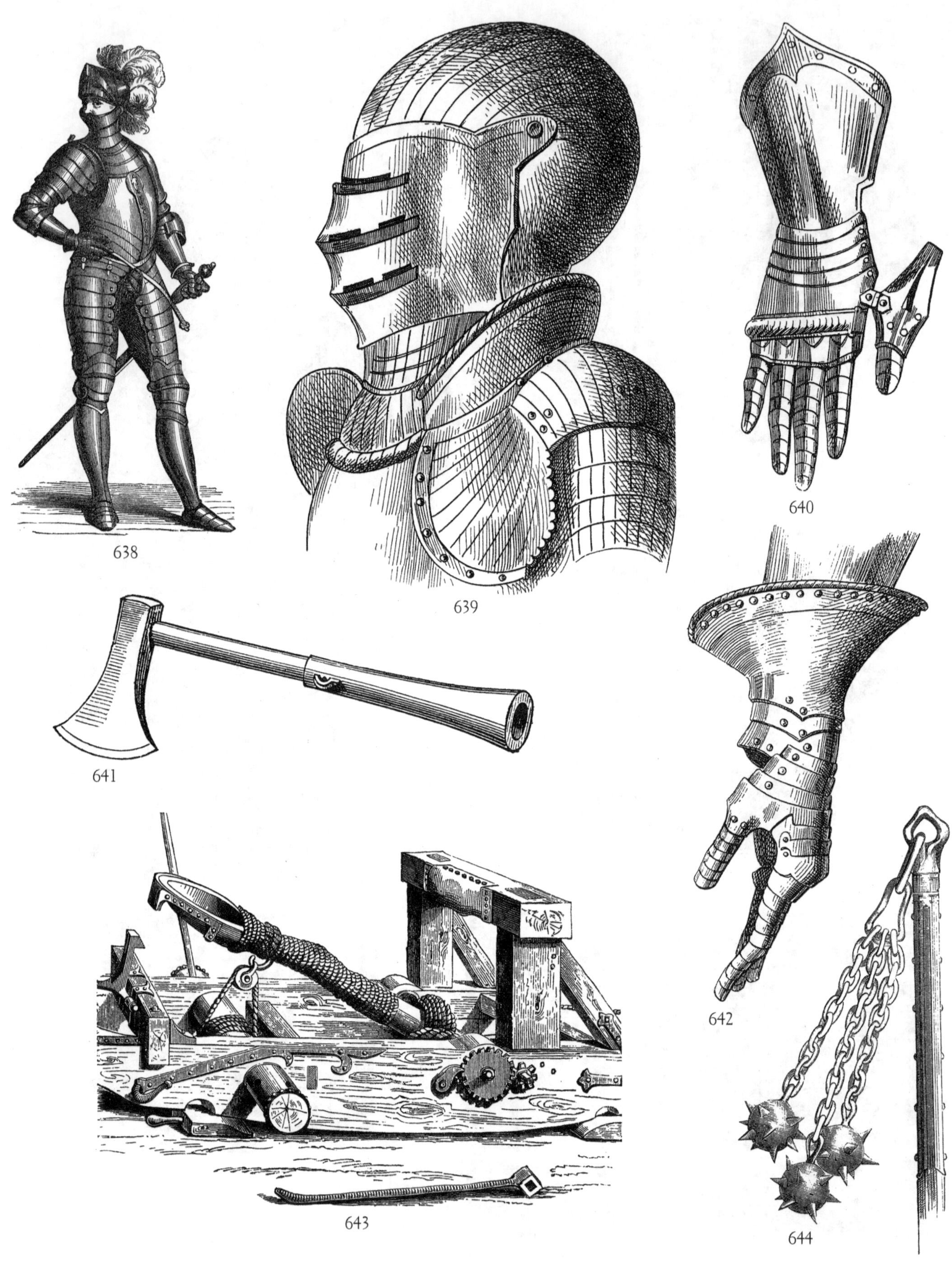

638. Knight in complete armor, 1590. **639.** Helmet, 13th century. **640.** French gauntlet, 15th century. **641.** German axe with gun in handle, 1393. **642.** French gauntlet, 15th century. **643.** Mangonneau, an engine of the War of the Fifteenth Century. **644.** Mace.

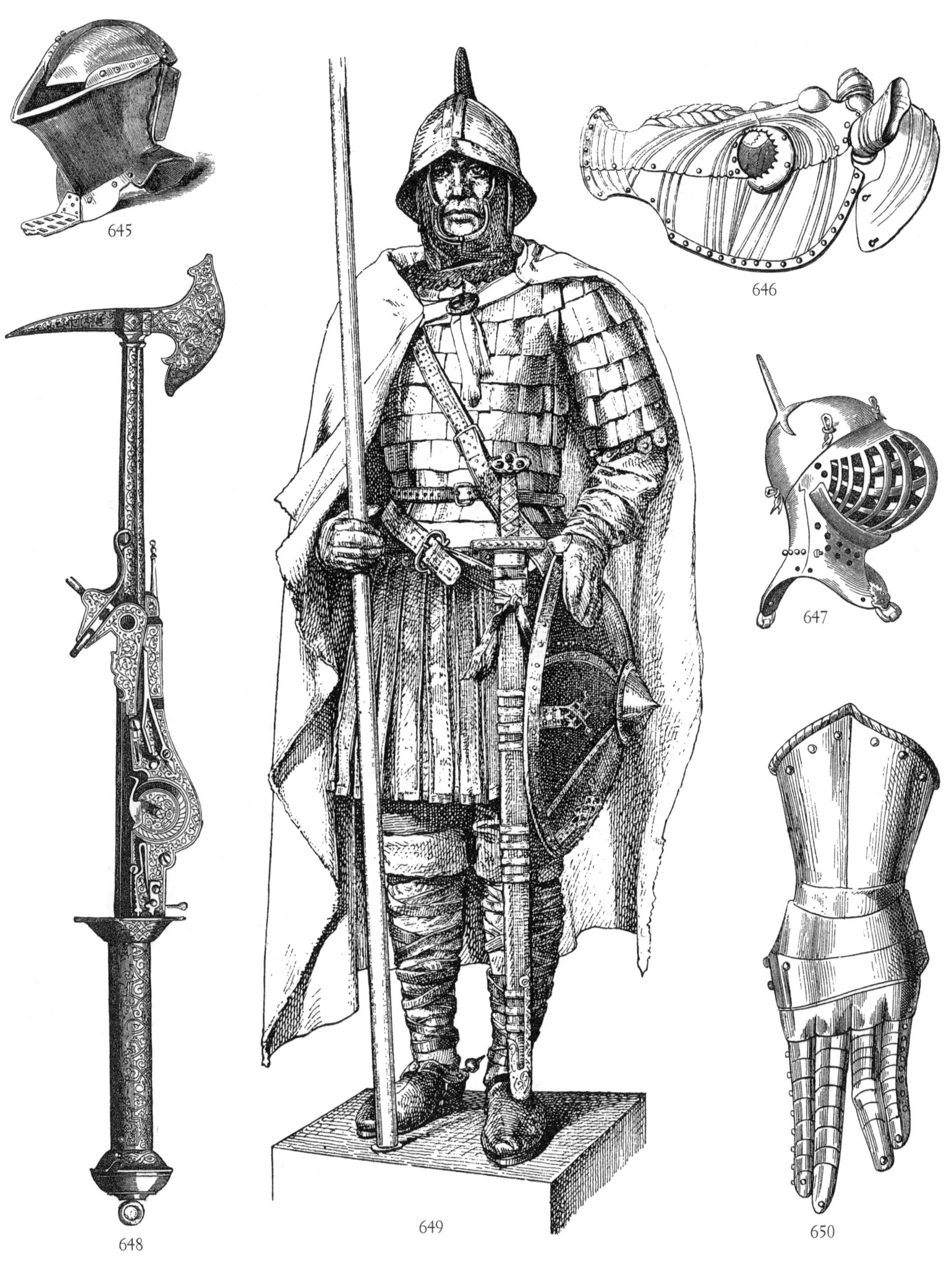

645. Tilting helmet, time of Henry VII. **646.** English champfrein. **647.** Armor, 15th century. **648.** Battle-axe and pistol, 16th century. **649.** Knight, 9th century. **650.** French gauntlet, 15th century.

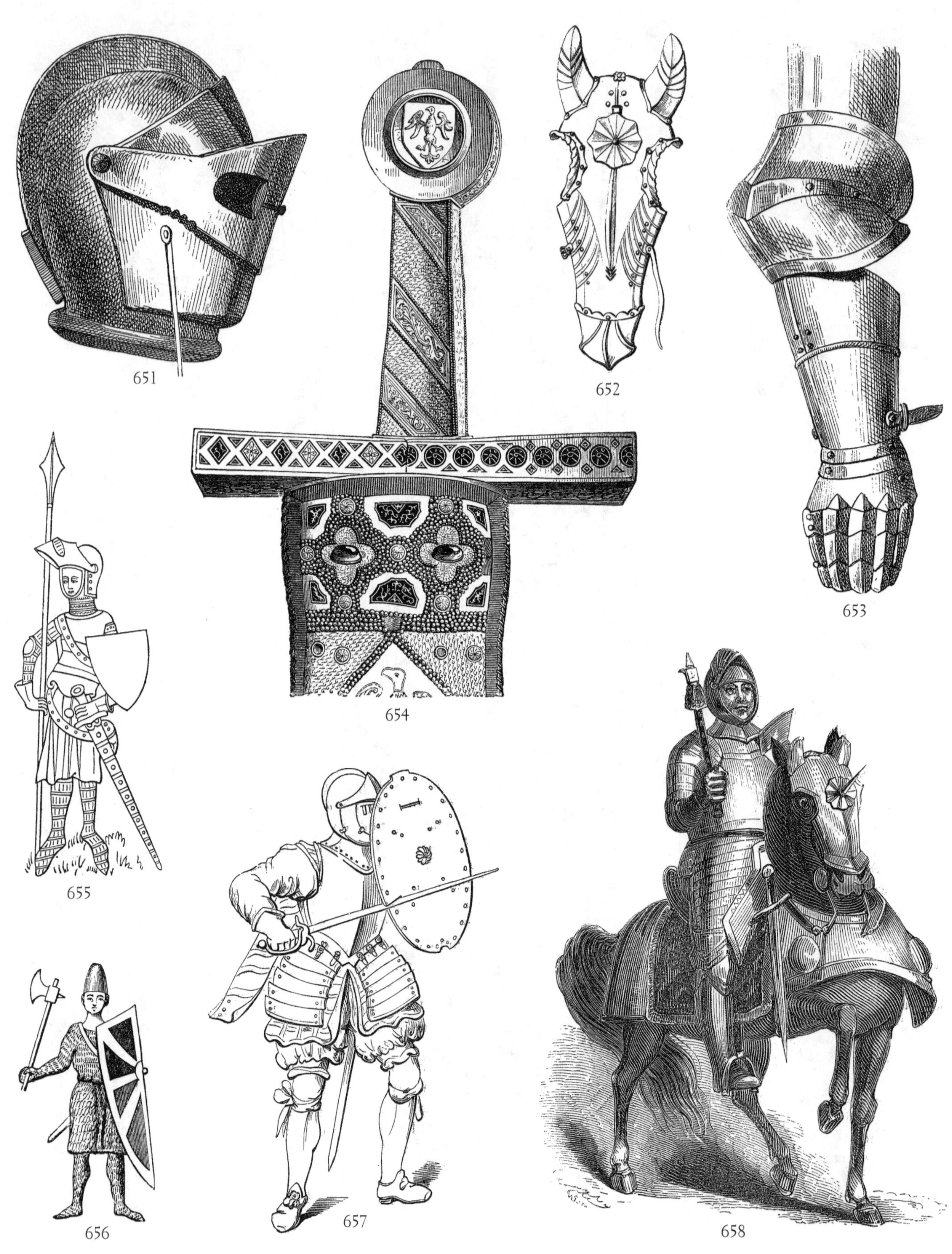

651. French helmet, 15th century. **652.** English champfrein. **653.** Arm piece. **654.** Sword of Charlemagne. **655.** Knight. **656.** Jean Sansterre, seal. **657.** Infantry armor. **658.** Henry VIII.

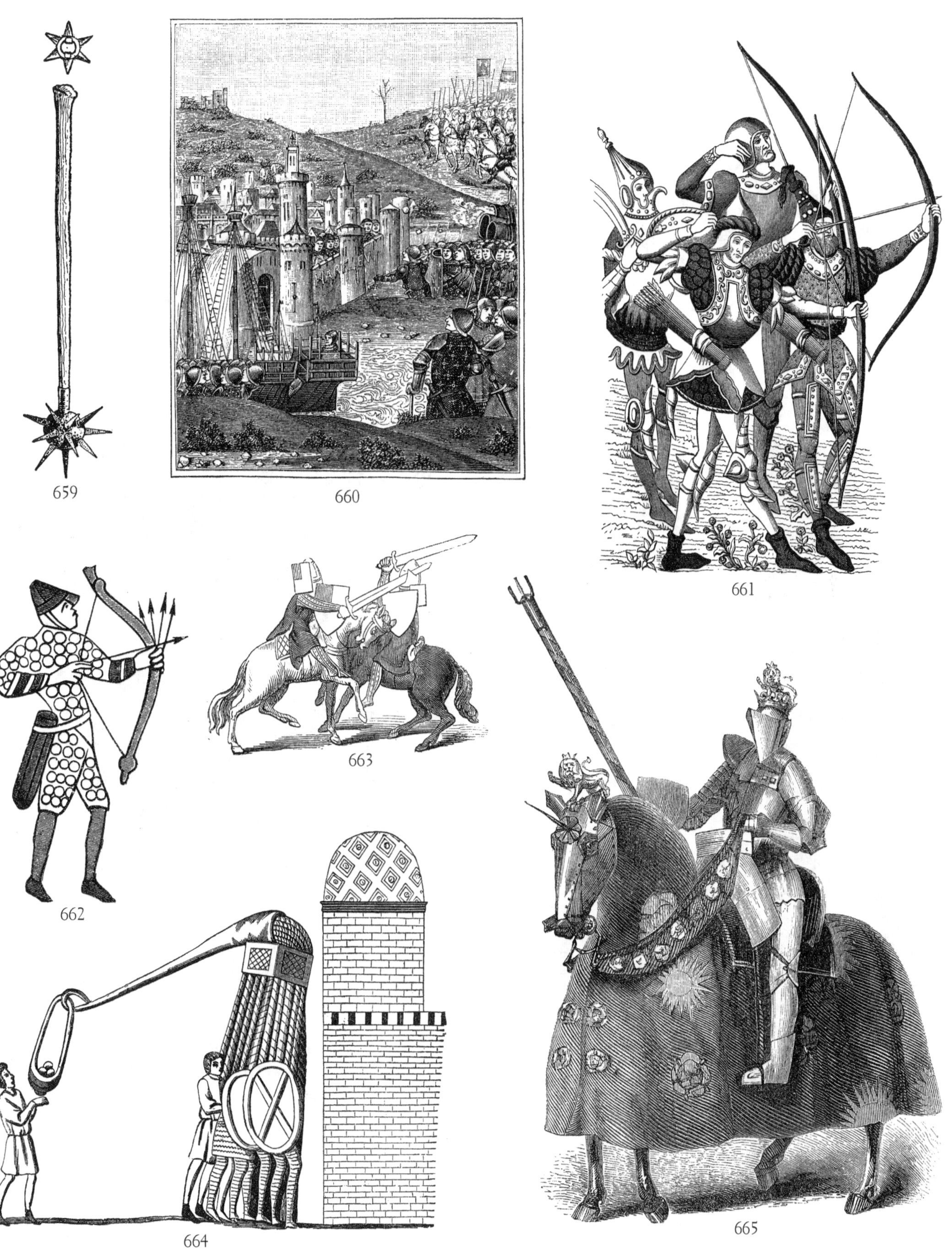

659. Morning-star mace, 15th century. **660.** King Charles sets out to besiege the town of Harfleur; 15th century manuscript. **661.** Frank archers, 15th century. **662.** Norman archer. **663.** Knights combating. **664.** Engine for hurling stones. **665.** Edward IV.

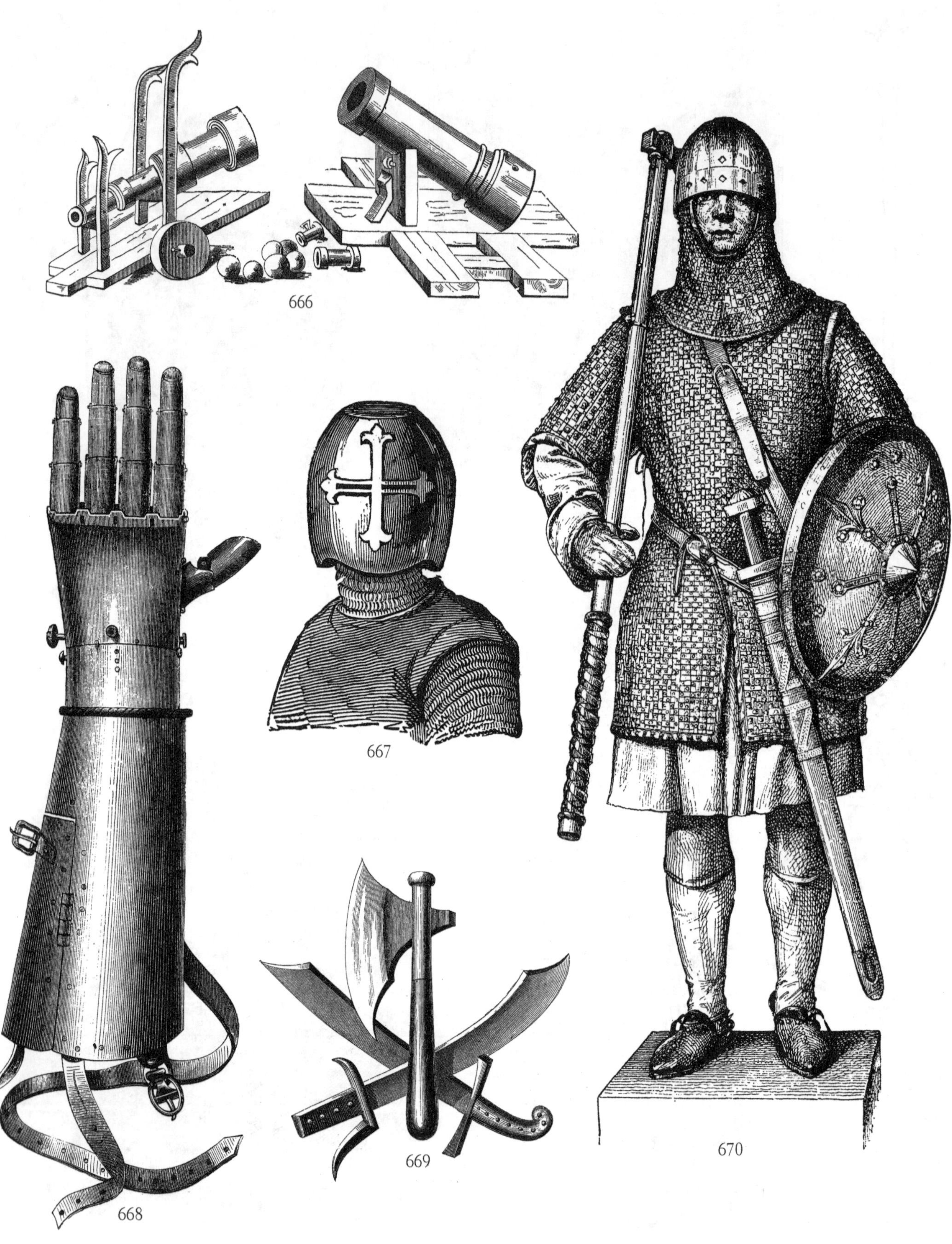

666. Bombards on fixed and rolling carriages. **667.** Helmet, 13th century. **668.** Gauntlet. **669.** Various arms, 15th century. **670.** Armor, 10th century.

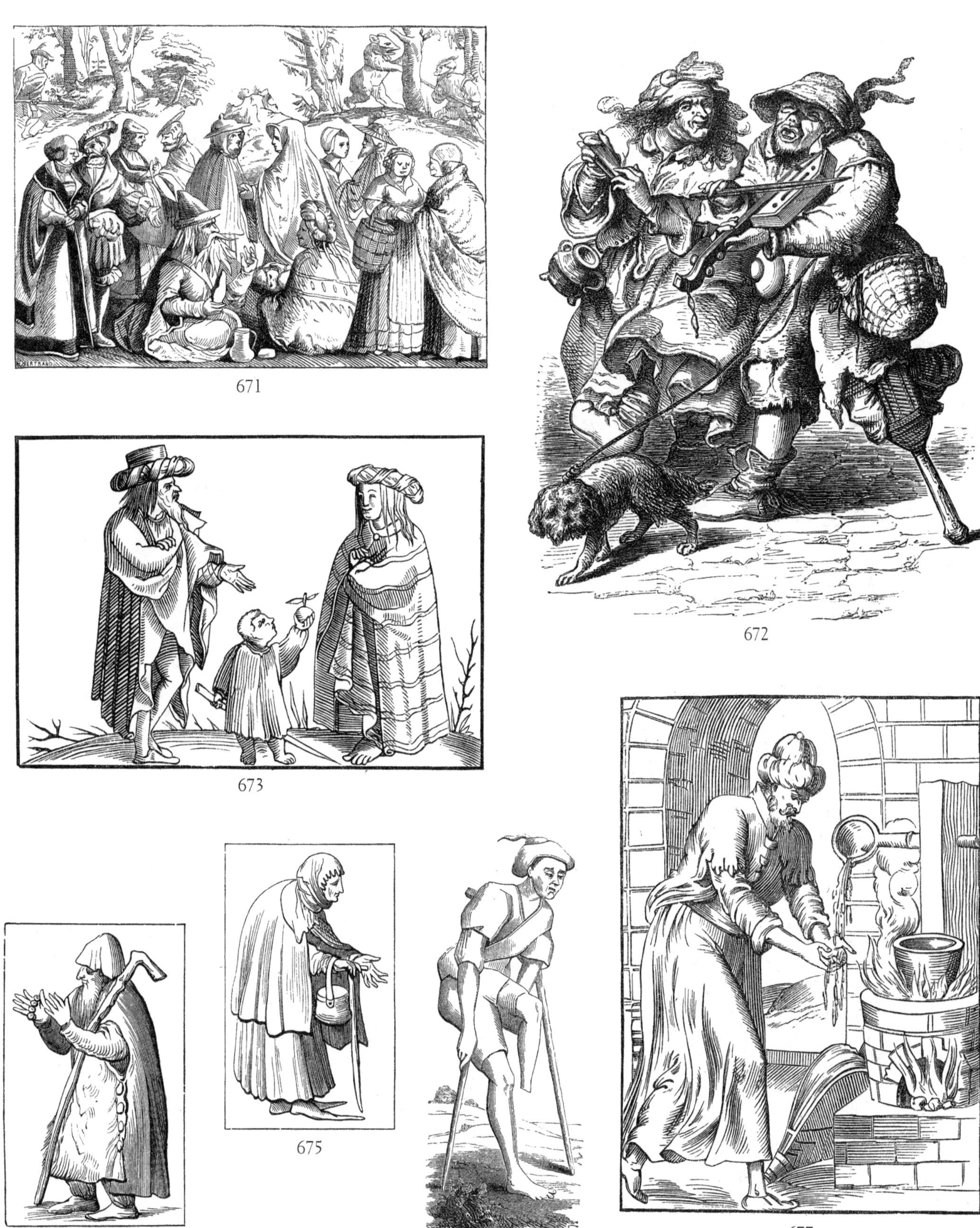

671. Gypsies fortune telling. 672. Beggar playing the fiddle, and his wife accompanying him with the bones. 673. Gypsy family. 674. From the *Cosmographie Universelle.* 675. From the *Cosmographie Universelle.* 676. Drille or narquois. 677. Gypsy who used to wash his hands in molten lead.

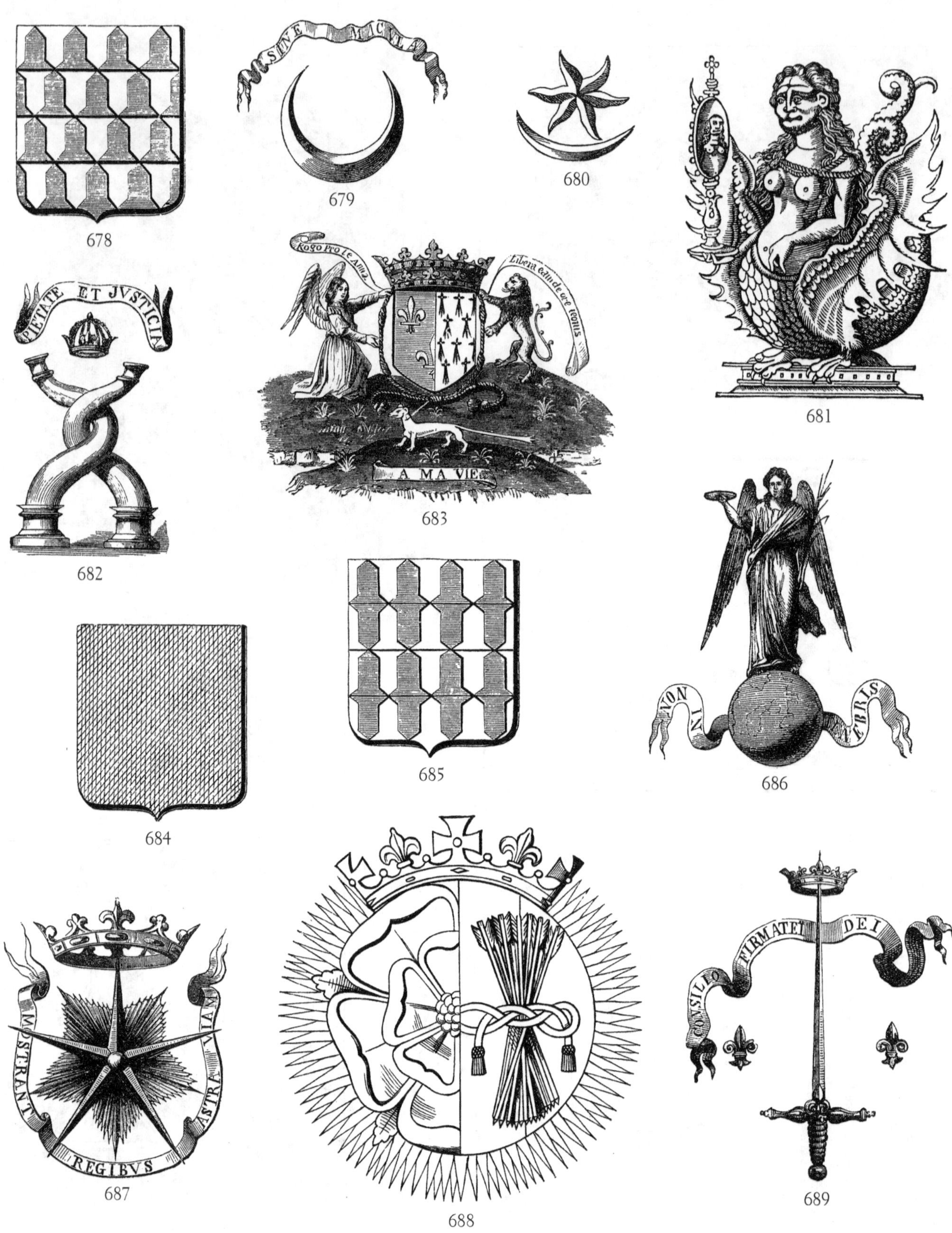

678. Heraldic mark, Vair. **679.** Piccolomini family, crescent with motto. **680.** Richard Cœur-de-Lion, King of England, emblem. **681.** The siren, token of Gérard Morrhy, printer at Paris, 1551. **682.** Device of Charles IX, King of France. **683.** The arms of Anne of Brittany, Queen of France. **684.** Heraldic mark, Tenne range. **685.** Heraldic mark, Counter-vair. **686.** Martin I, King of Aragon, emblem. **687.** John II, King of France, emblem with motto. **688.** Emblems of Mary Tudor, Queen of England. **689.** Emblem of family of Joan of Arc, composed by Charles VII, 1429.

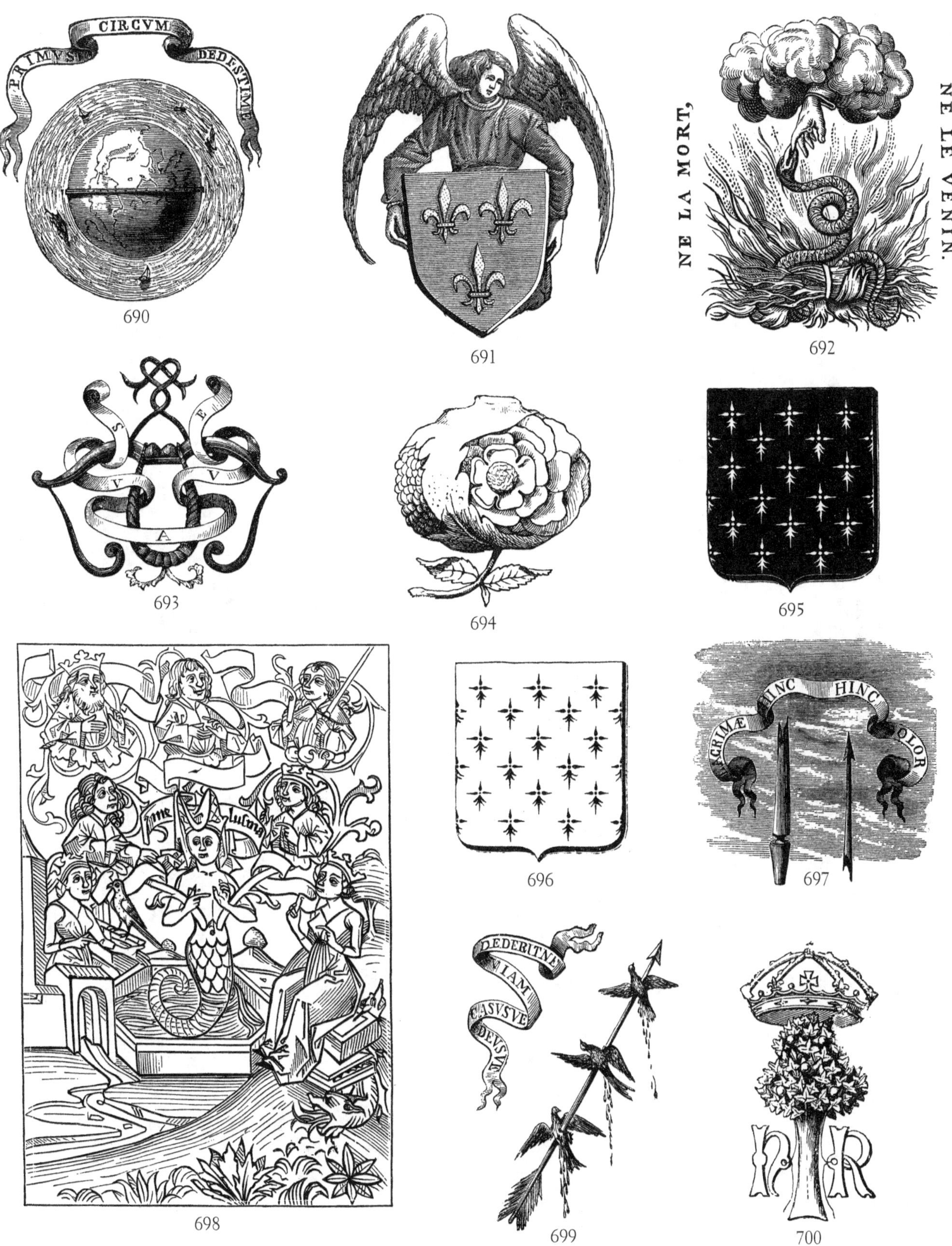

690. Emanuel, King of Portugal, emblem with motto. **691.** Arms of France. **692.** Token of Michel Fezandat, printer at Paris, 1552. **693.** Device of Pope Leo X. **694.** Emblem of Katherine of Aragon, first wife of Henry VIII. **695.** Heraldic mark, Ermines. **696.** Heraldic mark, Ermines. **697.** Device of Catherine de' Medicis, Queen of France, during her widowhood. **698.** The Fay Mélusine, 1480. **699.** Godfrey de Bouilon, Duke of Lorraine, King of Jerusalem (1099) with spread-eagle. **700.** Device of Henry VII, King of England.

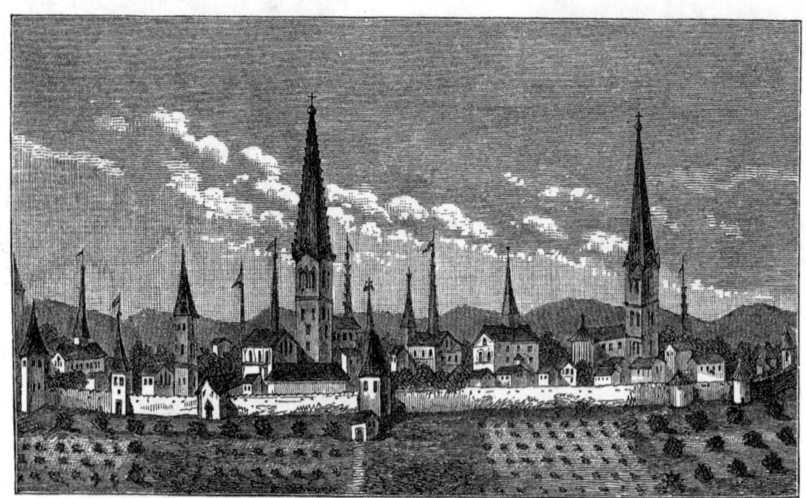

701

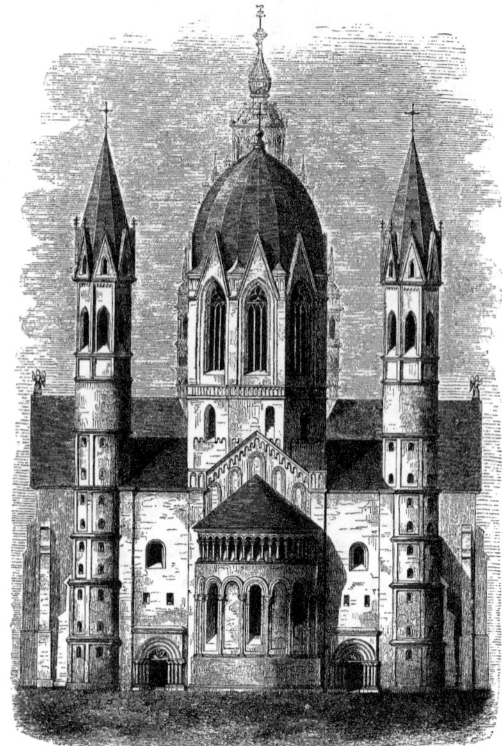

702

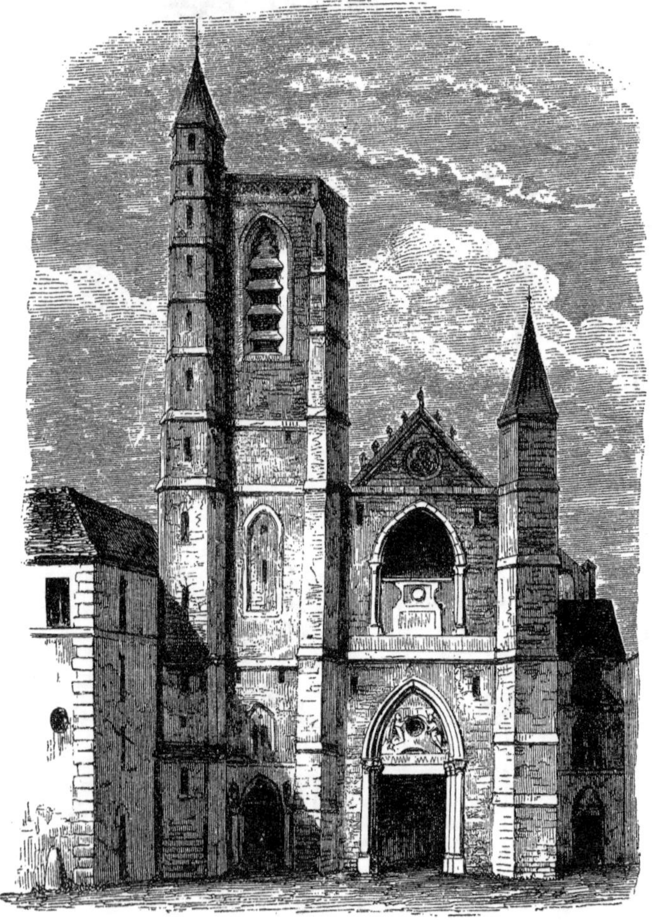

703

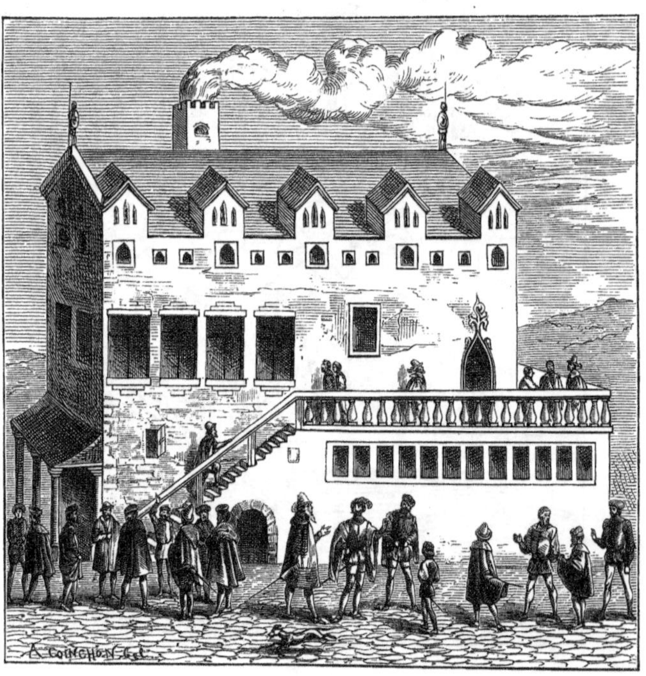

704

701. View of the town of Dortmund. **702.** Mayence Cathedral, 12th and 13th centuries. **703.** Ancient church of St. Paul-des-Champs, Paris, restored and rebuilt in the thirteenth century. **704.** Hotel of the chamber of accounts in the courtyard of the palace, Paris; *Cosmographie Universelle*, 1552.

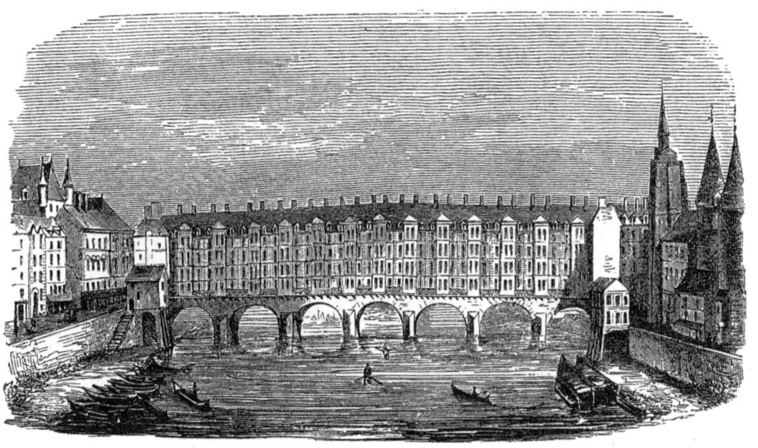
705

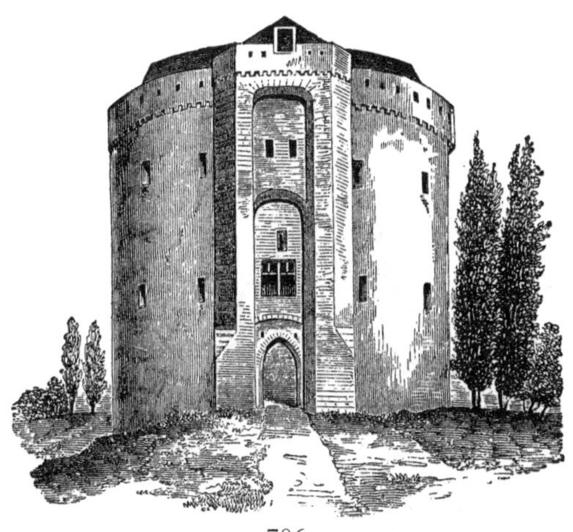
706

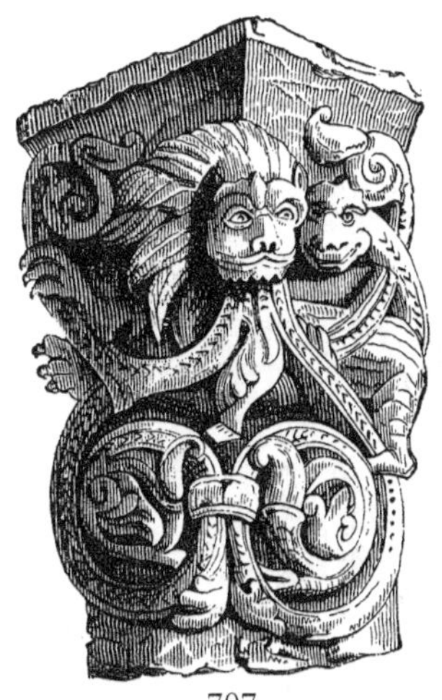
707

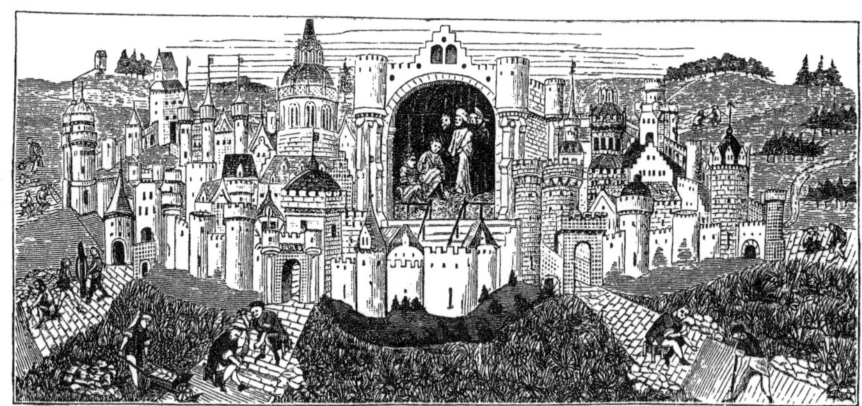
708

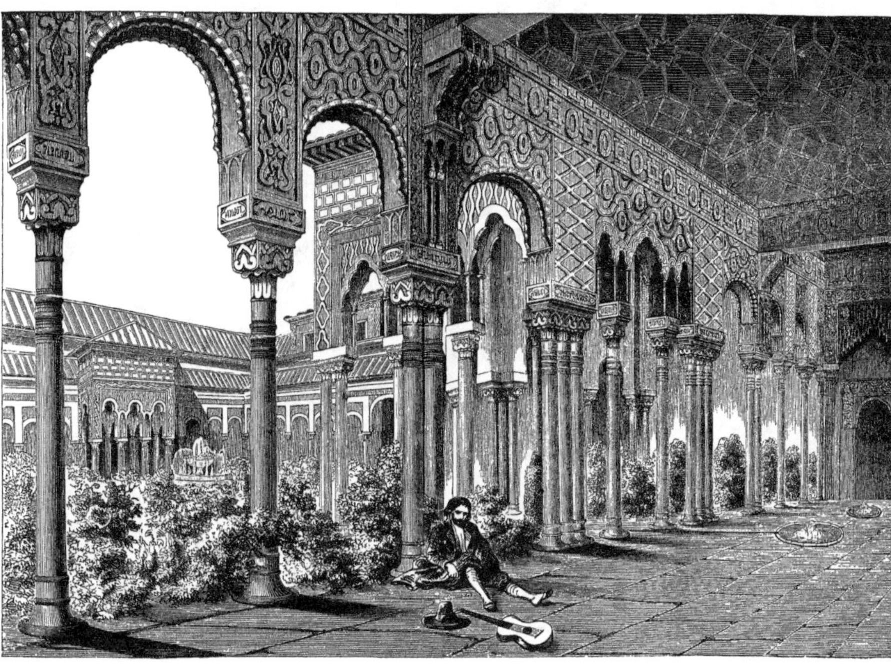
709

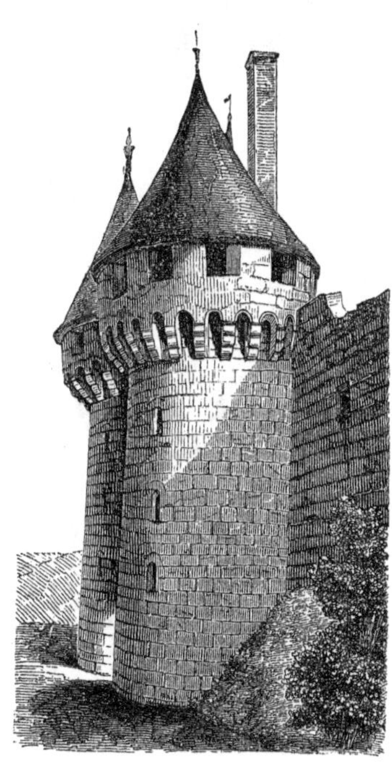
710

705. View of the ancient Pont aux Changeurs. **706.** Porte de Hal, Brussels. **707.** Capital of a column, abbey of St. Geneviève. **708.** Brunehaut superintending the making of the seven roads, which led from the city of Bavay. **709.** Interior of the palace of the Alhambra, Granada, 13th century. **710.** Castle of Nogent-le-Rotrou.

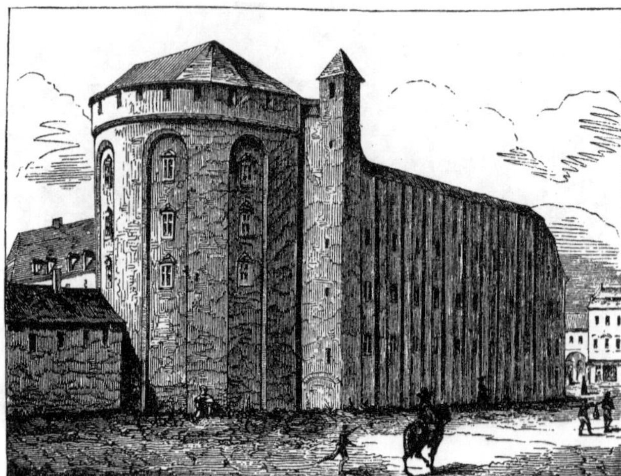
712

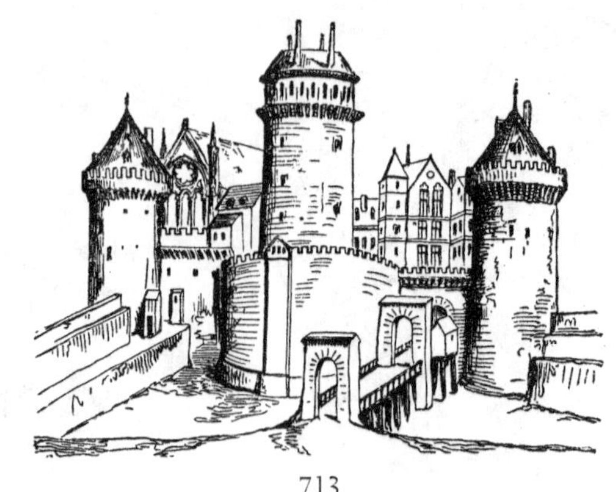
713

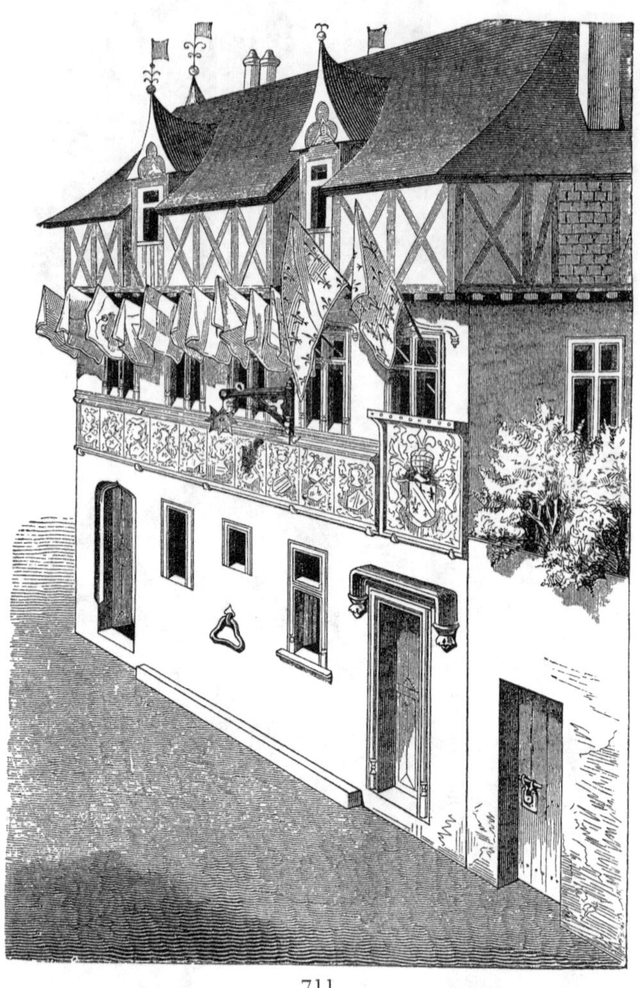

711

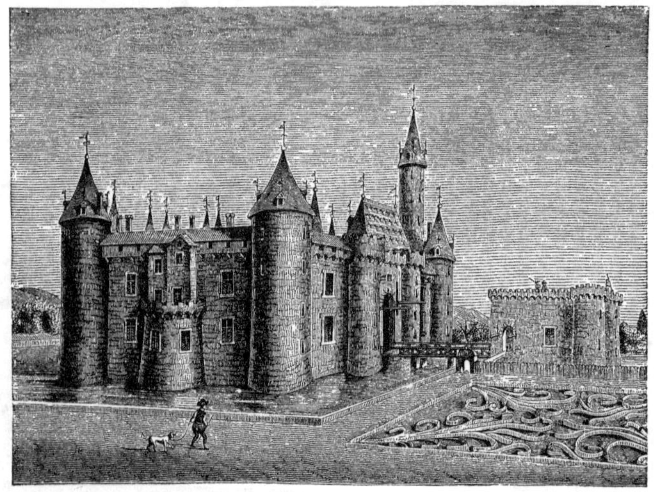
714

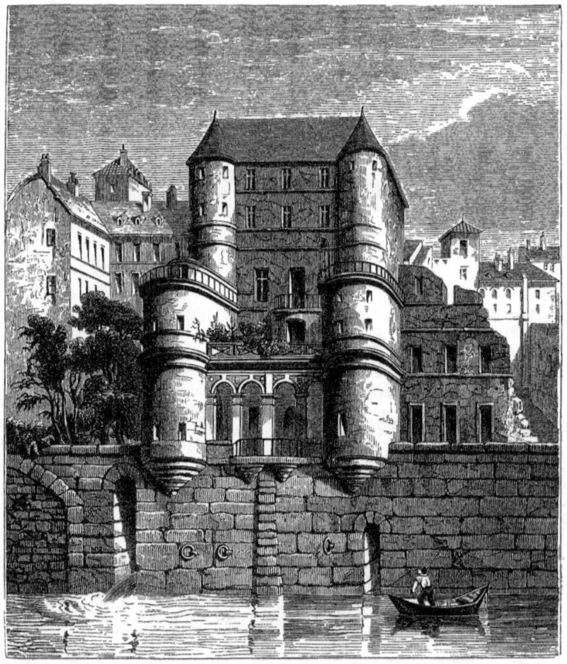

715

711. Lords and barons exhibit their nobility by displaying their banners and coats-of-arms from the windows of the Heralds' Lodge. **712.** Basilica of Constantine, Trèves, transformed into a fortress in the Middle Ages. **713.** The castle of Coucy in its ancient state; 13th century manuscript. **714.** Ancient castle of Marcoussis, 13th century. **715.** Hôtel des Ursins, Paris, now destroyed.

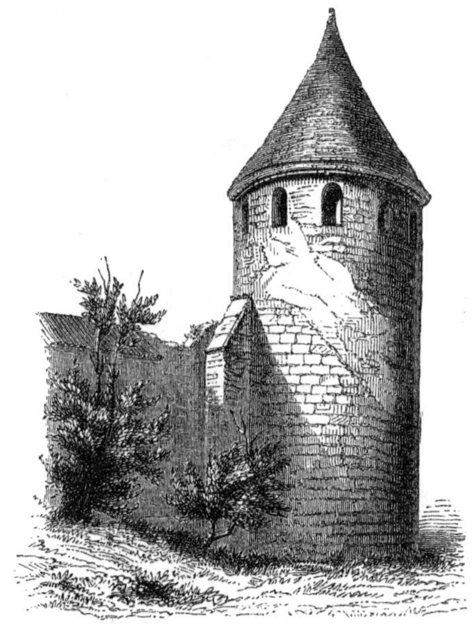

716

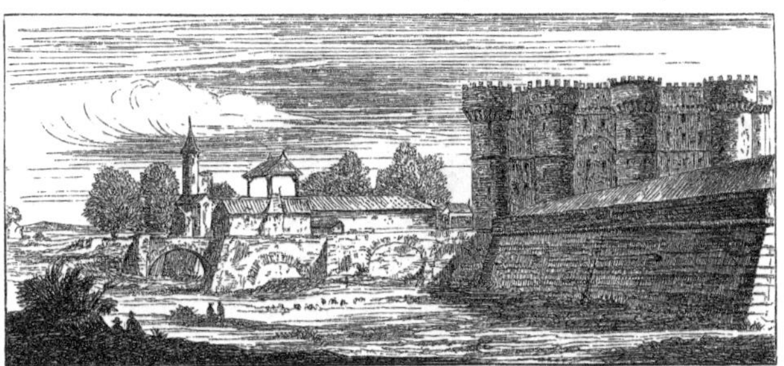

717

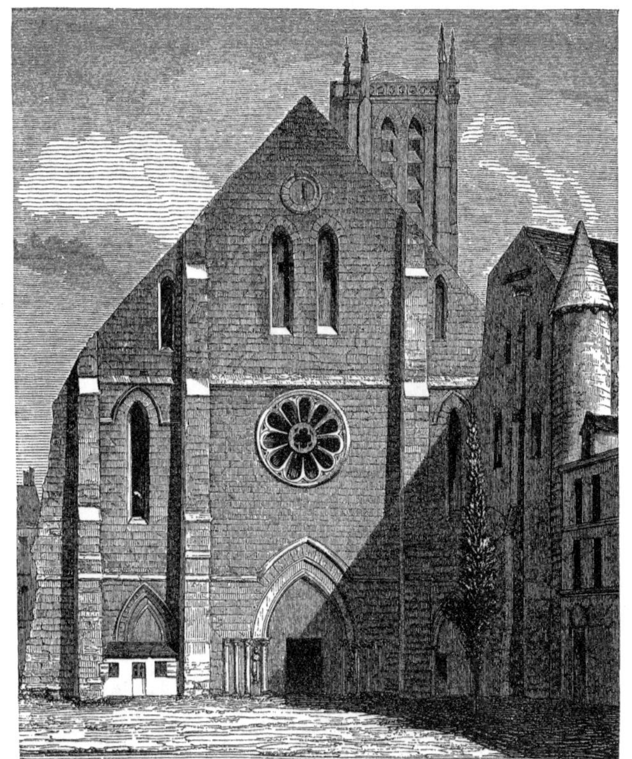

718

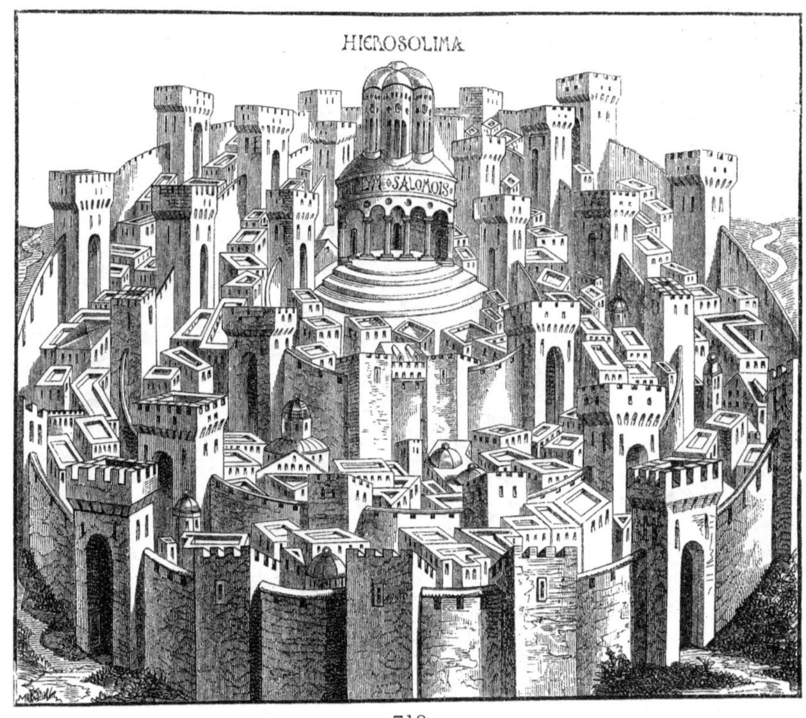

719

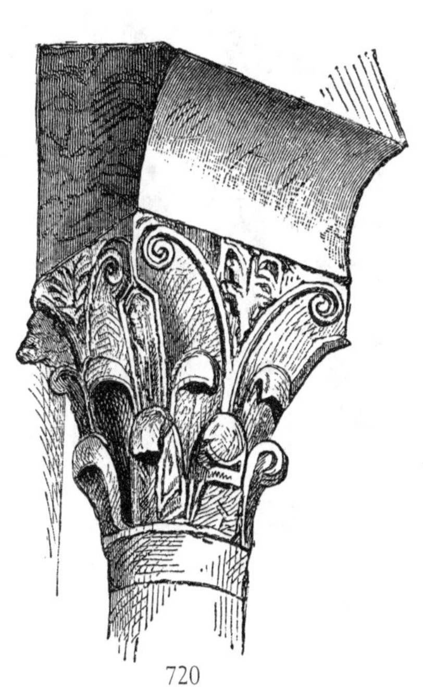

720

716. Tower of the castle of Sémur. **717.** Bastille. **718.** Front of the ancient church of the Abbey of Sainte-Geneviève, Paris, now destroyed. **719.** View and plan of Jerusalem. **720.** Vestige of the architecture of the Goths at Toledo, 7th century.

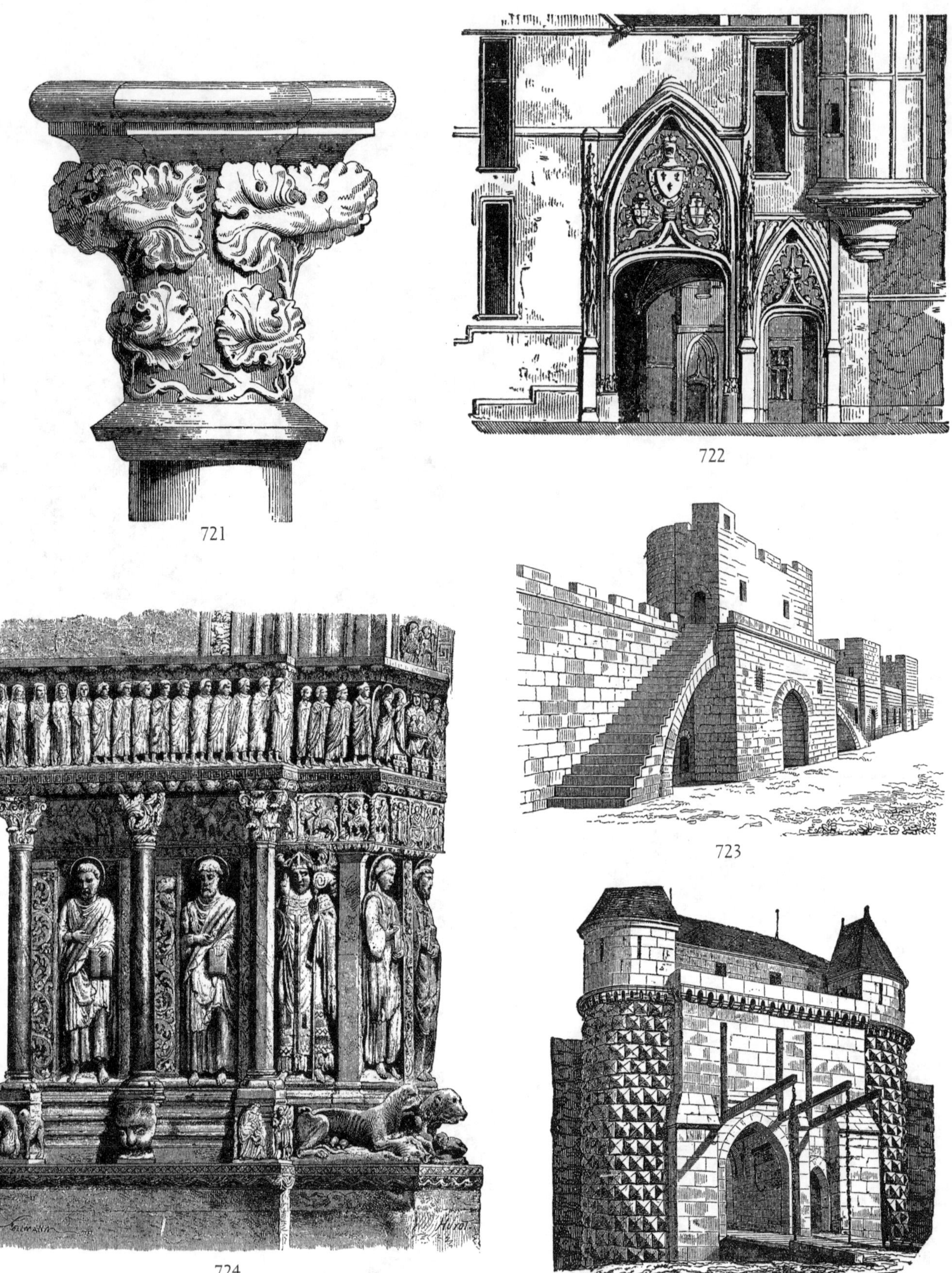

721. Capital in the church of the Célestins, destroyed. **722.** Doorways of the Hôtel de Sens, Paris. **723.** Ramparts of the town of Aigues-Mortes. **724.** Details of the Portal of St. Trophimus, Arles, 12th century. **725.** Gate of St. John, with drawbridge.

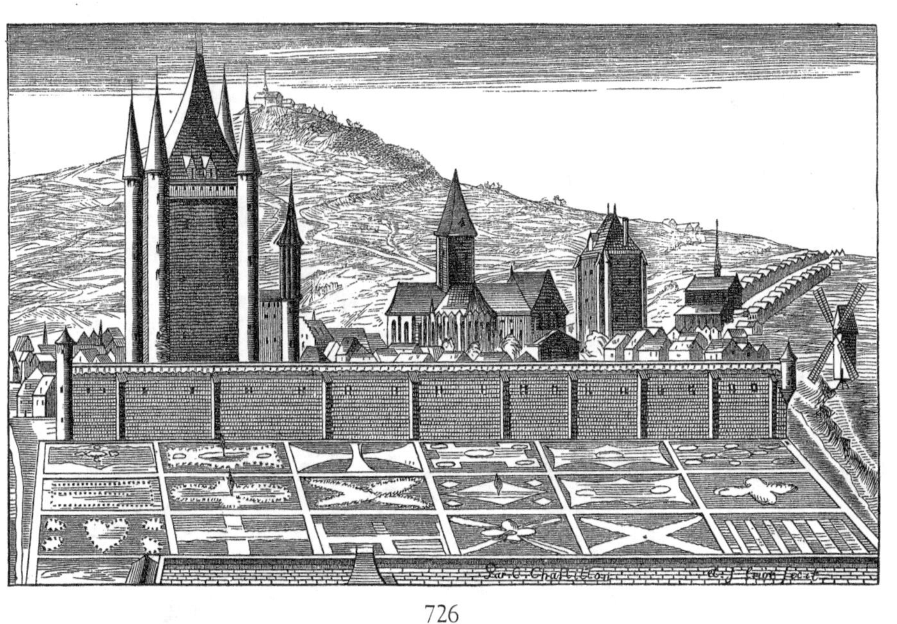

726

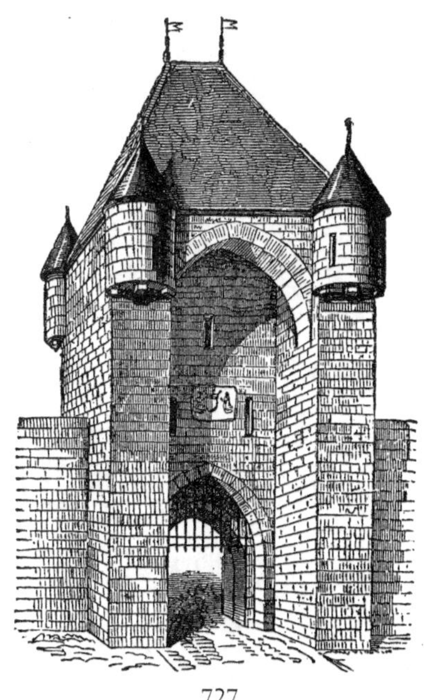

727

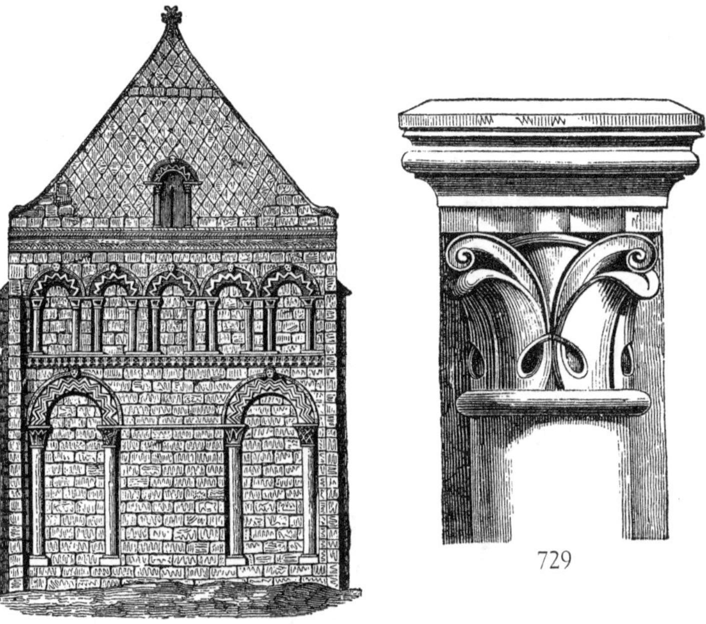

728

729

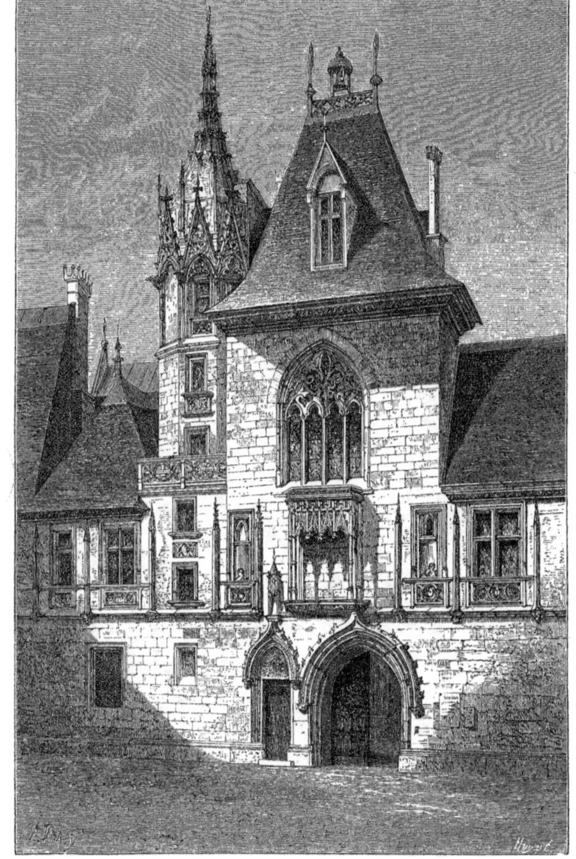

731

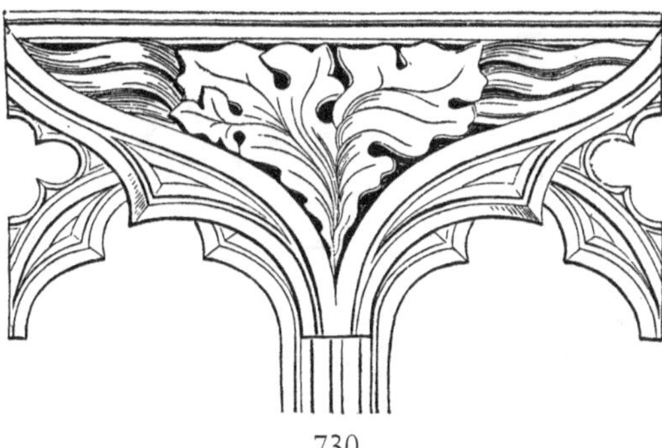

730

726. Tower of the temple in Paris. **727.** Gate of Moret. **728.** Remains of the church of Mouen, in Normandy. **729.** Capital of a column in the church of St. Julien the Poor. **730.** Design on the stalls in the church of St. Benoît-sur-Loire. **731.** House of Jacques Cœur at Bourges.

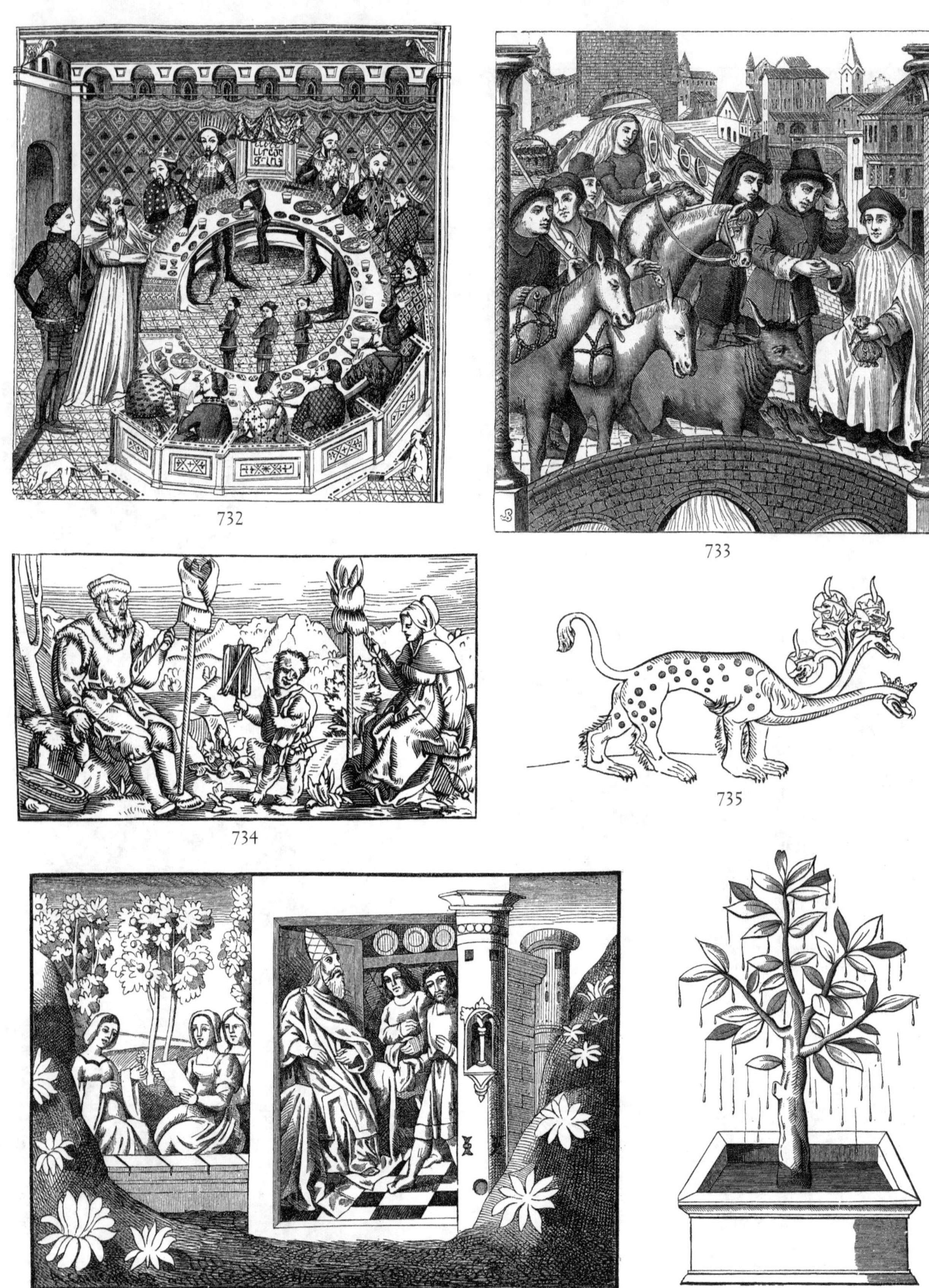

732 733 734 735 736 737

732. Round table of King Artus of Brittany, 14th century. **733.** Paying toll on passing a bridge, 15th century. **734.** Sedentary occupations of the peasants, 1552. **735.** Fantastic figure seen in the sky in the sixteenth century. **736.** The Old Man of the Mountain giving orders to his followers, 15th century manuscript. **737.** The Tree of Life, or the Weeping-tree, planted in the states of Prester John.

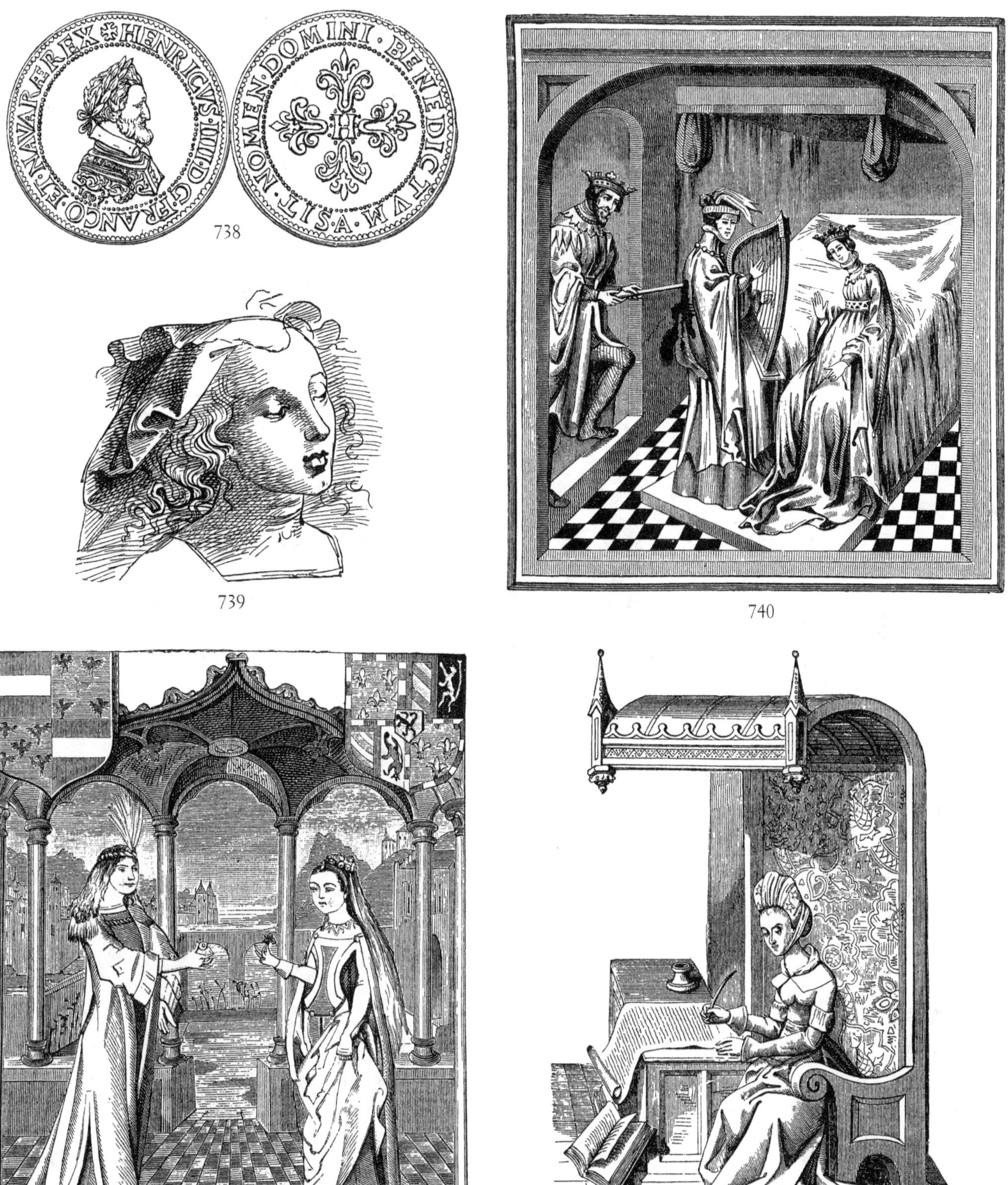

738. Silver franc. **739.** Sketch of the Virgin of Alba, Raphael. **740.** King Mark stabbing Tristan in the presence of Ysolt. **741.** Betrothal interview between Archduke Maximilian and Mary of Burgundy at Ghent, 15th century. **742.** Christine de Pizan, contemporary of Charles V and Charles VI, 15th century.

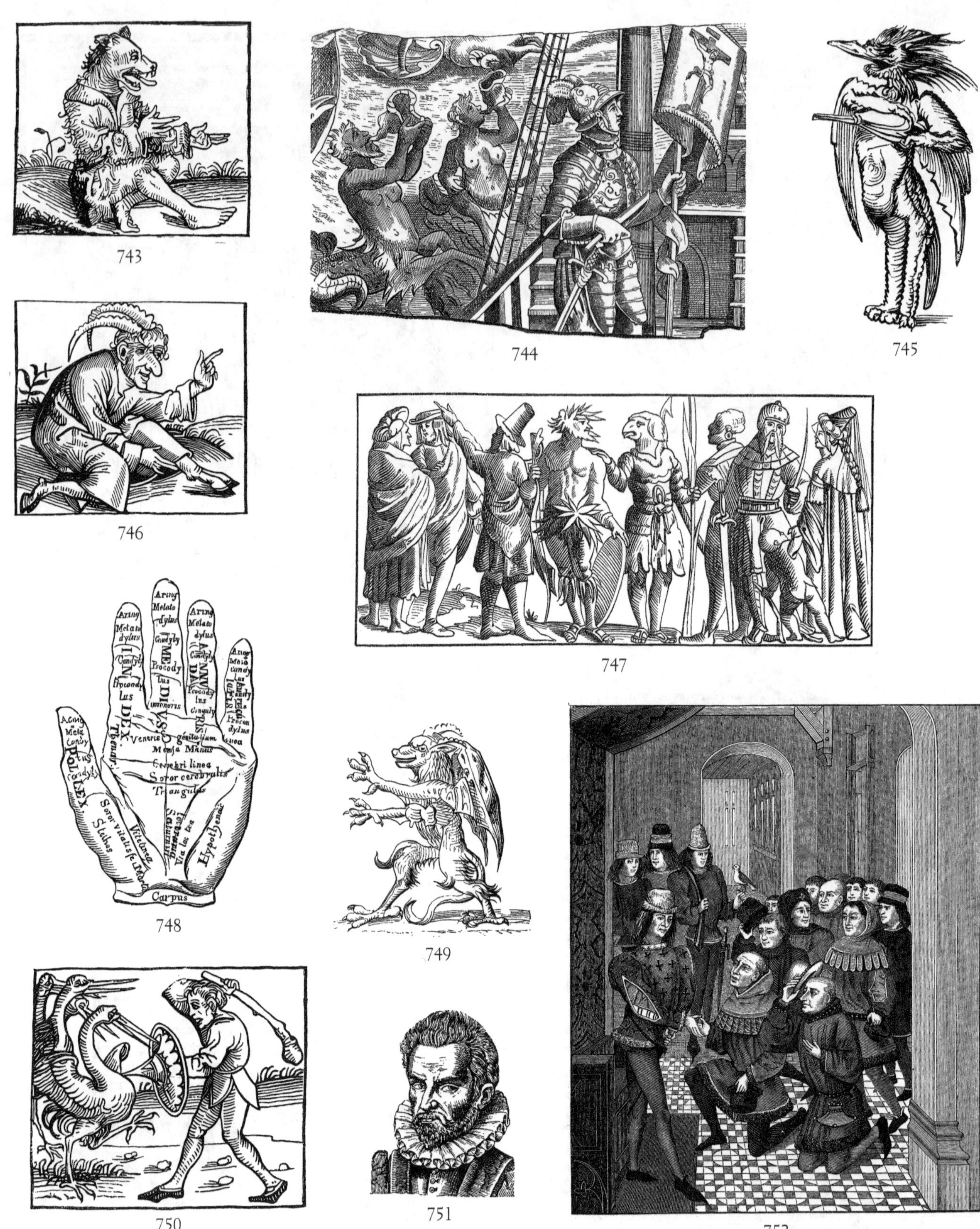

743. Monster born from the deluge. **744.** Columbus on board his ship during his first voyage to the west. **745.** Fantastic figure seen in the sky in the sixteenth century. **746.** Monster born from the deluge. **747.** Families and the barbarians. **748.** Specimen of the left hand, with horoscopic denominations. **749.** Fantastic figure seen in the sky in the sixteenth century. **750.** Monsters born from the deluge. **751.** Portrait of Robert Garnier. **752.** The deputies of the burghers of Ghent, in revolt against their sovereign, 1397.

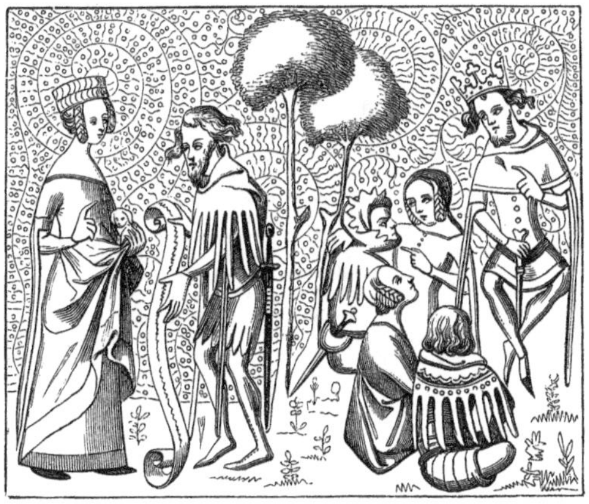

753

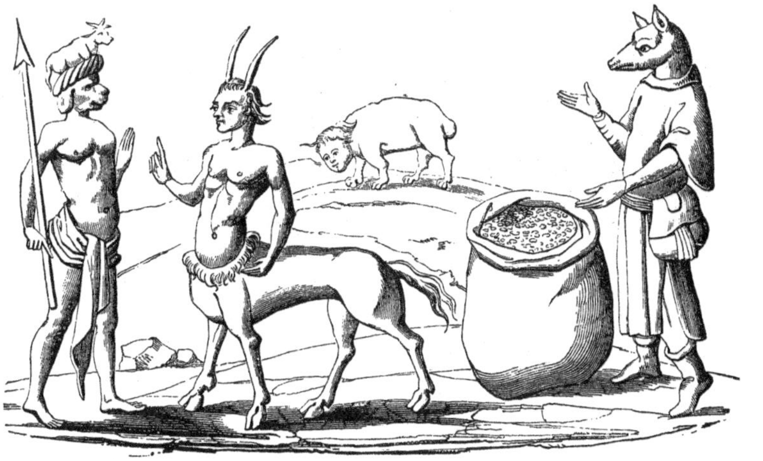

754

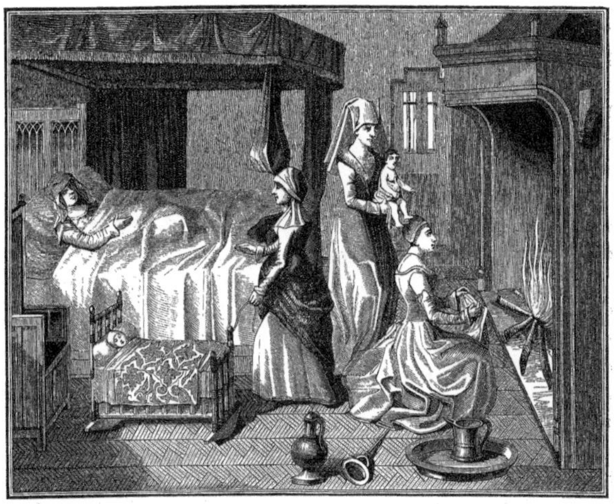

755

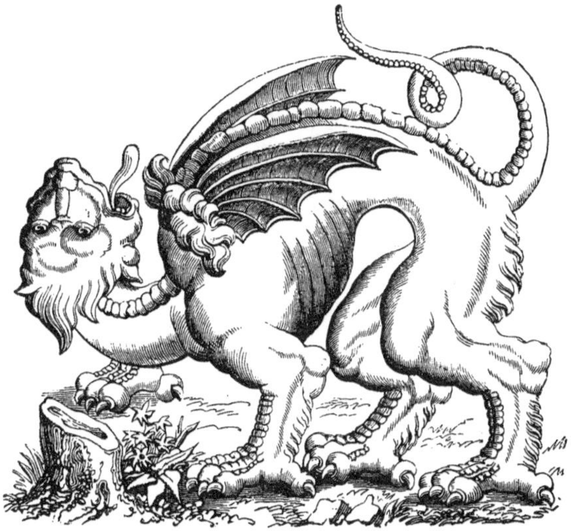

756

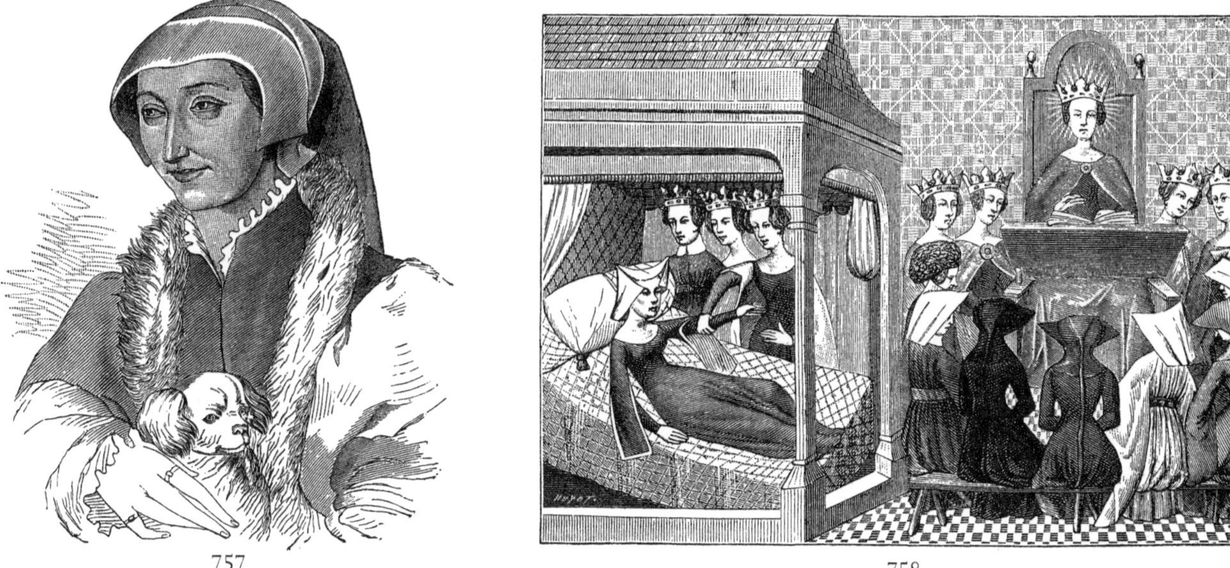

757

758

753. Court of love in Provence. **754.** The Man-dog, the Man-wolf, and the Man-pig, *Livres des Merveilles du Monde*, 14th century. **755.** The newborn Child, 15th century manuscript. **756.** Gargouille (gargoyle). **757.** Portrait of Marguerite de Valois, Queen of Navarre. **758.** The Three Virtues (Reason, Uprightness, and Justice), 1405.

www.ingramcontent.com/pod-product-compliance
Lightning Source LLC
LaVergne TN
LVHW061248100826
845148LV00008B/1066

* 9 7 8 0 4 8 6 4 6 0 1 2 3 *